SERIALIZATION AND THE NOVEL IN MID-VICTORIAN MAGAZINES

Examining the Victorian serial as a text in its own right, Catherine Delafield re-reads five novels by Elizabeth Gaskell, Anthony Trollope, Dinah Craik, and Wilkie Collins by situating them in the context of periodical publication. She traces the roles of the author and editor in the creation and dissemination of the texts and considers how first publication affected the consumption and reception of the novel through the periodical medium. Delafield contends that a novel in volume form has been separated from its original context, that is, from the pattern of consumption and reception presented by the serial. The novel's later re-publication still bears the imprint of this serialized original, and this book's investigation into nineteenth-century periodicals both generates new readings of the texts and reinstates those which have been lost in the reprinting process. Delafield's case studies provide evidence of the ways in which *Household Words*, *Cornhill Magazine*, *Good Words*, *All the Year Round* and *Cassell's Magazine* were designed for new audiences of novel readers. *Serialization and the Novel in Mid-Victorian Magazines* addresses the material conditions of production, illustrates the collective and collaborative creation of the serialized novel, and contextualizes a range of texts in the nineteenth-century experience of print.

T0331498

The Nineteenth Century Series
General Editors' Preface

The aim of the series is to reflect, develop and extend the great burgeoning of interest in the nineteenth century that has been an inevitable feature of recent years, as that former epoch has come more sharply into focus as a locus for our understanding not only of the past but of the contours of our modernity. It centres primarily upon major authors and subjects within Romantic and Victorian literature. It also includes studies of other British writers and issues, where these are matters of current debate: for example, biography and autobiography, journalism, periodical literature, travel writing, book production, gender, non-canonical writing. We are dedicated principally to publishing original monographs and symposia; our policy is to embrace a broad scope in chronology, approach and range of concern, and both to recognize and cut innovatively across such parameters as those suggested by the designations 'Romantic' and 'Victorian'. We welcome new ideas and theories, while valuing traditional scholarship. It is hoped that the world which predates yet so forcibly predicts and engages our own will emerge in parts, in the wider sweep, and in the lively streams of disputation and change that are so manifest an aspect of its intellectual, artistic and social landscape.

Vincent Newey
Joanne Shattock
University of Leicester

Serialization and the Novel in Mid-Victorian Magazines

CATHERINE DELAFIELD

Routledge
Taylor & Francis Group

LONDON AND NEW YORK

First published 2015 by Ashgate Publishing

2 Park Square, Milton Park, Abingdon, Oxfordshire OX14 4RN
52 Vanderbilt Avenue, New York, NY 10017

Routledge is an imprint of the Taylor & Francis Group, an informa business

First issued in paperback 2019

Copyright © 2015 Catherine Delafield

Catherine Delafield has asserted her right under the Copyright, Designs and Patents Act, 1988, to be identified as the author of this work.

All rights reserved. No part of this book may be reprinted or reproduced or utilised in any form or by any electronic, mechanical, or other means, now known or hereafter invented, including photocopying and recording, or in any information storage or retrieval system, without permission in writing from the publishers.

Notice:
Product or corporate names may be trademarks or registered trademarks, and are used only for identification and explanation without intent to infringe.

British Library Cataloguing in Publication Data
A catalogue record for this book is available from the British Library

The Library of Congress has cataloged the printed edition as follows:
Delafield, Catherine.
  Serialization and the novel in mid-Victorian magazines / by Catherine Delafield.
    pages cm. — (The nineteenth century series)
  Includes bibliographical references and index.
  ISBN 978-1-4724-5090-6 (hardcover: alk. paper)

  1. English fiction—19th century—History and criticism. 2. Literature publishing—Great Britain—History—19th century. 3. Serialized fiction—Great Britain—History and criticism. 4. Authors and publishers—Great Britain—History—19th century. I. Title.
  PR878.P78D45 2015
  823'.809—dc23
                                                                        2014038423

ISBN 978-1-4724-5090-6 (hbk)
ISBN 978-0-367-88090-3 (pbk)

Contents

List of Figures   *vii*
Acknowledgements   *ix*
List of Abbreviations   *x*

Introduction: Rereading the Novel   1

1   Serialization and the Nineteenth-Century Periodical   5

2   Authorship and the Serialized Novel   23

3   Serialization and the Periodical Editor   47

4   The Periodical and the Serialized Novel   73

5   The Serialized Novel   93

6   The Afterlife of the Serialized Novel   161

Appendices   *185*
Bibliography   *195*
Index   *207*

List of Figures

2.1   Opening page of *The Moonstone*, *All the Year Round*, 4 January 1868, 73.   31

5.1   'A Black Sheep,' Illustration opening Chapter 4 of *Lovel the Widower*, *Cornhill Magazine* 1 (1860): 385.   108

5.2   J.E. Millais, 'Lord Lufton and Lucy Robarts,' *Cornhill Magazine* 1 (1860): facing page 449.   109

5.3   J.E. Millais, Illustration for R. Monckton Milnes, 'Unspoken Dialogue,' *Cornhill Magazine* 1 (1860): facing page 194.   111

5.4   J.E. Millais, '"Mark,' she said, 'the men are here,"' *Cornhill Magazine* 3 (1861): facing page 342.   112

5.5   J.E. Millais, 'Was it not a lie?' *Cornhill Magazine* 1 (1860): facing page 691.   114

5.6   'Water-newt,' *Studies in Animal Life*, *Cornhill Magazine* 1 (1860): 291.   115

5.7   '*Campanularia* polyp,' *Studies in Animal Life*, *Cornhill Magazine* 1 (1860): 683.   116

5.8   Frederick Sandys, 'Legend of the Portent,' *Cornhill Magazine* 1 (1860): opposite page 617.   117

5.9   J.E. Millais, Illustration accompanying Chapters 5–6 of *Mistress and Maid*, *Good Words* 3 (1862): 161.   126

5.10   J.E. Millais, Illustration accompanying Chapters 21–23 of *Mistress and Maid*, *Good Words* 3 (1862): 609.   129

5.11   Simeon Solomon, Illustration for William Robertson, 'The Veiled Bride,' *Good Words* 3 (1862): 592.   130

5.12   J.E. Millais, Illustration accompanying Chapters 24–25 of *Mistress and Maid*, *Good Words* 3 (1862): 673.   132

5.13   Matthew Lawless, Illustration for [Dora Greenwell], 'The Bands of Love,' *Good Words* 3 (1862): 632.   133

5.14   Edward Hughes, 'Her clever fingers were passing over it rapidly,'
        Chapter 5, *Poor Miss Finch*, *Cassell's Magazine*, 9 September
        1871, 25.   151

5.15   Mary Ellen Edwards, 'Perchance it gave but a jealous glimpse,'
        illustration for H.G.B. Hunt, 'Found – A Veil,' *Cassell's
        Magazine*, 9 September 1871, 17.   152

5.16   Edward Hughes, 'Traced with a finger dipped in blood,'
        Chapter 11, *Poor Miss Finch*, *Cassell's Magazine*, 23 September
        1871, 57.   153

5.17   Mary Ellen Edwards, 'Stood at Gaze,' illustration for 'Over the
        Snow,' *Cassell's Magazine*, 2 December 1871, 209.   157

5.18   Mary Ellen Edwards, 'Flower-crowned hair with the berries
        between,' illustration for 'Led Captive,' *Cassell's Magazine*,
        16 December 1871, 241.   157

5.19   Mary Ellen Edwards, 'The buds of the crocus gay,' illustration
        for 'The Crocus,' *Cassell's Magazine*, 13 January 1872, 305.   157

5.20   Mary Ellen Edwards, 'Grasped in thy whiter hand,' illustration
        for William Sawyer, 'The Snowdrop,' *Cassell's Magazine*,
        3 February 1872, 353.   158

5.21   Edward Hughes, 'Miss Batchford rose to her feet,' Chapter 45,
        Poor Miss Finch, *Cassell's Magazine*, 3 February 1872, 361.   158

6.1   J.E. Millais, Frontispiece to *Good Words for 1862*.   179

Acknowledgements

I would like to acknowledge the efforts of staff at the British Library and the University of Leicester Library in locating material, as well as the unseen compilers of Dickens Journals Online who have helped to make this research possible. The illustrations were scanned and restored by Nick Walker. Some parts of the argument relating to Dinah Craik's *Mistress and Maid* have already appeared in 'Marketing Celebrity: Norman Macleod, Dinah Mulock Craik, and John Everett Millais in Alexander Strahan's *Good Words*,' *Victorian Periodicals Review* 46 (2013): 255–78 which is used with permission.

I am grateful to Janice Allan, Beth Palmer and Shafquat Towheed for their interest in earlier drafts of some sections of the book; also to Alexis Easley for her welcome feedback and suggestions. Both the anonymous Ashgate reader and editor Ann Donahue have provided practical and supportive comments, and I would like to thank Joanne Shattock for her encouragement. Finally, as in everything, thank you to George.

List of Abbreviations

AYR	*All the Year Round*
CassM	*Cassell's Magazine*
CIFP	*Cassell's Illustrated Family Paper*
CM	*Cornhill Magazine*
Collins, *Letters*	Collins, Wilkie. *The Letters of Wilkie Collins*, edited by William Baker and William M. Clarke. 2 vols. Basingstoke: Macmillan, 1999.
Collins, *The Public Face*	Collins, Wilkie. *The Public Face of Wilkie Collins: The Collected Letters*, edited by William Baker, Andrew Gasson, Graham Law and Paul Lewis. 4 vols. London: Pickering and Chatto, 2005.
Dickens, *Letters*	Dickens, Charles. *The Letters of Charles Dickens*, edited by Graham Storey, Kathleen Tillotson and Madeline House. 12 vols. Oxford: Clarendon Press, 1965–2002.
DJO	*Dickens Journals Online*. http://www.djo.org.uk.
DMVI	*A Database of Mid-Victorian Wood-Engraved Illustration*. http://www.dmvi.cf.ac.uk.
Gaskell, *Letters*	Gaskell, Elizabeth. *The Letters of Mrs Gaskell*, edited by J.A.V. Chapple and Arthur Pollard. 1966. Reprint, London: Mandolin, 1997.
Gaskell, *Further Letters*	Gaskell, Elizabeth. *Further Letters of Mrs Gaskell*, edited by John Chapple and Alan Sheldon. Manchester: Manchester University Press, 2000.
GW	*Good Words*
HW	*Household Words*
Slater, *Charles Dickens*	Slater, Michael. *Charles Dickens*. New Haven: Yale University Press, 2009.
Trollope, *Autobiography*	Trollope, Anthony. *Autobiography*. 1883. Reprint, London: Oxford University Press, 1950.
Trollope, *Letters*	Trollope, Anthony. *The Letters of Anthony Trollope*, edited by N. John Hall. 2 vols. Stanford: Stanford University Press, 1983.

Introduction:
Rereading the Novel

Elizabeth Gaskell wrote to publisher George Smith in 1860, 'I wish Mr Trollope would go on writing *Framley Parsonage* forever. I don't see any reason why it should ever come to an end'.[1] She had been reading month by month a new novel by Anthony Trollope serialized in Smith's newly launched periodical, *Cornhill Magazine*. Serialization was the process by which many nineteenth-century novels were published prior to their appearance in discrete volume form. Gaskell was not reading *Framley Parsonage* as a text which was fixed between covers; rather she was experiencing a novel which was both emerging from the throes of composition and functioning within the boundaries of a magazine. Any reading of the closed volume edition of a novel is thus a rereading of a text no longer interacting directly with the material and cultural frameworks which shaped the responses of the original serial readers. *Serialization and the Novel in Mid-Victorian Magazines* examines this original format of the novel as a serial by re-placing novels in the magazines which formed their original context. This approach prioritizes and then reads the serial as a text in its own right to shed new light on the nineteenth-century novel.

This book uses as case studies five novels serialized within periodicals which were designed for the new reading public of the mid nineteenth century. *Serialization and the Novel in Mid-Victorian Magazines* illustrates the contribution of three significant discourses within the 'multi-vocal discourse' of the periodical as defined by Laurel Brake and Julie Codell: namely those of the author, editor and periodical.[2] The five core texts for the discussion are Elizabeth Gaskell's *Cranford* (*Household Words*, 1851–53), Anthony Trollope's *Framley Parsonage* (*Cornhill Magazine*, 1860–61), Dinah Craik's *Mistress and Maid* (*Good Words*, 1862) and Wilkie Collins's *The Moonstone* (*All the Year Round*, 1868) and *Poor Miss Finch* (*Cassell's Magazine*, 1871–72). The vertical categories[3] of authorship, editing and the periodical are discussed in Chapters 2 to 4 and the horizontal progression of the serialized novel is treated in Chapter 5. Chapter 6 uses the 'after-life' of the serial to evaluate the serials against the fixed texts of the novels in order to assess the special impact of serialization within a periodical.

---

[1]   Elizabeth Gaskell to George Smith, 1 March 1860, Gaskell, *Letters*, 602.

[2]   Laurel Brake and Julie Codell, 'Encountering the Press,' in *Encounters in the Victorian Press*, ed. Laurel Brake and Julie Codell (Basingstoke: Palgrave Macmillan, 2004), 2.

[3]   This term is coined by Laurel Brake, 'Writing, Cultural Production and the Periodical Press in the Nineteenth Century,' in *Writing and Victorianism*, ed. J.B. Bullen (Harlow: Longman, 1997), 55.

In this book, a context for the serial in a magazine is established by examining the verbal and visual interactions which took place during the serialization. Mark Turner describes periodicals as 'essentially dialogic' and Deborah Wynne discovers 'new reading practices' in the 'dialogic form of the periodical press'.[4] Dialogues take place during the serialization of a novel between editor and contributor, between fiction and non-fiction and, at an external interface, between the periodicals themselves. Wynne debates how the 'lateral' reading of accompanying material 'supplemented and intensified the experience of reading' and Andrew Maunder defines the 'synchronic or inner relations' of the periodical created by the interspersed articles and serialized novels.[5] The role of illustrations and other visual material was significant in the composition and consumption of the novel as was the 'station' given to the serial within each issue. The text might also be valorized and consumed according to a hierarchy supplied by the editor or publisher; or the editor might lead the reader to a text positioned later in order to promote the consumption of particular items contained within the issue. Considering the mid-Victorian magazines studied here, for instance, *Cornhill Magazine* used patterns of alternation where few items other than the Editor's 'Roundabout Papers' were fixed in terms of position. *Good Words* kept its fiction within bounds by leading off with serious articles and concluding with recommendations for scripture reading whilst *All the Year Round* was almost invariably led by an instalment of a fictional serial. The novel's form and original reading context were shaped also by the incidence of publication whether monthly or weekly. Dickens, for example, complained on his own account about 'reading in … Teaspoons'[6] when he was writing *A Tale of Two Cities* which was being serialized weekly in *All the Year Round* as opposed to appearing in the more substantial instalments of the monthly format. The ongoing discussion of the contents between issues and the onward circulation of the magazine were, however, significant features of the serial as a reciprocal marketing tool. Inside an issue, the context of the serial and its relationship with connective texts or other interfaces were themselves localized factors in the original experience of the novel.

Norman Feltes sees traces of 'the concrete mediations of the historical' in the production of the novel[7] and the mediation of the serial is one of those 'modes of production' traceable in the text. This study addresses the influence of the material

---

[4]   Mark Turner, *Trollope and the Magazines: Gendered Issues in Mid-Victorian Britain* (Basingstoke: Macmillan, 2000), 7; Deborah Wynne, *The Sensation Novel and the Victorian Family Magazine* (Basingstoke: Palgrave, 2001), 3; 166; 167.

[5]   Wynne, 21; Andrew Maunder, '"Monitoring the Middle-Classes": Intertextuality and Ideology in Trollope's *Framley Parsonage* and the *Cornhill Magazine* 1859–60,' *Victorian Periodicals Review* 33 (2000): 53.

[6]   He wrote: 'you can better perceive my design by seeing it all together, instead of reading it in what Carlyle … calls "Teaspoons"' (Charles Dickens to Mrs William Howitt, 28 August 1859, Dickens, *Letters*, vol. 9, 113).

[7]   Norman. N. Feltes, *Modes of Publication of Victorian Novels* (Chicago: University of Chicago Press, 1986), x.

conditions of production and reception, illustrating the collective and collaborative creation of the novel and of the periodical. Analyses of the periodicals' structure, their language, illustrations, competing discourses and intertextual impact are the means of interrogating the novels in their contemporary context. This book reads, restores and rereads a range of texts as part of the nineteenth-century experience of print. As background to the role of the serial in the nineteenth-century periodical, Chapter 1 provides an overview of serialization. It also proposes a model for examining the serial as narrative. Chapters 2 to 4 take a vertical section or thematic view of the three voices within the periodical and more specifically within the five core magazines. These chapters analyse the serialized novel against the other competing narratives of publication grouped around the author, editor and periodical, stakeholder groups in the serial experience. In these chapters, the representative serials are assessed by isolating the voices in the multi-vocal discourse in order to broaden an understanding of collaboration in serial production. Chapter 4 provides a targeted introduction to those periodicals in which the novels appeared, noting the ways in which the novel was contextualized by the magazine within its overall output. This also includes the interaction of the serial with poetry, non-fiction serials, illustrations, the advice column and the editorial address.

Chapter 5 interrogates each core novel as a serialized text within a periodical series. The extended case studies in this chapter identify significant new readings of both novels and periodicals by highlighting the practices of collaboration and intertextuality arising from the consumption of the novel as a serial read in a context. The visual apprehension of the serial including the impact of the layout of the periodical and of the accompanying illustrations recapitulated and confirmed the text but also set up conflict and competition within the periodical series. This caused fluctuations in meaning between the serial as a text and the periodical as a text. The narrative growth of the story might be extended across the whole issue of a periodical but in addition, at the level of the series, the integration of the serial into the periodical was counterbalanced by the need to ensure that the periodical would carry on once that serial was concluded. It becomes clear from such an analysis using the detail of the five core novels that the process of serialization impacted on the serial itself and that the novels created were responses to periodical writing as well as to novel writing.

Finally, Chapter 6 examines the afterlife of the serialized novel by comparing the volume editions of both the core novels and the periodicals with their original serialized versions. The boundaries of the novel text were redrawn by the volume edition of the novel and were also restated in a new context by the volume edition of the periodical in which the reprinted serial then appeared. Robert Patten has pointed out that 'privileging the volume edition over the periodical issue distorts the nature of the fiction and the history of the book'.[8] The novel in its revised

---

[8] Robert Patten, 'Dickens as Serial Author: A Case of Multiple Identities,' in *Nineteenth-Century Media and the Construction of Identities*, ed. Laurel Brake, Bill Bell and David Finkelstein (Basingstoke: Palgrave, 2000), 137.

volume format still bears the imprint of its serialized original and the investigation into the periodicals which follows here both generates new readings and reinstates those which have been lost in the reprinting process.

The periodical was a 'time-released text'[9] which paradoxically denied its own importance by being date-stamped and expendable whilst at the same time pointing beyond itself to other numbers and other texts.[10] The composition and reception of novels within magazines was influenced during serialization by the process of reading, by reviewers and by audience feedback. In revisiting the serial as a timed text, this study can offer only selective discussion of the consumer of that text, and as Andrew King notes, there are dangers inherent in adopting a high-culture view of readers. King draws attention to the scarcity of studies of low prestige, high circulation titles.[11] There is an implied reader who has left some mark on the composition and reception of the novel but his or her influence can only be inferred. It is clear, however, that family magazines were designed to offer a stable and respectable niche in which to consume fiction and that the branding of the periodicals as a domestic reading space ensured the repeat and ongoing purchase of the publisher's output.

Lecturing in Edinburgh on 28 January 1870, Anthony Trollope explained pragmatically that 'the web of complex interactions uniting the writer, the reader and his publisher will have inevitable effects on the finished product, repercussions which must be considered in any complete evaluation of the work'.[12] In their ground-breaking study, Linda Hughes and Michael Lund demonstrate that 'publication format became an essential factor in creating meaning'.[13] This creation of meaning will be revived here through an analysis of the placement of the novels within the periodicals which gave them to the reading public of the nineteenth century. *Serialization and the Novel in Mid-Victorian Magazines* builds on existing critical approaches and research in order to provide an interpretative model for the novel as it originally appeared to readers like Gaskell: unfinished, unending and in a context.

---

[9]   Brake, 'Writing, Cultural Production and the Periodical Press,' 66.

[10]   See Margaret Beetham, 'Towards a Theory of the Periodical as a Publishing Genre,' in *Investigating Victorian Journalism*, ed. Laurel Brake, Aled Jones and Lionel Madden (Basingstoke: Macmillan, 1990), 26. Wynne describes periodicals as 'sites of simultaneity' (20).

[11]   Andrew King, *'The London Journal', 1845–83: Periodicals, Production and Gender* (Aldershot: Ashgate, 2004), 5; 16. See also, Jonathan Rose, 'Rereading the English Common Reader: A Preface to a History of Audiences,' *Journal of the History of Ideas* 53.1 (1992): 47–70.

[12]   Anthony Trollope, 'On English Prose Fiction as a Rational Amusement,' in *Four Lectures by Anthony Trollope*, ed. Morris L. Parrish (London: Constable, 1938), 91–124; quoted in Guinevere L. Griest, *Mudie's Circulating Library* (Newton Abbot: David and Charles, 1970), 2.

[13]   Linda K. Hughes and Michael Lund, *The Victorian Serial* (Charlottesville: University Press of Virginia, 1991), 2.

Chapter 1
Serialization and the Nineteenth-Century Periodical

The use of instalments was intrinsic to the development of the novel form in the nineteenth century. The serial had been associated with lower forms of literature but the instalment system became essential to the production process and to the economics of publishing for publishers, authors and editors. This chapter provides firstly some background to the serialization of the novel within the nineteenth-century periodical by discussing broader attitudes to serialization before moving on to the relationship between serial and periodical. This is then followed by a brief overview of the novels and magazines which form the core texts for the study as a whole. Finally there is a discussion of the periodical context for the serial including the use of illustration and of the paratexts which acted as boundaries in the serialization process.

Serialization in the Nineteenth Century

The serialization of a new work of fiction, in a periodical or by publishing in parts, meant that a novel was being read at intervals over a period of time. This had an impact on that novel in terms of both its composition and its reception. For the author it was essential to keep elements of the plot under discussion and to make characters recognisable when they reappeared from instalment to instalment. The author and his publisher also gained the benefit of the novel's being talked about by readers from week to week and month to month. The published parts used moments of tension or anticipation to encourage repeat buying. At the same time there was a danger of stereotyping or simplifying characters, and critics were scathing of the overuse of coincidence, crisis and padding.

The serialization of the novel in the nineteenth century derived in part from practices developed in the eighteenth century to service many types of literature.[1] Robert D. Mayo has pointed out that the potential audience for a serialized work in a magazine was only about two hundred thousand in 1800 and that such fiction during the period 1740 to 1815 was 'trashy, affected, and egregiously sentimental'.[2] A few decades later, a much larger audience of readers was being conditioned to approach the respectable consumption of fiction and other educational material

---

[1]   See R.M. Wiles, *Serial Publication in England before 1750* (Cambridge: Cambridge University Press, 1957).

[2]   Robert D. Mayo, *The English Novel and the Magazine 1740–1815* (London: Oxford University Press, 1962), 353; 351.

through reading in parts. Allan Dooley has suggested that serial publication in the nineteenth century grew as a result of the shortage of type to set up the pages of the novels. [3] Production in parts meant, however, that publishers could afford to produce literature and that consumers could afford to read and collect it. Robert Patten describes the serialization process as 'democratizing' book reading and book buying,[4] and the evolution of part publication and of the magazine printing of serials demonstrates how the two forms of serialization were to some extent co-dependent in popularizing the reading of fiction.

This apparent alliance between commercial imperatives and the new reading public in the mid nineteenth century was, however, heavily criticized by reviewers of the period. The *Spectator* commented of the first instalment of *Nicholas Nickleby* that there was 'just enough to serve as a meal to the mob of readers',[5] and in March 1843, John Wilson Croker in the *Quarterly Review* predicted 'early oblivion' for the serialization of new fiction.[6] *The Pickwick Papers* had first appeared monthly from April 1836 until November 1837 and, in his Preface to the cheap volume edition of 1847, Dickens reported: 'My friends told me it was a low, cheap form of publication by which I should ruin all my rising hopes'.[7] In the Preface to the first collected *Pickwick* of 1837, Dickens described his 'general design' as simple enough to appear in 'this detached and desultory form'. His success in that form, in both monthly parts and weekly periodical parts, gave him the authority to develop a structure beyond the 'gentle and not unnatural progress of adventure'[8] which characterized *Pickwick*. Much later he used that authority to write a 'Postscript in lieu of Preface' to *Our Mutual Friend*, dated 2 September 1865. In this, he explained the difficulty of his design for that novel, originally serialized in 20 parts:

> it would be very unreasonable to expect that many readers, pursuing a story in portions from month to month through nineteen months[9] will, until they have it before them complete, perceive the relations of its finer threads to the whole pattern which is always before the eyes of the story-weaver at his loom.

───────────

   [3]   Allan Dooley, *Author and Printer in Victorian England* (Charlottesville: University Press of Virginia, 1992), 148. See also Simon Eliot, 'The Business of Victorian Publishing,' in *The Cambridge Companion to the Victorian Novel*, ed. Deirdre David (Cambridge: Cambridge University Press, 2001), 55.

   [4]   Robert L. Patten, *Charles Dickens and His Publishers* (Oxford; Clarendon, 1978), 45. Patten lists twelve reasons for the growth of serialization during the thirty years after *The Pickwick Papers* (54).

   [5]   *Spectator* 11 (31 March 1838) 304; repr., *Dickens: The Critical Heritage*, ed. Philip Collins (London: Routledge and Kegan Paul, 1971), 69.

   [6]   *Quarterly Review* 71 (1843), 502–28; repr., Collins, ed., 137.

   [7]   Charles Dickens, *The Pickwick Papers*, ed. Robert L. Patten (1972; repr., Harmondsworth: Penguin, 1986), 45.

   [8]   Dickens, *The Pickwick Papers*, 41.

   [9]   The last part was, as usual, a double number.

He then harked back to his original success twenty years before:

> Yet, that I hold the advantages of the mode of publication to outweigh the disadvantages, may be easily believed of one who revived it in the Pickwick Papers after long disuse, and has pursued it ever since.[10]

Where Dickens saw publishing in parts as a craft, critics saw the form of the serial as counter-creative. In 1855, a reviewer in the *North British Review* protested that 'Art will not endure piecemeal generation'.[11] Although complimenting *David Copperfield*, a writer in the *Prospective Review* in 1851 observed that 'The serial tale … is probably the lowest artistic form yet invented … which affords the greatest excuse for unlimited departures from … consistency, completeness and proportion'.[12] The *Morning Advertiser* in 1852 insisted that 'the instalment system … is by no means conducive to a fair estimate of the ability of a fiction-writer, or the coherence and construction of his story'. The reviewer reinforced the viewpoint of the critics of high culture by describing serialization as 'a series of spasmodic efforts at fixed intervals, rather than the performance of continuous and homogeneous work, in which the due proportion of its parts shall be symmetrically contrived'.[13] Reviewing the volume edition of *Framley Parsonage*, the *Westminster Review* commented that 'the habit of writing a story in periodical instalments is almost always fatal to that coherence and proportion without which no work can lay claim to any really artistic merit'.[14] The anonymous reviewer objected to novel-writing on this model as a type of industrial production like 'Manchester goods … retailed at so much per yard'.[15] The cottage industry conjured up by Dickens was transmuted into mass production and commercial exchange.

Where authors could see artistic control, critics identified commercialization and lack of direction. Anthony Trollope himself called it the 'rushing mode of publication' but the *Westminster Review* differentiated George Eliot's publication in parts, observing that 'she makes those pauses and gives us those breaks which are so necessary for repose in the enjoyment of a work of art'.[16] *Middlemarch*, for instance, was scheduled to appear in eight half volumes at two-monthly intervals

---

[10]   Charles Dickens, *Our Mutual Friend*, ed. Stephen Gill (1971; repr., Harmondsworth: Penguin, 1982), 893.

[11]   *North British Review* (1855), 350; quoted in Kathleen Tillotson, *Novels of the Eighteen-Forties* (1954; repr., Oxford: Oxford University Press, 1961), 39.

[12]   '*David Copperfield* and *Pendennis*,' *Prospective Review* 7 (1851), 158.

[13]   *Morning Advertiser*, 3 July 1852, 3; quoted in Brahma Chaudhuri, 'Dickens's Serial Structure in *Bleak House*,' *The Dickensian* 86, no. 2 (1990): 71.

[14]   Unsigned notice of *Framley Parsonage*, *Westminster Review* 76 (1861), repr., *Trollope: The Critical Heritage*, ed. Donald Smalley (London: Routledge and Kegan Paul, 1969), 131.

[15]   Unsigned notice of *Framley Parsonage*, 134.

[16]   Trollope, *Autobiography*, 138; unsigned review of *Middlemarch*, *Westminster Review* n. s. 39 (1872): 276–7.

corresponding to the 'books' within the novel.[17] *Daniel Deronda* appeared monthly from February to September 1876, maintaining this half-volume length for each instalment. Reviewing the first part of the novel, the *London Globe and Traveller* went further in distinguishing Eliot from other authors of part-work serials: 'George Eliot may be published in parts, but she writes with a view to the effect of the whole. Dickens made every part a little whole in itself; ... he reads better piece-meal. Thackeray's characters were like our acquaintance [and we] cared for their society more than their history'.[18] It seems that the association with Eliot whose parts comprised substantial portions of her novels could elevate the status of the part-work serial. The *Non Conformist* of 21 February 1872 acknowledged, again with reference to *Middlemarch*, that 'a separate publication makes more pretension [than monthly instalments in magazines], and is not to be ... cavalierly treated'.[19]

The overtly commercial, repeat-buying arrangement of a periodical seems thus to have made the production treadmill of serialization more prominent in the minds of critics. In addition, periodical serialization had a long association with lower forms of literature and poor production values. Dickens mentions in his 1847 preface to *The Pickwick Papers* the shilling numbers of 'interminable novels' sold by pedlars around the country.[20] Although this might suggest that his claims of having revived the practice are rather exaggerated, by the mid nineteenth century he and many other novelists had honed their deployment of this part-work process.

For nineteenth-century critics, the serial – and especially the serial within a periodical – threatened the boundaries of art. It appeared effectively to be authored by a group or collective within the pages of the periodical issue. Laurel Brake has observed that the authorship of a serial is 'collective ... [through] intertextuality and editing' and Mary Hamer calls it 'a group activity'.[21] John Sutherland now regards novels as 'the outcome of collaboration, compromise or commission'[22] whereas contemporary reviewers maintained the view that literature was to be valued by (their) absolute artistic standards of individualized authorship and not by the needs or fluctuations of the market. Anonymity or attribution to the group was viewed by contemporary critics as contrary to an expressed need for ownership

---

[17]   In the event the parts appeared in December 1871, February, April, June and (at the end of) July 1872 and concluded in October, November and December 1872.

[18]   *London Globe and Traveller*, 31 January 1876, 6; quoted in Carol A. Martin, *George Eliot's Serial Fiction* (Columbus: Ohio State University Press, 1994), 238–9.

[19]   Quoted in Martin, 202.

[20]   Dickens, *The Pickwick Papers*, 44.

[21]   Laurel Brake, *Print in Transition, 1850–1910: Studies in Media and Book History* (Basingstoke: Palgrave, 2001), 18; Mary Hamer, *Writing by Numbers: Trollope's Serial Fiction* (Cambridge: Cambridge University Press, 1987), 1.

[22]   John Sutherland, *Victorian Novelists and Publishers* (London: Athlone Press, 1976), 6.

and identification. In addition, new serialized fiction was dangerously incomplete and appeared not to be shaped or sculpted. The serial within a magazine also enjoyed horizontal integration with other embedded texts and was in competition and dialogue with these other texts. Such a serial existed in a form that was not bounded and absolute. Finally, it could not be a work of art precisely because it was date-stamped and apparently ephemeral so that in spite of its collection into a whole, the serial would always betray the marks of its composition and the contingency of its original evolution.

In 1859, the critic E.S. Dallas wrote a series of articles entitled 'Popular Literature' in *Blackwood's Edinburgh Magazine* which highlighted the ephemeral, miscellaneous and popular character of the periodical and of fiction serialized in a magazine. The first two articles in this series were subtitled 'The Periodical Press' and appeared in January and February 1859; 'Tracts' followed in May and 'Prize Essays' in December.[23] Dallas described periodical literature as 'essentially a popular literature' and he highlighted the 'manifold forces' of speed of production allied with increased literacy, indicating that the accumulation of popular literature had caused it to gain 'critical value'. It had become 'a mine of wealth' rather than 'a collection of curiosities'. [24] He saw this popularity actually resulting from the periodical being miscellaneous and 'a creature of the day' produced for 'the appreciation not of the few, but of the many'.[25] He also countered that: 'Even in the issue of works which are not of an ephemeral nature … publishers find the advantage of serial publication'.[26] He was referring here to reprints of novels and reference works sold in parts which, from their origins in the eighteenth century, had gained greater impetus in the early nineteenth century as a result of the growth in the reading public. Dallas reminded the readers of *Blackwood's* that their own magazines used a wide range of subjects as 'cause and effect of popularity': 'there will be an essay on fly-fishing immediately after an exposure of the weaknesses of the Turkish empire, or a tale of the most exalted love after a long dissertation on the nebular hypothesis'.[27]

A little over two years later, Dallas revisited this discussion when he used a review of the three-volume edition of *Great Expectations* to defend the serialization of that novel in a periodical. He differentiated between the monthly and weekly formats and nonetheless concluded that 'the weekly form of publication is not incompatible with a very high order of fiction'.[28] The 1860s produced a wider

---

[23]   [E.S. Dallas], 'Popular Literature – The Periodical Press,' *Blackwood's Edinburgh Magazine* 85 (1859): 96–112; 180–95; 'Popular Literature – Tracts,' *Blackwood's Edinburgh Magazine* 85 (1859): 515–32; 'Popular Literature – Prize Essays,' *Blackwood's Edinburgh Magazine* 86 (1859): 681–89.

[24]   [Dallas], 'Popular Literature – The Periodical Press,' 101; 99; 96.

[25]   [Dallas], 'Popular Literature – The Periodical Press,' 101.

[26]   [Dallas], 'Popular Literature – The Periodical Press,' 101.

[27]   [Dallas], 'Popular Literature – The Periodical Press,' 101.

[28]   [E.S. Dallas], '*Great Expectations*,' *The Times*, 17 October 1861, 6.

range of novels appearing as serials in periodicals which could be promoted to this 'high order' in spite of the fact that their original production and dissemination was tainted by association with the penny journals of the earlier part of the century and with the alternate 'popular literature' in wide circulation. Part of this success was attributable to the affordability and availability of serials which Dallas had described in 1859. It was also a matter of the familiarity that both part works and periodicals came to have within readers' lives. Dickens himself drew attention to the illusion of passing time created by serialization in one of his later letters when he described a serial as 'a story nine or ten months long'.[29] After Dickens's death the *Illustrated London News* trivialized 'the feeling of continual dependence on the living author' who thus became 'personally indispensable' to his readers 'just as if we received a letter or a visit at regular intervals from a kindly observant gossip'.[30] There was thus a sense of shared time and shared experience which has modern-day equivalents in the soap opera.[31] In terms of magazine publication, Laurel Brake points out that the day of issue for a nineteenth-century periodical created a linked community of readers,[32] the ultimate in contingent experience and shared temporality at a time when opportunities for communication and the wider promulgation of knowledge were beginning to be exploited.

Broadly it is undisputed that the number of readers and their access to print increased markedly in the nineteenth century as a result of education, print technology and increased urbanization. The seminal discussion is still that of Richard Altick in *The English Common Reader*, although Jonathan Rose expresses concern that the lack of direct, representational evidence means that any study can only be partial and is often far from impartial.[33] The production of serials and of novels was influenced not just by the number of readers but also by the act of reading. Hughes and Lund conclude that it is necessary to consider 'the impact of reading strategies on the production of meaning' and Andrew King has pointed out that meaning is created by readers through their interaction with texts.[34] Other critics see the nature of reading changed by the location for that reading and by the company kept by the reader to the extent that meaning is 'contingent … on

---

[29]   Charles Dickens to Mrs Brookfield, 24 January 1866, Dickens, *Letters*, vol. 9, 144.

[30]   'The Late Charles Dickens,' *Illustrated London News*, 18 June 1870, 639.

[31]   See Jennifer Hayward, *Consuming Pleasures: Active Audiences and Serial Fictions from Dickens to Soap Operas* (Lexington: University of Kentucky Press, 1997).

[32]   Brake, *Print in Transition*, 11.

[33]   Richard Altick, *The English Common Reader: A Social History of the Mass Reading Public, 1800–1900* (Chicago: University of Chicago Press, 1957); Jonathan Rose, 'Rereading the English Common Reader: A Preface to a History of Audiences,' *Journal of the History of Ideas* 53 (1992): 47–70.

[34]   Linda K. Hughes and Michael Lund, *The Victorian Serial* (Charlottesville: University Press of Virginia, 1991), 276; Andrew King, *'The London Journal', 1845–83: Periodicals, Production and Gender* (Aldershot: Ashgate, 2004), 11. King builds on the earlier study and discusses eight elements of periodical production (King, 49–81).

the materiality of the text'.[35] The experience of actually seeing the novel in a magazine is assessed in a later discussion in this book. In Chapter 5 the 'material framework'[36] of individual serials is a major element in the process of re-placing and rereading the serials in their original context and intertext.

Contemporary critics appear to have found it distasteful that the new nineteenth-century readership was in a direct and ongoing commercial relationship with the periodical through which the novel was being produced. Christopher Kent suggests that this arose in part because the incomplete serialization implied subordination to an editor and thus to the commercial imperatives of the periodical, and Bill Bell observes that the 'serial commodity-text' was seen to be 'compromised by the mediation of its new productive frame ... [and] overdetermined ... by the constraints of readerly expectation and productive convention'.[37] The periodicals in their turn created other imperatives for reading and repeat purchase. A magazine like the *Cornhill* might be linked with 'social differentiation' with fiction as a reward for shared values.[38] In the process of this identification with the text, there was also seepage between the reader's life and the life of that text. Mark Turner asserts that the reader could in effect alter the text and Kathleen Tillotson observes that there was a special type of contract existing between the author of the serial and his reader precisely because the ending might not be written.[39] The serial occupied a place within the number of the periodical and its accompanying matter. Each issue looked forward both to the future completion of the serial and the ongoing life of the series which contained it. While the story unfolded there was always the possibility of alternative endings and readings as well as influence over the serial from reviews or reader feedback.

As will be demonstrated through the discussion of editorship in Chapter 3, the periodical series and the serial within it were operating both in parallel

---

[35] James Raven, Helen Small and Naomi Tadmor, 'Introduction,' *The Practice and Representation of Reading in England* (Cambridge: Cambridge University Press, 1996), 12. See also Tom Keymer, 'Reading Time and Serial Fiction Before Dickens,' *Yearbook of English Studies* 30 (2000): 34–45 and Nicholas Dames, *The Physiology of the Novel* (Oxford: Oxford University Press, 2007), 25–70.

[36] Hughes and Lund, *The Victorian Serial*, 9.

[37] Christopher Kent, 'Victorian Periodicals and the Constructing of Victorian Reality,' in *Victorian Periodicals: A Guide to Research*, vol.2, ed. J. Don Vann and Rosemary T. Van Arsdel (New York: MLA, 1989), 2; Bill Bell, 'Fiction and the Marketplace: Towards a Study of the Victorian Serial,' in *Serials and their Readers 1620–1914*, ed. Robin Myers and Michael Harris (Winchester: St Paul's Bibliographies, 1993), 128; 129.

[38] Andrew Maunder, '"Discourses of Distinction": The Reception of the *Cornhill Magazine* 1859–60,' *Victorian Periodicals Review* 32 (1999): 240; Stephen Elwell, 'Editors and Social Change: A Case Study of *Once a Week* (1859–80),' in *Innovators and Preachers: the Role of the Editor in Victorian England*, ed. Joel H. Wiener, (Westport, Ct.: Greenwood Press, 1985), 39.

[39] Mark Turner, *Trollope and the Magazines: Gendered Issues in Mid-Victorian Britain* (Basingstoke: Macmillan, 2000), 15; Tillotson, 26.

and in conflict. Louis James suggests that the 'format itself becomes a form of communication ... a way of conditioning our response', [40] and the novel serialized within the periodical offers up a number of paradoxes as 'a form of communication'. The serialized instalment appeared as a periodical piece similar to the texts within which it was embedded. At the same time, that instalment had to be differentiated from occasional pieces and other serials because of its participation in the wider task of completing a narrative stretching over longer periods of time. The individual issues of the periodical and instalments of the serial might appear to operate under the control of the editor, but at the same time the novel itself was dependent on contingency and affected by the conditions of production, the availability of material and the circumstances under which the text was read. At the outer boundary of the novel, the need to close the individual serial challenged the reader's relationship with the ongoing periodical series. In addition, the periodical series might itself be re-launched, and perhaps change format or binding to encourage collection of the periodical without regard to the serial being followed within. Through their collective physical appearance on the reader's shelf, the individual issues became symbolic of both an ongoing relationship and the shared values of readership. In this way the reading of the periodical was not only about education and amusement but might also be about display, control and ownership.

The periodical was open-ended and boundless as a text but it also operated weekly or monthly within the boundaries of page limit, type layout and costs. By reinstating these boundaries and so rereading the novel in its original context *Serialization and the Novel in Mid-Victorian Magazines* endeavours to recover the creative paradox of the novel, both open and closed within in its original and commercial periodical space.

Novels Serialized in Magazines of the Mid Nineteenth Century

This book rereads five novels which were serialized in periodicals over a twenty-year period: Elizabeth Gaskell's *Cranford* (*Household Words*, 1851–53), Anthony Trollope's *Framley Parsonage* (*Cornhill Magazine*, 1860–61), Dinah Craik's *Mistress and Maid* (*Good Words*, 1862) and Wilkie Collins's *The Moonstone* (*All the Year Round*, 1868) and *Poor Miss Finch* (*Cassell's Magazine*, 1871–72). A table of dates including those of other contemporary serials is provided at Appendix 1. A range of other texts is also used for the purposes of illustration. This includes *Bleak House*, which was being issued in parts during the appearance of *Cranford*, *Hard Times*, which appeared in *Household Words* in 1854, *North and South* (also in *Household Words* in 1855) and *A Tale of Two Cities*, which launched

---

[40]   Louis James, 'The Trouble with Betsey: Periodicals and the Common Reader in Mid Nineteenth-Century England,' in *The Victorian Periodical Press: Samplings and Soundings*, ed. E.J. Shattock and Michael Wolff (Leicester: Leicester University Press, 1982), 351.

All the Year Round in 1859. Anthony Trollope's *The Small House at Allington* which also appeared in *Cornhill Magazine* (1862–64) and *The Last Chronicle of Barset* which was issued in parts in 1867 provide a context for the Barsetshire series discussed in Chapter 6. Collins's *Man and Wife*, which preceded *Poor Miss Finch* in *Cassell's Magazine* in 1869–70, serves to demonstrate the effect of the *Magazine* on the novelist's established style and the impact of this new periodical context. The instalments of these serials were retrospectively smoothed into new wholes when the novels were reprinted in volume form. As shown later, however, novelists continued to draw the attention of the readers of subsequent versions of the novel to the ongoing relationship created by the original serialization.

Each of the novels in periodicals originated as part of a miscellany to be read within an allocated weekly or monthly time frame while time passed in the life of the reader. Features such as the message of the magazine and the context for the serial indicate ways in which the novels came to have a competitive or comparative place within the mid nineteenth-century magazine. Thus *Mistress and Maid* had a targeted life within a household, literally to be read by mistress and maid whilst *Cranford* evolved in *Household Words* as a non-sequential serial located in discussions of other near-historical events or parodies of contemporary malpractice. Some of the magazines reviewed novels and offered advice to would-be writers who were both reading the serial and rereading the volume edition. Periodicals also marketed reprinted novels by their contributing authors and publicized related events such as Dickens's public readings, which were advertised within *All the Year Round* during the serialization of *The Moonstone*.

The five periodicals in which these novels were serialized had been launched to serve the maturing market for reading which had developed by the 1850s. A table of dates, prices and editors is supplied at Appendix 2. *Household Words* was launched in 1850 and adopted a journalistic style which emerged from Dickens's earlier experiences as a newspaper reporter and magazine writer. *Oliver Twist* had appeared irregularly as sketches in *Bentley's Magazine* from February 1837 to April 1839, and *The Old Curiosity Shop* evolved from within *Master Humphrey's Clock* beginning on 25 April 1840 before appearing weekly from 16 May until 6 February 1841.[41] *Cassell's Magazine* began under the title of *Cassell's Illustrated Family Paper* in 1853, providing educational articles and advice to accompany its pot-boiling fiction. *Cornhill Magazine* and *All the Year Round* which succeeded *Household Words* were specifically established as vehicles for fiction in 1859–60. *Good Words* was founded at about the same time and was a religious paper with an evangelical voice which presented fiction and illustrations as educational. *Cassell's Magazine* evolved from the *Family Paper* as a response to the fiction market in the late 1860s but retained the readership and reputation of its predecessor, and eventually returned to an updated version of that original format as *Cassell's Family Magazine* in 1874. These periodicals all demonstrated an awareness of their family readership. As early as 1844 the first volume of *The Family Herald*

---

[41] Slater, *Charles Dickens*, 93–124; 158–74.

had claimed that 'great poets have written many things we would not print ... A periodical for the public must be more discreet than a bound book'.[42] This was because the accompanying material was targeting a family audience. Ease of access to unsuitable texts would be frowned upon and had the potential to damage circulation. Reading was also believed to be appropriate only during leisure time on a Sunday, and this limited the place of fiction for family consumption in the periodical. *The Graphic* weekly illustrated newspaper remarked sternly in 1875 in a review of other magazines: 'The serial stories in the *Leisure Hour*, besides being very readable, are always thoroughly wholesome, which cannot be said of all serial stories in these days'.[43]

The novels in this study have been chosen because of their origins as serials in the context of magazines. *Cranford* was an unplanned, incidental serial; *Framley Parsonage* and *The Moonstone* were planned but written by authors with very different experience of serialization; *Mistress and Maid* and *Poor Miss Finch* were targeted at a specific magazine audience. This selection is inevitably based on *post hoc* factors which have made the texts significant both in themselves and as works representative of the careers of their authors. *Cranford* became Gaskell's first serialized novel retrospectively when the sketches were collected together in 1853 and the progression of the individual pieces illustrates Gaskell's involvement with Dickens as editor. Of her other novels, *Mary Barton* had already appeared as a three-volume novel in 1848 whilst *Ruth* was published in 1853 and *Sylvia's Lovers* in 1863. *North and South* was serialized weekly in *Household Words*, and *Cousin Phillis* and *Wives and Daughters* monthly in *Cornhill Magazine*.[44] In the case of Anthony Trollope, *Framley Parsonage* launched one of the most famous family magazines of the century but the novel was also part of a series itself already in progress. Trollope's previous novels had been published in volume form but he would prove himself ready to explore all forms of publication in the 47 novels he produced during his writing career.[45] *Mistress and Maid* was a novel with a purpose whose success was dependant on the sequence of Craik's publications in the wake of her enormously popular *John Halifax, Gentleman* of 1856. The serial appeared in 1862 when 'the Author of *John Halifax, Gentleman*' was a household name. Although she had been long associated with periodicals such as *Chambers's Edinburgh Journal*, *Mistress and Maid* was Craik's first serialized novel and she would go on to be serialized in *Macmillan's Magazine* and *St Pauls* as well as

---

[42]   *The Family Herald*, 17 February 1844; quoted in Sally Mitchell, 'The Forgotten Woman of the Period: Penny Weekly Family Magazines of the 1840s and 1850s,' in *A Widening Sphere: Changing Roles of Victorian Women*, ed. Martha Vicinus (1977; repr., London: Methuen, 1980), 43.

[43]   *The Graphic*, 9 January 1875, 42.

[44]   See Appendix 1.

[45]   For a summary of Trollope's publications, see the Appendix to Hamer, *Writing by Numbers*.

producing other novels in volume form.[46] After Wilkie Collins's fourth novel *The Dead Secret* was serialized in *Household Words* in 1857, all his 17 subsequent novels appeared in periodicals.[47] After the muted response to *Armadale* serialized in the *Cornhill* (1864–66), *The Moonstone* restored Collins's popularity by returning to the style of his earlier serial, *The Woman in White*. With the two novels which followed *The Moonstone* – including *Poor Miss Finch* – he sought a new audience in the relaunched *Cassell's Magazine* and thence, for his subsequent novels, still other readers including those of *The Graphic*, *Belgravia* and a range of provincial newspapers.[48]

Graham Law identifies a 'fundamental economic doubleness about the periodical form'[49] in that it was both random and piecemeal but at the same time complex and calculated. Robert Patten writes that serialization affects the convention of single authorship, the genre of fiction, its self-containedness and the timing of the story's reception.[50] The serial is part of a 'larger collaborative project' and is influenced by its ongoing reception and position within topical subject matter or passing events.[51] It is influenced also by the closest accompanying matter, its textual framing and its illustrations.

Illustration and the 'Threshold'

The concept of illustration within serialized fiction was originally closely associated with the category of 'cheap literature'. In *Blackwood's*, Dallas described his subject matter for 'Popular Literature' as 'a multitude of journals and serials, most of them profusely illustrated, and all of them devoted to fiction, published at a penny or less and intended for the most ignorant of readers'.[52] Three of the five core texts for this study were originally serialized in illustrated magazines. Chapter 5 will consider both the illustrations accompanying the serial and those accompanying the textual material in which that serial was embedded. In order to provide a context for this discussion of the individual novels, the section which follows here discusses the ways in which illustrations were deployed. The discussion broadens out to include the idea of the textual threshold which is relevant to the visual display of the serial

---

[46] *The Woman's Kingdom* appeared in *Good Words* in 1868; *A Brave Lady* in *Macmillan's Magazine* in 1869–70 and *Hannah* in *St Paul's* in 1871.

[47] See Graham Law, *Serializing Fiction in the Victorian Press* (Basingstoke: Palgrave, 2000), 171; 184.

[48] See Graham Law, 'Wilkie in the Weeklies: The Serialization and Syndication of Collins's Late Novels,' *Victorian Periodicals Review* 30 (1997): 244–5.

[49] Law, *Serializing Fiction*, 35.

[50] Robert L. Patten, 'Dickens as Serial Author: A Case of Multiple Identities,' in *Nineteenth-Century Media and the Construction of Identities*, ed. Laurel Brake, Bill Bell and David Finkelstein (Basingstoke: Palgrave, 2000), 140.

[51] Patten, 144; 150.

[52] [Dallas], 'Popular Literature – The Periodical Press,' 100.

within the magazine. This section considers the idea of paratextual framing and its contribution to a visual experience of the contents of the periodical within the 'enabling space'[53] of print.

It was Dickens who made illustration respectable in his monthly part serializations although his serials within periodicals were not illustrated for the simple reason that the weekly *Household Words* and *All the Year Round* did not carry illustrations. In the first half of the century illustration was based on caricature as used in *The Pickwick Papers* and *Nicholas Nickleby*. After the 1850s, illustrations adopted the style of English genre painting, which addressed itself more closely to the representation of the action of the novel.[54] Reviewing Gustave Doré's illustrations for *Don Quixote*, a columnist in *All the Year Round* complained in 1867 that 'our own book-artists of the new school give us well-executed pictures about nothing.'[55] George Eliot wrote to Frederick Leighton who had illustrated *Romola* in *Cornhill Magazine* in 1862: 'I am convinced that illustrations can only form a sort of overture to the text. The artist who uses the pencil must otherwise be tormented to misery by the deficiencies or requirements of the one who uses the pen, and the writer on the other hand, must die of impossible expectations.'[56] Illustrations might thus be viewed as opportunities for separation between novelist and artist despite the co-ordinated visual experience of the reader. Judith Fisher maintains, however, that periodicals of the second half of the century prioritized the text,[57] a process made possible by the changing timescales of production.

The idea of a collaboration has been taken up more readily among literary commentators who have described the illustrator as the first critic of a novel with the illustration itself as an *aide memoire*, so that 'graphic criticism' and an 'expanded text' are produced through the inclusion of illustrations. [58]As Mary Elizabeth Leighton and Lisa Surridge have indicated in their recent studies, however, the illustrations were themselves an element of the plot. [59] The illustrations in their context affected the narrative and were intrinsic to the first reading experience of the novel. Some of the serials under discussion were not illustrated when they

---

[53]   Margaret Beetham, 'Towards a Theory of the Periodical as a Publishing Genre,' in *Investigating Victorian Journalism*, ed. Laurel Brake, Aled Jones and Lionel Madden (Basingstoke: Macmillan, 1990), 25.

[54]   See Judith L. Fisher, 'Image Versus Text in the Illustrated Novels of William Makepeace Thackeray,' in *Victorian Literature and the Victorian Visual Imagination*, ed. Carol T. Christ and John O. Jordan (Berkeley: University of California Press, 1995), 60–87.

[55]   'Book Illustration,' *AYR*, 10 August 1867, 155.

[56]   George Eliot, *The George Eliot Letters*, ed. Gordon S. Haight, vol. 4 (New Haven: Yale University Press), 55–6.

[57]   Fisher, 61.

[58]   Elizabeth Cayzer, 'Dickens and his Late Illustrators: A Change in Style: "Phiz" and *A Tale of Two Cities*,' *The Dickensian* 86, no. 3 (1990): 140; 131; Arlene M. Jackson, *Illustration and the Novels of Thomas Hardy* (Macmillan: Basingstoke, 1981), xiii; xi.

[59]   Mary Elizabeth Leighton and Lisa Surridge, '"The Plot Thickens": Towards a Narratology of Illustrated Serial Fiction in the 1860s,' *Victorian Studies* 51 (2008): 65–101.

were republished as volumes whilst others acquired illustrations in reprinted formats. This highlights that there is a potential rereading which will take place when the novel reappears in its volume form. Thus the volume edition of *Mistress and Maid* published by Hurst and Blackett in 1863 was not illustrated apart from a frontispiece which was supplied from Millais's *Good Words* illustrations.[60] *The Moonstone* was illustrated in *Harper's Weekly Magazine* where it was serialized in parallel with its non-illustrated appearance in *All the Year Round*.[61] Having appeared un-illustrated in Bentley's 1872 edition, *Poor Miss Finch* was reunited with its magazine illustrations when the novel was reprinted by Chatto and Windus in 1875 but the serial was still widely available with its original illustrations and other periodical matter in the reprint of *Cassell's Magazine* for 1871–72.

In terms of the periodicals themselves, *Cornhill Magazine* was illustrated from its first appearance whereas *Cassell's Magazine* developed its style of illustration through its other incarnations. *Good Words* followed the *Cornhill* in using illustration but also picked up the educative power of pictures from the earlier *Cassell's Illustrated Family Paper*. Critics discuss the physical appearance of illustrations by differentiating between decorative capitals and vignettes as opposed to single-page or integrated half-page illustrations.[62] This should not ignore the importance of the reception conditions of any illustration which may carry a connoted message or counter narrative. Phillip Alllingham observes that illustrations condition reader-response and 'may connote more than the text denoted', and for Patricia Anderson, the 'connoted' message of an illustration may be recovered from the combined impact of its literal appearance, its place within an accompanying commentary and is cumulative symbolic or social context.[63] Brian Maidment describes how single-page images create 'a "counter" or "meta" narrative to the main text', and Judith Fisher draws attention to the 'countervoices' of image and text and the ways in which these two components destabilize each other.[64]

Cornhill Magazine used single detached images for *Framley Parsonage* making the separated illustrations a significant part of the reading experience of the fictional serial. The 'connoted' message of illustrations across the serialization was also created through visual references which can be identified running across

---

[60]   Originally published in February 1862.

[61]   See Mary Elizabeth Leighton and Lisa Surridge, 'The Transatlantic *Moonstone*: A Study of the Illustrated Serial in *Harper's Weekly*,' *Victorian Periodicals Review* 42 (2009): 207–40.

[62]   See Brian Maidment, *Reading Popular Prints 1790–1870*, 2nd ed. (Manchester: Manchester University Press, 2001), 9; Fisher, 85, note 6.

[63]   Philip Allingham, 'Robert Barnes' Illustrations for Thomas Hardy's *The Mayor of Casterbridge* as Serialised in *The Graphic*,' *Victorian Periodicals Review* 28 (1995): 32; Patricia Anderson, *The Printed Image and the Transformation of Popular Culture 1790–1860* (Oxford: Clarendon Press, 1991), 58–60.

[64]   Fisher, 61; 72.

the accompanying factual serials and poems. [65] The *Cornhill*'s longer production schedule also allowed the integration of other visual features such as the capitals which set the comic tone of Thackeray's own fiction and of his 'Roundabout Papers' as editor. *Good Words* and *Cassell's Magazine* used the embedded half-page illustration on the first page of each instalment of novel-text. [66] The resulting 'counter narrative' is particularly marked in the serialization of Collins's novels not only in the illustrations for the serial itself but also at points where the novel is set against illustrations for the accompanying poems in the numbers of *Cassell's Magazine*. The combined verbal and visual units[67] across the issues of the magazine produce a reinterpretation of the novel through the competitive discourse which can be rediscovered in that serial context.

Brian Maidment points out that these illustrations should not be regarded as 'failed paintings'[68] but it is nonetheless clear that both the *Cornhill* and *Good Words* relied to some extent on the recognition of John Everett Millais as a painter in his contribution to these periodicals and to *Framley Parsonage* and *Mistress and Maid* among other serialized novels. George Smith suggested Millais as illustrator for *Framley Parsonage* on 20 January 1860, and Trollope wrote enthusiastically back to him on 12 February: 'Should I live to see my story illustrated by Millais nobody would be able to hold me.'[69] Looking back in his *Autobiography*, Trollope called Millais's contribution 'conscientious': 'In every figure that he drew it was his object to promote the views of the writer whose work he had undertaken to illustrate, and he never spared himself any pains in studying that work, so as to enable him to do so.'[70] As so often in the retrospective of his life, Trollope was gilding the lily since at the time he expressed concerns that Millais was not devoting enough time to the serial particularly when he discovered that the illustration for Chapter 16 of *Framley Parsonage* represented the very last line of the chapter.[71] In his *Autobiography* Trollope carried on the illusion of fruitful cooperation[72] but Michael Mason claims that serial assignments were less important to Millais. Mason regards serial illustrations not as active collaborations

---

[65]   The separation may, however, have been necessary because of type-setting and production schedules; see Chapter 5 for further discussion.

[66]   During *Man and Wife* the illustration was sometimes embedded in the second page of text.

[67]   See Stuart Sillars, *Visualisation in Popular Fiction 1860–1960: Graphic Narratives, Fictional Images* (London: Routledge, 1995), 21. He identifies the 'dual discourse … produced by an illustrated text' (Sillars, 1).

[68]   Maidment, 10.

[69]   Anthony Trollope to George Smith, 12 February 1860, Trollope, *Letters*, vol. 1, 97.

[70]   Trollope, *Autobiography*, 148.

[71]   Anthony Trollope to George Smith, 16 May 1860; 27 May 1860, Trollope, *Letters*, vol. 1, 104. This was the famous bustle illustration 'Was it not a lie?' which appeared in June 1860.

[72]   He claimed, '[I] have had my own early ideas impressed indelibly on my memory by the excellence of his delineations' (Trollope, *Autobiography*, 148).

but merely a 'dignifying treatment of the mundane',[73] a statement which tends to prioritize art above the context of its creation. Removing the illustrations from the context of the periodical or ignoring that context disrupts the generation of meaning and indeed tries to produce that sense of the illustration as a 'failed painting'.

It is the change in context or readerly viewpoint which reprioritizes illustration over text and *vice versa*. Other recent critics are divided between the theories of illustrations as works of art and as collaborations with the text of the novel or serial. Simon Cooke's recent study provides lavish illustrations divorced from the serials themselves and describes these illustrations as 'embellishments for literature'.[74] Peter W. Sinnema suggests that periodical illustration is 'invested with meaning not explicitly acknowledged in either words or pictures'.[75] *Serialization and the Novel in Mid-Victorian Magazines* will rather take a literary standpoint based on David Skilton's counter view that illustrations should be studied as 'bimodal works of art' as a means of analysing the production of meaning.[76] There is indeed a new set of signs and signifiers created by the illustrated serial in context which will be integrated during Chapter 5 into those further sets created by the other collaborators in the serial: the author, editor and periodical.

Illustrations were designed to be seen within the periodical issue and the reading of the serial within the periodical demonstrates the contingent result of reading in a context. Although Gerard Genette makes no reference to the serial or periodical, he supplies an already existing terminology for the narrative form of the periodical in his *Paratexts: Thresholds of Interpretation*, first published in 1987. Genette draws attention to the 'degree of materialization' surrounding the printed book, and defines 'paratexts' as the 'accompanying productions [which] ensure the text's presence in the world'.[77] These include 'spatial categories' or 'peritexts'[78] which are elements of contextualization such as the prefaces discussed in Chapter 6 of *Serialization and the Novel in Mid-Victorian Magazines*. Critics

---

[73]   Michael Mason, 'The Way We Look Now: Millais' Illustrations to Trollope,' *Art History* 1 (1978): 332; 328; 313. He adds that the illustrations did not influence the text because the novel was completed (Mason, 325) but *Framley Parsonage* is one of the exceptions to Trollope's practice since the novel was still being written when the serialization was underway.

[74]   Simon Cooke, *Illustrated Periodicals of the 1860s: Contexts and Collaborations* (London: British Library, 2010), 17. As reasons for studying illustration, he lists also the artist's contribution, the illustration's value as art and its technical and traditional impact.

[75]   Peter W. Sinnema, *Dynamics of the Printed Page: Representing the Nation in the 'Illustrated London News'* (Aldershot: Ashgate, 1998), 81.

[76]   David Skilton, 'The Centrality of Literary Illustration in Victorian Visual Culture: The Example of Millais and Trollope from 1860 to 1864,' *Journal of Illustration Studies* (December 2007), http://jois.uia.no/articles.php?article=30, para. 2 of 24.

[77]   Gérard Genette, *Paratexts: Thresholds of Interpretation* (1987; repr., trans. Jane E. Lewin, Cambridge: Cambridge University Press, 1997), 3; 1.

[78]   Genette, 5.

have pointed out that periodical discourse is competitive and offers 'ideological, visual and linguistic juxtapositions'.[79] Genette describes the peritext as being 'in the service of the text'[80] but the serial within a periodical may not always be allowed to harmonize or function in comfort with the juxtaposed material. In the serialized novel, new categories of peritext appear through accompanying material which acts along with the periodical's own format as a super-preface or even an anti-preface to the novel.

Narrative theory might also consider the periodical framework of the serialized novel as an extradiegetic narrative. The novel became part of a weekly or monthly closed text at the same time as providing a forward-looking open-ended narrative with its planned future closure. Publication in parts has been described as 'a level of narrative in itself' with the competing articles acting as part of a 'narrative contestation'.[81] For reasons of repeat purchase, the periodical exploited the divisions which marked both the delimitation from and the threshold with other complementary reading material which was presented within the periodical frame. The influences of the framework and of that original reading encounter then continued to be signalled in the authors' prefaces supplied for the reprinted volumes which in turn act as new, revised frameworks or peritexts.

The function of authorship offers a further extradiegetic frame created by the author both as novelist and as serialist constructing the original text within the boundary of the editor/publisher's mission. The seriality of authorship as discussed in Chapter 2 considers the messages brought inside the pages of the periodical by authorial identity, a function termed the 'epitext' or knowledge of the author by Genette.[82] Editorial practice varied in its approach to the naming or anonymity of contributors, but both these practices allowed the periodicals to project the sense of group authorship under the umbrella of the magazine title. Trollope's authorial voice mirrored that of the other unnamed serial authors in the *Cornhill* such as Thackeray, George Sala and G.H. Lewes. Strahan and Macleod at *Good Words* were careful to demonstrate the breadth of their support from churchmen by naming them, and were able to promote their novelist Craik as an additional

---

[79]   Andrew Maunder, '"Monitoring the Middle-Classes": Intertextuality and Ideology in Trollope's *Framley Parsonage* and the *Cornhill Magazine* 1859–60,' *Victorian Periodicals Review* 33 (1999): 45; Maura Ives 'A Bibliographical Approach to Victorian Publishing,' in *Literature in the Marketplace: Nineteenth-Century British Publishing and Reading Practices*, ed. John O. Jordon and Robert L. Patten (1995; repr., Cambridge: Cambridge University Press, 2003), 275.

[80]   Genette, 12.

[81]   W.J. McCormack, '"Never Put Your Name to an Anonymous Letter": Serial Reading in the *Dublin University Magazine, 1861–1869,' YES* 26 (1996): 114; H. Porter Abbott, *The Cambridge Introduction to Narrative* (Cambridge: Cambridge University Press, 2002), 151. Shlomoth Rimmon Kenan summarizes narrative levels based on the work of Genette and Mieke Bal (*Narrative Fiction: Contemporary Poetics* (2nd ed., London: Routledge, 2003), 92–100).

[82]   Genette, 3.

preacher under her commercial pseudonym. Collins with his wide experience of serialization used multiple fictional narrators in *The Moonstone* and this structure imitated the editorial technique used for the surrounding material in *All the Year Round*.

Within his ten separate 'peritextual' or 'spatial' categories, Genette also includes the zone of the publisher,[83] which has special significance for the material production of the serialized novel in a periodical. Strahan's emphatically named *Christian Guest* was a precursor to *Good Words*, and the titles of the magazines themselves had paratextual functions such as those of *Good Words* and *Household Words* seeking periodical entrance to family reading events. Genette's book-publishing terminology also offers a bibliological definition of the concept of seeing a serialized novel in context: 'More than a boundary or sealed border, the paratext is, rather, a *threshold*' or, as it is translated, a vestibule or fringe.[84] For nineteenth-century family magazines, the access to a domestic space over a 'threshold' using the cultivated intertext of publisher, periodical, author and illustrator was part of a calculated strategy to gain readership through respectability. In terms of the nineteenth-century periodical, reference to the paratext as a vestibule or entrance to the domestic space renders the terminology even more apt since the elements of material framing within a respectable text made periodicals welcome guests in the family home under the guise and guidance of a chaplain like Norman Macleod, an educator like John Cassell and a popular novelist like Dickens.

In addition to the influence of author, editor and periodical, the serial shared at its most basic typographical level the layout, headings and paragraph markings of the periodical in which it was embedded. The appearance of other elements, even columns and headpieces, played a role in the contextual positioning of the serial. Access to the novel was through the visual display on the page using the spatial impact of words and of framing devices including the printed name of the editor, the signatures of the illustrator and engraver, and the associations of the other named or "unnamed" authors. Such features are not found in the volume edition published later in another series or publishing context, and the re-evaluation of the original appearance of the serial must consider ways in which the authors and narrators of the novels performed within that outer frame of the magazine issue which is unseen in the later volume edition.

The serialized novel was thus embedded or intercalated[85] in other serials both fictional and non-fictional which would reinforce, echo or contrast the situations and characters of the novel. The novel provided a connective textual and visual pattern over a longer horizontal timeframe but the links with other material within the periodical offered additional intertextual commentary. The main discussion of this intertextuality can be found in Chapter 5. It should be noted, however, that

---

[83] Genette, 5; 16.

[84] Genette, 2. By 'bibliology', he (through his translator) denotes the book's 'material construction' (16).

[85] See Rimmon Kenan, 91.

Cranford appeared with many other running subjects over three years, a period nearly four times as long as a regular weekly serialized novel. *Framley Parsonage* was set against the editor's own *Lovel the Widower* and *The Four Georges*, and *Mistress and Maid* dramatized the situation of reading from the scriptures which were both a serial and an implied commentary within the same periodical. As this study will demonstrate, the actions of the eponymous *Poor Miss Finch* were re-emphasized in an informal parallel serial linked between magazine issues by an illustrator rather than an author.

The novelists within periodicals were identified by their own style and by their previous works. They were also writing to meet the demands of the periodical's readership policed by the editor and publisher of the periodical. The novelists and serialists were engaged in the performance of their own authorship, which is where this investigation of the serialized novel in mid-Victorian magazines must begin.

Chapter 2
Authorship and the Serialized Novel

In a material sense, the serialized novel was embedded in the text of the periodical, and authorship of such a novel thus created a mediated identity for an author who was writing not just as an individual but under contract and in a group. The author of a text within another text had responsibilities to an editor and a publisher, to the ideological commitments of the periodical itself and to the magazine's audience. The following chapter explores this web of connection using the concepts of prior authorship and of the group authorship of the serialized novel. It assesses the collaborative composition of the novel serialized in a periodical using the core texts as well as a number of complementary novels which were periodical serials and part works. Authorship is investigated through examples of naming and attribution, and by the use of prior authorship as identity. The chapter then addresses both group authorship across the contents of the periodical and group authorship by the narrators of the serialized novels themselves.

The authors of the five core novels played a variety of parts in the evolution of the magazines for which they wrote. They also brought with them associations which were exploited within the serialization process by the five serializing periodicals. This discussion will review authors as characters or personae constructed for periodical and serial consumption such as Dinah Craik, 'the author of *John Halifax, Gentleman*' or Wilkie Collins, 'author of *The Woman in White*'. Identity and attribution are flexible concepts within the periodical, and there were within the periodicals gradations of naming and anonymity. An author might be anonymized on the page within the periodical issue but then indexed by name in the reprinted volume edition of that periodical. The identity of the pseudonymous author might be publicized by name or attribution during the ongoing marketing of the magazine week by week or month by month although no direct attribution was made for the serialized instalments. In considering the authorship of serialized novels within the periodical, this chapter explores the role of naming and attribution related to the magazines' policies of identifying or demarking their contributors. This demarcation is linked to the use of prior authorship as an identity for periodical contributors, and the argument demonstrates how prior authorship is both a further refinement of identity and a halfway point between naming and complete anonymity. The chapter then discusses the group authorship of the periodical and the interaction between its contributors. It also explores ways in which this group authorship of the periodical is mirrored by the fictional narrators of the serial, doubly enclosed within both novel and periodical. A final section then looks at the branding or vertical category of authorship for the authors of the core texts. The overall effect of the serial within the periodical can thus be differentiated from the novel reprinted in volume format. The original serial context demonstrates these competing discourses and at the same time the dialogic effect of the novel within the periodical.

Naming and Attribution

Authorship within the periodicals under discussion had a variety of forms. The authors of the serials might simply be named as Collins was in *Cassell's Magazine*. This assumed that prior authorship had already identified the author as a relevant and appropriate contributor to the periodical or to other forms of publishing. The naming of the author might be an attribution such as 'the author of *John Halifax, Gentleman*' which linked the author with her prior authorship. The author might also be genuinely anonymous in terms of the material text of the periodical as Trollope was in *Cornhill Magazine*. Despite the question of whether an author could remain truly anonymous during serialization for a period of up to two years, naming and anonymity were part of the publishing strategy which underpinned the rationale of the periodical title itself.

The range of writing demanded for the family audience was unlikely to be fulfilled by a single author, and periodicals therefore developed a number of strategies for the deployment of the concept of authorship. Contributors had to be seen to possess the expertise required for individual articles and to have the authority to meet the publisher's twin objectives of education and amusement. There was thus physical separation between those articles both by attribution and by the typographical devices which contributed to the visual display of the periodical and to the arrangement of the articles which surrounded the serial. The difference between authors was also maintained by using markers of attribution which might be names or official titles or other devices such as the positioning or serial recurrence of material.

Naming and anonymity was thus a localized tool for the publisher of the serial. Laurel Brake observes that anonymity such as that used in *Household Words* and *Cornhill Magazine* gives an 'illusion of homogeneity' so that any attribution is actually disruptive or 'splinters the text'.[1] In many cases an author's identity was an open secret and it was the approach of the periodical which dictated how this authorship was deployed within the pages of the magazine or in material which was drawn into the overarching series which was the magazine title itself. Attribution separated a contributor from his fellows whereas anonymity established the category of the periodical as author. In the examples under discussion, this was clearly truer of *Cornhill Magazine* at the time of its launch when contributors remained anonymous than it was of *Household Words* and *All the Year Round* where each page other than the first was always headed with the name of Charles Dickens. *Cassell's Magazine* retained the name of its founder in its overall title even after John Cassell's bankruptcy and death because of his association with the

---

[1] Laurel Brake, *Print in Transition, 1850–1910: Studies in Media and Book History* (Basingstoke: Palgrave, 2001), 4.

educational and moral objectives of the publishing house. In *Good Words*, Norman Macleod was also named on every page but this was balanced by the attribution of other authors who wrote with his apparent authority. This was exemplified in his announcement of the serialization of *Mistress and Maid* in December 1860 where it was advertised that ten clergymen including Macleod himself would write a 'series of papers for family reading' called 'Our Sunday Evenings'. Macleod was able to publicize the names of a range of contributors including those of these fellow clergymen. The three female contributors were named in a different way: Craik through 'John Halifax' at the head of the advertisement followed by the clergymen with their 'Series of Papers for Family Reading', then the 'Unknown Author' of 'Memoirs of an Unknown Life' and finally 'J.B.' who will contribute 'Illustrations of Scripture'. [2] 'J.B.' was the Scottish illustrator Jemima Blackburn – a 'cunning artist' according to *Notes and Queries* – whose *Photographic Illustrations of Scripture* of 1854 had 'excited so much attention and admiration in the world of Art'.[3] She had been a contributor to *Good Words* already in 1860 but would be supplanted by Millais for the major scriptural illustrations of 'The Parables' in 1863. The 'Unknown Author' remains unknown. The strategy of naming and attribution in *Good Words* was itself a marker of the overt acceptance of responsibility for the opinions contained within the periodical and for indicating the support its contents received across a wide spectrum of churchmen.[4]

Authorial character and its 'epitext' was an important factor in the placement of a writer within a periodical and in the ongoing relationship with the audience across issues within the periodical series. As editor of two of the periodicals under discussion Dickens appeared to have been very conscious of the naming phenomenon and deployed his own name as novelist freely when he was author of the serial. In considering how 'Boz' migrated into 'Charles Dickens' in the 1830s, Rob Allen observes that 'the representation of authorship in serial fiction was dependant [on] ... the materiality of textual production'.[5] If the periodical depended on its successful serials then the names and prior authorship of the novelists were significant for the periodicals' ongoing success. The serial authors were part of a multi-vocal discourse but at the same time they were expendable commodities since the periodicals would continue to function without them. It is also clear from the examples of the core texts that the boundaries between popular serials required careful handling by magazine editors in terms of promoting authors whose popularity had an impact on circulation. Thus George Smith was keen to agree a new serial with Trollope as *Framley Parsonage* ended and Cassell's

2   [Norman Macleod], 'Note by the Editor,' *GW* 1 (1860): 796.

3   *Notes and Queries*, 5 January 1856, 19.

4   See Patricia Thomas Srebrnik, *Alexander Strahan: Victorian Publisher* (Ann Arbor: University of Michigan Press, 1986), 41; this is discussed further in Chapter 3.

5   Rob Allen, '"Boz versus Dickens": Paratext, Pseudonyms and Serialization in the Victorian Literary Marketplace,' in *From Compositors to Collectors: Essays on Book-Trade History*, ed. Matthew Day and John Hicks (London: British Library, 2012) 180.

overlooked some of the problems over *Man and Wife* in order to accommodate *Poor Miss Finch*. Conversely, the progression between serial novels in *All the Year Round* was fraught with issues for Dickens and actually shaped his own work when *Great Expectations* had to appear in 1861 to restore sales of the periodical.

Gerard Genette discusses the author as 'the guarantor of the text' who is himself introduced by a publisher,[6] but there are additional layers of authority in periodical publishing since the novel was embedded in other texts. The serialized novel was given a context by the work of other writers, other publications being advertised by the publisher and by cross-referencing within the magazine issue. The author was also re-presented as a constructed character in his own right based both on previous works and on the characteristic publication traits of the periodical itself including the use of naming or anonymity. There was a publishing practice of naming which characterized the authors of the core texts since they had alternate personae as factual reporters within the pages of the periodicals for which they wrote and were also at different stages of their novel-writing careers. Laurel Brake has suggested that writing in a periodical occurs outside 'the framework of authorship' creating a counterpoint to the vertical category of author,[7] but the naming or non-naming of a novelist during the serialization of a novel was an area in which this cumulative or prior knowledge of an author was manipulated. Any discussion of authorship should not ignore the additional discrepancy between the author in his or her own person and the author as a character constructed as a serial writer.

Prior Authorship

Andrew King has highlighted the ways in which star names functioned as brands in penny weekly magazines such as *The London Journal* so that 'the by-line effectively defined the name as a category of fictional experience, rather than as the creator owner of an individual work'.[8] In employing Dinah Craik to write a serial for *Good Words*, publisher Alexander Strahan in particular exploited the category into which Craik's prior authorship had placed her. When the novel *Mistress and Maid* began to appear in January 1862, a year later than originally advertised, the text was plainly attributed with prior authorship in mind as being by 'the Author of "John Halifax, Gentleman"'. This was a "name" which Craik had already been using for six years as a result of the phenomenal success of her 1856 novel *John*

---

6   Gérard Genette, *Paratexts: Thresholds of Interpretation* (1987; repr., translated by Jane E. Lewin, Cambridge: Cambridge University Press, 1997), 46. He also discusses naming, anonymity and pseudonymity (37–55).

7   Laurel Brake, 'Writing, Cultural Production and the Periodical Press in the Nineteenth-Century,' in *Writing and Victorianism*, ed. J.B. Bullen (Harlow: Longman, 1997), 55.

8   Andrew King, *'The London Journal', 1845–83: Periodicals, Production and Gender* (Aldershot: Ashgate, 2004), 119.

Halifax, Gentleman and the attribution was itself part of her authorial persona as a writer of further novels and of articles within *Chambers's Edinburgh Journal*.[9]

Naming through prior authorship was clearly a vital part of Craik's representation as a writer. Attempting to stave off criticism from other Evangelicals about 'Sunday reading', Macleod explained that the contents of his magazine would 'reflect the every-day life of a good man'.[10] This aim was fulfilled in part by the invocation of Craik's persona as 'the Author of "John Halifax, Gentleman"' at the beginning of every episode of *Mistress and Maid: A Household Story* in each issue of *Good Words* for 1862. The appeal to a 'good man' was further reinforced horizontally across issues of the periodical through Craik's other contributions, and vertically (in Brake's denotation) to a range of other periodicals before that. Her 'Autumn Psalm for 1860' appeared in *Good Words* in season around the time of her original employment by Strahan and a week later he advertised the novel for the first time.[11] In 1861 two of her poems were published to keep her authorial identity in the minds of readers of the magazine and perhaps in lieu of the novel which had to be deferred for a year.[12]

During the serialization of *Mistress and Maid*, this persona was particularly reinforced and cross-referenced in May and June 1862 for a periodical audience which was then reading the fifth and sixth instalments of the novel. *Mistress and Maid* was set in the 1830s. In the April 1862 instalment, Craik pinpointed the date on which the Leaf sisters decide to leave Stowbury as that of Victoria's coronation in 1837 which 'is now twenty-four years ago'.[13] As 'the Author of *John Halifax, Gentleman*' Craik contributed the poem 'Until her Death' to the May issue of *Good Words*.[14] In that month's instalment of the serial, she referred to women's rights at an earlier period and in terms of Craik's sustained identity, this echoed some of her own discussion in *A Woman's Thoughts About Women*, originally published as a series of articles in *Chambers's Edinburgh Journal* between 2 May and 19 December 1857. Craik then observed in the May instalment that '[i]n those days women's work and women's rights had not been discussed so freely as at present.'[15] In *A Woman's Thoughts About Women*, she had extolled domestic womanhood but reminded her readers that 'above and before all, they are to be *women* – women

---

[9]   *A Life for a Life* appeared in 1859 using the name of 'the Author of "John Halifax, Gentleman"'. *A Women's Thoughts About Women* (London: Hurst and Blackett, 1857) and *Studies from Life* (London: Hurst and Blackett, 1861) reprinted articles from *Chambers's Edinburgh Journal* under the same authorship.

[10]   [Macleod], 'Note by the Editor.'

[11]   [Dinah Craik], 'Autumn Psalm for 1860,' *GW* 1 (1860): 777–8. The advertisement appeared in the next (weekly) issue on page 796.

[12]   [Dinah Craik], 'The Coming of the Spring,' *GW* 2 (1861): 224; 'The First Lookout on the World,' *GW* 2 (1861): 392.

[13]   *GW* 3 (1862): 230.

[14]   [Dinah Craik], 'Until Her Death,' *GW* 3 (1862): 312.

[15]   *GW* 3 (1862): 292.

whose character is of their own making, and whose lot lies in their own hands.'[16] She had emphasized that the only right in women's rights is 'the right of having something to do' which she applied in the 1860s to the situation of the fictional Leaf sisters in *Mistress and Maid*.[17] In addition to her serial instalment, Craik was employed to write an editorial for the following June issue of *Good Words*, providing her 'Five Shillings' Worth of the Great World's Fair'.[18] In her article, Craik further reprised the persona she adopted in *Chambers's Edinburgh Journal* in order to describe a visit to the Great International Exhibition.

Craik was the only non-clergyman to supply an opening article or editorial during 1862. The implication was that such a reputable author could be safely trusted with the lead item and be interchangeable with a clerical figure. The other leads were all supplied by Macleod himself, apart from two in November and December by the Irish Presbyterian minister William Fleming Stevenson. As reinforcement for her role as a substitute for these churchmen, Craik had been described in a review of her novel *A Life for a Life* in the *Saturday Review* in 1859 as an author with a 'decorous and feminine way of giving sermons', and by 1869 *The Graphic* was calling her 'a preacher in disguise'.[19] Sally Mitchell describes Craik's novels of the 1860s as 'disregarded by literary history',[20] but Craik's intertwined novel-writing periodical persona was exploited in *Good Words* by publisher Alexander Strahan to enhance the appeal and reinforce the seriousness and religious bias of his periodical. Mitchell adds that Craik 'maneuvers (sic) the stereotypes supplied by her society in an attempt to give authority to women's values.'[21] The serialized novel put Craik's ideas in *A Woman's Thoughts About Women* into a fictional context and it was a significant part of her success that she had earned the right and the place to air such views in print through the fictional authority and popularity of 'the author of *John Halifax, Gentleman*'.

In the first sixteen numbers of *Cornhill Magazine* Anthony Trollope was not named as the author of *Framley Parsonage* in any of the novel's instalments but he was known to be its author. Trollope's prior authorship in 1860 during the serialization of the novel was not just an association with his own earlier novels in what would become the Barsetshire Chronicles but rather with the output of his mother Frances Trollope. On 10 March 1860 *Bell's Weekly Messenger* complained after three instalments of his serial that 'Mr Trollope's *Framley Parsonage* savours of all the vulgarity of one of his mother's novels, and is full of absurd references

---

[16]   [Craik], *A Women's Thoughts*, 344.

[17]   [Craik], *A Women's Thoughts*, 6.

[18]   [Dinah Craik], 'Five Shillings' Worth of the Great World's Fair,' *GW* 3 (1862): 321–7.

[19]   '*A Life for a Life*,' *Saturday Review*, 10 December 1859, 709; 'Who writes all the bad novels?' *The Graphic*, 25 December 1869, 75.

[20]   Sally Mitchell, *Dinah Mulock Craik* (Boston: Twayne, 1983), 59.

[21]   Mitchell, 59.

to high life of which he can have no cognisance'.[22] There were also references in the serial to characters from previous Barsetshire novels such as the Grantlys from *The Warden* and *Barchester Towers* who are seeking a husband for their stately daughter Griselda, and the patent medicine heiress Miss Dunstable as well as to Dr Thorne and Mary and Frank Gresham from *Dr Thorne*. In January 1861 there was an illustration of 'Mrs Gresham and Miss Dunstable' who are relatively minor characters in *Framley Parsonage*. Trollope both assumed a familiarity with the plot of *Dr Thorne* and provided enough information in the serial to attract new readers to the story of Mary and Frank 'all of which have been narrated in the county chronicles of Barsetshire, and may now be read by men and women interested therein'.[23] Using his persona as narrator, he suggested in the fifth instalment of *Framley Parsonage* 'I almost fear that it will become necessary, before this history be completed, to provide a map of Barsetshire for the due explanation of all these localities.'[24] Such commentary reinforced his previous authorship but also made practical use of it in the composition of the serial in progress.

Just as Barsetshire made its periodical debut in *Cornhill Magazine* after having a life elsewhere, the village of Cranford had also evolved before its first appearance within the pages of *Household Words*. Jenny Uglow sees *Cranford* as 'the final stage in a process of recollection gradually transmuted into fiction'[25] and, like Craik, Gaskell was using material which marked her authorship albeit it was subsumed in the early 1850s within the group authorship of the periodical under Dickens. It was at a pivotal moment of recollection that 'Cranford' was created leading out of the semi-factual reporting of her earlier 'The Last Generation in England' and the three-part story 'Mr Harrison's Confessions'.[26] The magazines which published these pieces did not have a wide circulation and the stories were not reprinted with an attribution until 'Mr Harrison's Confessions' appeared in *Lizzie Leigh and other Tales* in 1855 and 'The Last Generation' in the modern Oxford edition of *Cranford* in 1972. 'Mr Harrison's Confessions' used the pre-*Cranford* setting of Duncombe but it was clearly a version of Gaskell's Knutsford as was Hanbury in 'My Lady Ludlow' which was serialized in *Household Words* in 1858.

When *Cranford* appeared in *Household Words* as an occasional serial the prior authorship of *Mary Barton* published in 1848 would have been available

---

[22]   *Bell's Weekly Messenger*, 10 March 1860, 6; quoted in Andrew Maunder, '"Discourses of Distinction": The Reception of the *Cornhill Magazine* 1859–60,' *Victorian Periodicals Review* 32 (1999): 252.

[23]   *CM* 3 (1861): 62.

[24]   *CM* 1 (1860): 525. In Chapter 4 of his *Autobiography* he claimed that he 'made a map of the dear county.'

[25]   Jenny Uglow, *Elizabeth Gaskell: A Habit of Stories* (London: Faber and Faber, 1993), 279.

[26]   'The Last Generation in England,' *Sartain's Union Magazine*, July 1849; 'Mr Harrison's Confessions,' *Ladies' Companion and Monthly Magazine*, February to April 1851.

as an indicator for the periodical reader, but no attribution was made. Although Gaskell was apparently prioritized as a contributor in the very earliest scheme for Dickens's new periodical when it was launched in 1850, the available attribution had not been used either for her short story 'Lizzie Leigh' which appeared in the first number of *Household Words*. In this case, the material production of the text reprioritized editor and periodical over author since Dickens's prospectus for his magazine – his 'Preliminary Word' – ran over onto page two of the first issue on 30 March 1850. After becoming the first article in the periodical in issue one, the second and third parts of 'Lizzie Leigh' occupied the third and then the sixth stations and became part of that group authorship which was still functioning when the first parts of *Cranford* appeared the following year.

Wilkie Collins's identity also evolved through prior authorship but he found that he was not allowed to shake off the original tag of his 1859–60 success with *The Woman in White*. In 1869, during his period of writing for *Cassell's Magazine*, Collins asked the publishers for some adjustments to the typeface of an advertisement. He wanted it to read either '*The Woman in White* etc.' or else to refer to all his novels in the same size type. He explained that to do otherwise would lead to 'establishing comparisons … Don't let us encourage the public (for the sake of <u>Man and Wife</u>) in its one everlasting cry about me;– Ah! he may write what he pleases! He will never do anything again like the Woman in White'.[27] All of Collins's novels had appeared as serials within magazines since the publication of his fourth novel *The Dead Secret* in *Household Words* in 1857. For the novel immediately subsequent to *The Woman in White* – *No Name*, serialized in *All the Year Round* in 44 parts from 15 March 1862 – he was 'the Author of "The Woman in White," &c.' which appeared to acknowledge his works prior to *The Woman in White* by the additional ampersand. Although Dickens has been found to have disparaged his work in private, Collins's style and method matched closely the demands and confinement of the weekly serial format with its 'advertised limits'.[28] Despite his contribution to the success of Dickens's magazines, the material production of *The Moonstone*, Collins's last serial for *All the Year Round* demonstrates the subordination of individual authorship even when it could boost circulation. Under the terms of the magazine's non-naming policy, Collins was throughout the serialization of *The Moonstone* 'the Author of "The Woman in White," &c. &c' within a title page announcing the names of two periodicals ('All the Year Round … with which is incorporated Household Words'), the name of Shakespeare who was the author of the name of the periodical itself,[29] and the name of the editor: 'Conducted by Charles Dickens' (see Figure 2.1).

27   Wilkie Collins to Cassell, Petter and Galpin, 29 October 1869, Collins, *The Public Face*, vol. 2, 157.

28   The term was used by Gaskell in her note on the title page of the volume edition of *North and South* (see Chapter 6).

29   'The story of our lives from year to year' was slightly amended from a speech made by Othello (*Othello*, Act 1, Scene 3); 'the story of my life' told to Desdemona.

"THE STORY OF OUR LIVES FROM YEAR TO YEAR."—SHAKESPEARE.

ALL THE YEAR ROUND.

A WEEKLY JOURNAL.

CONDUCTED BY CHARLES DICKENS.

WITH WHICH IS INCORPORATED HOUSEHOLD WORDS.

N°· 454.]　　　SATURDAY, JANUARY 4, 1868.　　　[PRICE 2*d*.

THE MOONSTONE.

BY THE AUTHOR OF "THE WOMAN IN WHITE," &c. &c.

Prologue.

THE STORMING OF SERINGAPATAM (1799):
(Extracted from a Family Paper).

I.

I ADDRESS these lines—written in India—to my relatives in England.

My object is to explain the motive which has induced me to refuse the right hand of friendship to my cousin, John Herncastle. The reserve which I have hitherto maintained in this matter has been misinterpreted by members of my family whose good opinion I cannot consent to forfeit. I request them to suspend their decision until they have read my narrative. And I declare, on my word of honour, that what I am now about to write is, strictly and literally, the truth.

The private difference between my cousin and me took its rise in a great public event in which we were both concerned—the storming of Seringapatam, under General Baird, on the 4th of May, 1799.

In order that the circumstances may be clearly understood, I must revert for a moment to the period before the assault, and to the stories current in our camp of the treasure in jewels and gold stored up in the Palace of Seringapatam.

II.

One of the wildest of these stories related to a Yellow Diamond—a famous gem in the native annals of India.

The earliest known traditions describe the stone as having been set in the forehead of the four-handed Indian god who typifies the Moon. Partly from its peculiar colour, partly from a superstition which represented it as feeling the influence of the deity whom it adorned, and growing and lessening in lustre with the waxing and waning of the moon, it first gained the name by which it continues to be known in India to this day—the name of THE MOONSTONE. A similar superstition was once prevalent, as I have heard, in ancient Greece and Rome; not applying, however (as in India), to a diamond devoted to the service of a god, but to a semi-transparent stone of the inferior order of gems, supposed to be affected by the lunar influences—the moon, in this latter case also, giving the name by which the stone is still known to collectors in our own time.

The adventures of the Yellow Diamond begin with the eleventh century of the Christian era.

At that date, the Mohammedan conqueror, Mahmoud of Ghizni, crossed India; seized on the holy city of Somnauth; and stripped of its treasures the famous temple, which had stood for centuries—the shrine of Hindoo pilgrimage, and the wonder of the Eastern world.

Of all the deities worshipped in the temple, the moon-god alone escaped the rapacity of the conquering Mohammedans. Preserved by three Brahmins, the inviolate deity, bearing the Yellow Diamond in its forehead, was removed by night, and was transported to the second of the sacred cities of India—the city of Benares.

Here, in a new shrine—in a hall inlaid with precious stones, under a roof supported by pillars of gold—the moon-god was set up and worshipped. Here, on the night when the shrine was completed, Vishnu the Preserver appeared to the three Brahmins in a dream.

The deity breathed the breath of his divinity on the Diamond in the forehead of the god. And the Brahmins knelt and hid their faces in their robes. The deity commanded that the Moonstone should be watched, from that time forth, by three priests in turn, night and day, to the end of the generations of men. And the Brahmins heard, and bowed before his will. The deity predicted certain disaster to the presumptuous mortal who laid hands on the sacred gem, and to all of his house and name who received it after him. And the Brahmins caused the prophecy to be written over the gates of the shrine in letters of gold.

One age followed another—and still, generation after generation, the successors of the three Brahmins watched their priceless Moonstone, night and day. One age followed another, until the first years of the eighteenth Christian century saw the reign of Aurungzebe, Emperor of the Moguls. At his command, havoc and rapine were let loose once more among the temples of the worship of Brahmah. The shrine of the four-handed god was polluted by the slaughter of sacred animals; the images of the deities were broken in pieces; and the Moonstone was seized by an officer of rank in the army of Aurungzebe.

Powerless to recover their lost treasure by

Fig. 2.1　　Opening page of *The Moonstone*, *All the Year Round*, 4 January 1868, 73.

As demonstrated on the opening page of the serial, the hierarchy of typeface sizes from largest to smallest ran: All the Year Round, The Moonstone, Charles Dickens (in bold), Household Words, Shakespeare (whose name headed the title page each week), the text of the novel and finally 'the Author of "The Woman in White," &c. &c'. Collins's name was used for advertising within *All the Year Round* as, for instance, in the week before the serialization commenced: 'Next week will be commenced The Moonstone; a new serial story by Wilkie Collins'[30] but he was not named in the indexes to the collected volumes of the periodical where he remained 'the Author of "The Woman in White"'.

Since its launch *Cassell's Magazine* had used names as a means of identifying serial content, and with the completion of *The Moonstone*, the *Magazine* was ready to name Collins in return for an increase in its own readership. Two years after the correspondence with Cassell's over advertising, Collins was clearly named as the author of every instalment of *Poor Miss Finch* with no adumbration from other novels except in further advertising. The sources of tension in *Poor Miss Finch*'s original magazine serial context arose from the intertextual relationship with other material to be discussed in Chapter 5 but also from a conflict between the established reputations of both Collins and the House of Cassell.

These names or authorial constructs were being exploited to increase circulation by referring to texts already owned or discussed widely in other printed media as Collins's were. This covers access to texts outside the periodical across a wide range through part work or volume, owned, shared or borrowed. The persona of 'the author of *John Halifax, Gentleman*' or the 'author of *The Woman in White*' was being constructed through this prior knowledge and "named" for reasons of marketing. Trollope's prior authorship operated within the context of his previous novels which he drew upon because of the opportunity provided by Smith and Thackeray to contribute to the *Cornhill* at short notice, and the tone of the magazine was jointly developed in the context of group authorship as discussed below. In the case of *Household Words* and *All the Year Round*, Dickens was named both as author of his own fiction and as 'Conductor' on the running header which was printed above the text of other novelists' serials. He was named as author from the beginning of *All the Year Round* with the first instalment of *A Tale of Two Cities* whilst the immediately following *The Woman in White* was completely anonymized and unattributed at that period before Collins's fame was established. This invocation of prior authorship in its different forms reminded the reader that the serial was a repeated act of writing and therefore a trustworthy and worthwhile purchase. At the same time the appearance of the demarked author in the periodical suggested that the serial was something new by accumulating it within the author's advertised writing career, embedding it in miscellaneous material and issuing it as a weekly or monthly magazine.[31]

---

[30]   *AYR*, 28 December 1867, 72; see also *AYR*, 14 December 1867, 48.
[31]   This demonstrates a specialized use of prior authorship in the magazine context. The naming of authors based on prior authorship was not uncommon in volume editions of novels where, of course, Craik herself continued to be known as 'the Author of *John Halifax, Gentleman*' and Collins was identified with *The Woman in White*.

Group Authorship: the Periodical

It was the economics of producing a journal based on shared beliefs and targeted at the family audience which made the periodical miscellany of fiction, education and topical investigation attractive to publishers. The appearance of topical material in weekly or monthly numbers gave each instalment of a serial a function within the group authorship of the periodical. Robert Patten has suggested that '[s]erialization deconstructs the single author as sole creator, and does so as a part of a larger collaborative project within which the serial is framed.'[32] Laurel Brake argues that the periodical presents a type of collective authorship where all the writing operated within the 'codes of discourse' of the periodical. Group authorship thus affected the original presentation of the serial novel, and Brake adds 'at the very least it is not individualist'.[33] Group authorship was part of the context in which the serial was both composed and read under the collective supervision of author, editor and publisher. Louis James describes the periodical issue as 'a community of voices'[34] and this concept applied whether authorship was attributed or not; it was the co-existence of subject matter which indicated the combined 'community' even when Dickens and Macleod were named above other contributors. Brake and Julie Codell define this as a 'false unity', which makes it appear 'as if the journal itself were a single author'.[35]

Dickens was in effect elided with his magazines as if their titles were actually *Household Words Conducted by Charles Dickens* and *All the Year Round Conducted by Charles Dickens*. The short pieces which made up *Cranford* in the early 1850s were not attributed and, although they were divided by typographical markings from other material, they became part of the overall social critique which *Household Words* offered. *Cranford* was thus suspended without prioritization within the investigative journalism which characterized that periodical's 'code of discourse'. Dinah Craik's contributions to *Good Words* were identified through her non-name and the other contributors were named as part of Strahan's objectives for his magazine, both as a competitor with other illustrated weeklies and as a niche-marketed religious publication. *Cornhill Magazine* sought to use its own title as part of the naming process without the need to name the otherwise well-known contributors. George Smith and Thackeray presented the contents as a

---

[32]   Robert L. Patten, 'Dickens as Serial Author: A Case of Multiple Identities,' in *Nineteenth-Century Media and the Construction of Identities*, ed. Laurel Brake, Bill Bell and David Finkelstein (Basingstoke: Palgrave, 2000), 144.

[33]   Brake, *Print in Transition*, 18.

[34]   Louis James, 'The Trouble with Betsey: Periodicals and the Common Reader in Mid Nineteenth-Century England,' in *The Victorian Periodical Press: Samplings and Soundings*, ed. E.J. Shattock and Michael Wolff (Leicester: Leicester University Press, 1982), 352.

[35]   Laurel Brake and Julie Codell, 'Encountering the Press,' in *Encounters in the Victorian Press*, ed. Laurel Brake and Julie Codell (Basingstoke: Palgrave Macmillan, 2004), 1.

well-informed conversation around a table, an idea which Thackeray used in the prospectus for the magazine. Smith promoted his illustrious writers through both exterior marketing and clear subject matter which brought other writers under his influence in response to the strength of this material and – since Smith was well known for his generous payment – the promised reward. Authors learned to assess both the appropriateness of material and their own place within the group. Gaskell, for instance, contributed 'Curious if True' to the *Cornhill* in February 1860 and told Smith it was delayed 'because I want to make it as good as I can, & so only to write at it in my best moments'. As a contributor to the group authorship of periodicals, she could judge the tone of the magazines even before the first issue of the *Cornhill* appeared. She wrote to Smith that she could not offer him 'Lois the Witch' because it was 'not good enough for the C. M. ... but might be good enough for Household Words'.[36]

In terms of the *Cornhill* we can see how Trollope's approach echoed the style of other articles. In the first instalment of *Framley Parsonage*, Trollope called description 'the novelist's great difficulty' and he appeared to be plucking a name out of the air when he called Mark Robarts's future wife Fanny.[37] He revisited this problem in the fourth instalment when he developed the character of Lucy Robarts, complaining 'if one might only go on without these descriptions'.[38] In the third instalment of 'The Four Georges' which was originally a lecture tour given in 1855, Thackeray observed: 'We have to glance over sixty years in as many minutes. To read the mere catalogue of characters who figured during that long period would occupy our allotted time, and we should have all text and no sermon.'[39] In the same number of the periodical as the lament over description, George Sala reached the third instalment of 'William Hogarth' and admonished himself, 'I am wandering up and down the years as well as the streets'.[40] In October 1860, Trollope choreographed Miss Dunstable's party with its illustration of Lady Lufton and the Duke of Omnium, and he announced firstly that 'Lady Lufton is waiting for us in the ante-room' and then returned to Miss Dunstable: 'whom we should not have left for so long a time'.[41] This interaction within the group of periodical authors demonstrates how the novel's authorship and the group authorship of the periodical presented and shared the 'false unity' which created the characteristics of the *Cornhill* in its first four months of publication.

In the serial, these devices also reflected the need to recall the reader into the story between episodes and between the pieces accompanying it within the

[36] Elizabeth Gaskell to George Smith, 23 December 1859, Gaskell, *Letters*, 595. 'Lois the Witch' appeared in *All the Year Round* (8, 15 and 22 October 1859) during the serialization of *A Tale of Two Cities*.

[37] *CM* 1 (1860): 3.

[38] *CM* 1, 451.

[39] *CM* 2 (1860): 257.

[40] *CM* 1, 435.

[41] *CM* 2, 479.

periodical. Thus, for instance, the second paragraph of *Framley Parsonage* at the very opening of the magazine announced the themes of 'the first page or two of this narrative'.[42] In September 1860 the authorial voice of the novel asked 'my readers' to remember an incident which occurred in the July instalment.[43] Yet, in spite of these characteristic interpolations, the audience clearly found that the plot and characters of the serial were compelling within the periodical and indeed becoming part of their own lives. As we have seen, Gaskell wrote to George Smith that she could not bear for *Framley Parsonage* to end although she confessed after the early issues that she had 'not read the sensible & improving articles'.[44] *The Saturday Review* which reacted badly to the *Cornhill* as a matter of routine because the new magazine had poached some of its writers claimed to find objective comment difficult for similar reasons. The reviewer contended that *Framley Parsonage* had become 'an intimate of the drawing room – it has travelled with us in the train'.[45]

Group authorship in *Good Words* reflected the boundaried miscellany of content which Macleod proposed in December 1860. Macleod's editorial authorization was visible on every page and seemed to underline the single authorship which brought an intended 'unity' to the periodical. The effect of this 'unity' with its apparent control of material would later haunt him in 1863 when his fellow Evangelicals turned on him in the *Record*.[46] The naming of Macleod as leader of the group was vital to the mission of the magazine to promote 'Sunday reading for all the week' sandwiched between a religious introduction from the editor and family readings from scripture. This 'healthy recreation'[47] in the periodical format meant that 'the author of "John Halifax, Gentleman"' the prior author was grouped with a wide range of other contributors ranging from a working man to an archbishop but always with the object of promoting a religious viewpoint.[48] Craik's article on the Great International Exhibition was supplemented in August by 'An Exhibition Homily' which exhorted readers to be 'thankful for all the products of human skill and industry … if we will remember God the giver'.[49] An account of Norsemen was

[42]   *CM* 1, 1.

[43]   *CM* 2, 296.

[44]   Elizabeth Gaskell to George Smith, 1 March 1860; 23 December 1859, Gaskell, *Letters*, 602; 595.

[45]   *Saturday Review*, 4 May 1861; repr., *Trollope: The Critical Heritage*, ed. Donald Smalley (London: Routledge and Kegan Paul, 1969), 121.

[46]   See [Thomas Alexander], '"Good Words": The Theology of Its Editor and Some of Its Contributors Reprinted from the "Record" Newspaper' (London: Record Office, 1863); this is discussed in Chapter 3.

[47]   [Macleod], 'Note by the Editor.'

[48]   'What a Working Man Said the Other Day at the Opening of a Dissenting School in Hertfordshire by Himself' appeared in April (*GW* 3 (1862): 221–4) and 'Some Verses Written by a Working Man' in July (433–4). 'Short Papers by Archbishop Whately' appeared in January (30–31) and in April (197–9).

[49]   J. Llewellyn Davies, 'An Exhibition Homily,' *GW* 3 (1862): 399.

headed 'God's Hand in the Paddle Power of England' and Darwin was described as having 'a tendency to expel the Almighty from the universe' whilst '[d]eclining to receive light from above'.[50] The illustrators too participated in group authorship as when Craik's poem 'Until Her Death' was accompanied by Frederick Sandys's illustration of a skeleton offering a woman the habit of a nun.[51] The domestic scene of the poem 'Rung into Heaven' with its illustration by Matthew Lawless of three children in a bell tower belied the grim outcome of the poem where little Rose was killed by the church bells.[52]

Group authorship also took place in *Good Words* in 1862 through a range of intertextual references which reinforced unity. For instance in the April instalment of *Mistress and Maid*, Craik's three poor but genteel sisters were pictured at a train station having taken their first ever train journey. They have opted to travel 'cheerless and cushionless' in third class in order to stay with their maid.[53] Several of Craik's 'Studies from Life' which was reprinted from *Chambers* material in 1861 used the background of train travel and she described a 'railway terminus … as a first-rate academy'.[54] In 'War Sparkles', Craik travelled on a train with baggage for the Crimea and in 'Travelling Companions' she wrote that the second-class carriage 'furnish[ed] studies for many a novel-writer'[55] which she was able to employ in the serial. In the August issue of *Good Words* an article 'On Solitude' then complemented the experience of the Leaf sisters by decrying the impact of the railroad and telegraph on the simpler life.[56] In May 1862 Craik's reference to women's rights and to her own *A Woman's Thoughts About Women* chimed also with the piece immediately following, 'Old Maids and Young Maids' by that "unnamed" 'Unknown Author of "Memoirs of an Unknown Life"'. The fifth instalment of the novel (Chapters 10 and 11) occupied pages 289 to 297, and the article began immediately on page 298. The 'Old Maids' article discussed 'woman's mission' as an old maid, providing parallels with the experience of the Leaf sisters in the serial to which this piece offered a textual exterior frame as well as an expanded commentary. The ultimate in group authorship was achieved in the collected volume edition of *Good Words for 1862* which was re-presented as a memorial to Prince Albert as discussed in Chapter 6. Despite the naming of contributors, group authorship was actually about similarity within the 'Good

───────────

[50]   *GW* 3 (1862): 349–52; David Brewster, 'The Facts and Fancies of Mr Darwin,' *GW* 3(1862): 3; 8.

[51]   *GW* 3, 312.

[52]   *GW* 3,153–4.

[53]   *GW* 3, 231.

[54]   [Dinah Craik], *Studies from Life by the author of "John Halifax, Gentleman", "A Woman's Thoughts About Women", "A Life for a Life", "Nothing New" &c. &c.* (London: Hurst and Blackett, [1861]), 96.

[55]   [Dinah Craik], 'War Sparkles,' in *Studies from Life*, 94–120; 'Travelling Companions,' in *Studies from Life*, 171.

[56]   Aeneas Sage, 'On Solitude,' *GW* 3 (1862): 472–8.

words for all the week' strategy which proved that there was a religious slant on every subject.

Any assessment of the serial must consider how much the sense of group authorship affected the composition and reception of the novel serialized within the periodical. The interaction between the instalments of the serials and the surrounding material in individual numbers of the periodicals is discussed more fully in Chapter 5. Group authorship also included the contribution of the illustrators (to *Framley Parsonage*, *Mistress and Maid* and *Poor Miss Finch*) which is discussed in the context of the periodical and of the serial in Chapters 4 and 5.

Group Authorship: the Serial

Evidence of the effect of group authorship in the periodical also emerges, however, from the narrative method of the novels. The *Saturday Review*, reviewing the volume edition of *Poor Miss Finch*, found that 'There is the inevitable personage who acts annotator or chorus, and the book turns at last into the inevitable journal, although singularly enough, not till the third volume'.[57] The style of the serial was not always affected as obviously as this critic perceived but it is possible to trace the fictional group authorship employed by the serials. In their original context, the novels were read embedded in a community, group or "falsely unified" discourse. For Trollope, Gaskell and Craik this was a reaction to other styles of authorship in the periodical but for Collins the use of narrative devices was the result of a long career in periodical writing.

During the serialization of his earlier novel *The Woman in White*, Collins was not identified as author but remained anonymous as a staff writer within a group of anonymous contributors, nor was he named in the volume editions of *All the Year Round* for 1859–60. As the novel unfolded, however, the names of the narrators of the novel (Walter Hartright, the lawyer Mr Gilmore, Marian Halcombe, the housekeeper Mrs Michelson and Laura's uncle Frederick Fairlie) were highlighted on the line of text which would have been occupied by the name of the author, thus reflecting their own collective authorship of the novel. This practice of naming the narrators at the head of each instalment resumed in *The Moonstone* in 1868 with the added reference to *The Woman in White* in smaller type. The author who had learned his trade in the pages of *Household Words* and who had helped to establish the rationale of serialization in *All the Year Round* returned. That first success could be re-embedded in the text of 1868 through the established practice of attribution since every instalment of *The Moonstone* referred back to 'the Author of "The Woman in White"'. The Prologue to *The Moonstone*, a 'family paper' on the Storming of Seringapatam, could easily have been a standalone article from the pages of *All the Year Round*. The serialized novel had its overall editor in

---

[57] *The Saturday Review*, 2 March 1872, 282–3; repr., in *Wilkie Collins: The Critical Heritage*, ed. Norman Page (London: Routledge and Kegan Paul, 1974), 197.

Franklin Blake who employed his narrators to give evidence in strict sequence: the steward Gabriel Betteredge for thirteen instalments, then 'several Narratives' by Miss Clack, the lawyer Mr Bruff, Franklin Blake himself (containing the letter of the servant Rosanna Spearman), the doctor's assistant Ezra Jennings (through his journal), Blake again, Sergeant Cuff, the doctor Mr Candy and then Betteredge again. The serial concluded with an Epilogue in three voices. Three of these eight 'several Narratives' appeared with that Epilogue in the final instalment on 8 August 1868, effectively producing a group-authored periodical number in miniature.

Inside the novel, an impact was also created by the invocation of *Robinson Crusoe* in Betteredge's narratives. The analogy with the self-made man spoke to the reading matter associated with the middle- and working-class readers who were the audience for serials in the nineteenth century and added Defoe's character to the category of authorship. Overall, however, Collins demonstrated how his training as an author writing for a periodical had given him the ability to imitate the rhythm and register of the magazine. He drew on the semi-fictional style of other periodical contributors including himself to narrate the novel although, unlike the editor Dickens, he named his authors. This was another deployment of 'false unity' through which Collins effectively embedded *The Moonstone* in *All the Year Round* by making a virtue of the demarcation between contributors.

The effect of writing for a periodical on the narrative and authorship of a novel published in parts can also be traced using the example of *Bleak House* which appeared during the period when *Cranford* was commissioned, re-commissioned and written for *Household Words*. There are parallels in terms of narrative structure between the two serials which illustrate the co-dependence of forms as well as the influence of periodical writing on the longer serial. *Bleak House* was Dickens's ninth novel and the first to be wholly written when he was editor of his own periodical. It was composed between November 1851 and August 1853 and was published in monthly parts between March 1852 and September 1853.[58] Biographers have linked Dickens's experiences as a journalist with the events of the novel. The character of Inspector Bucket is regarded as a fictional version of the real-life detective policeman Charles Frederick Field who was himself fictionalized as 'Wield' in three journalistic pieces appearing in 1850.[59] Even before this, Dickens's co-editor Wills had contributed 'A Coroner's Inquest',[60] which reflected on incidents reminiscent of the inquest on Nemo in Chapter 11, the fourth instalment of *Bleak House* which appeared in June 1852. John Butt and Kathleen Tillotson describe the novel as 'a fable for 1852', using the ' dateable

---

[58]   Evidence is supplied by John Forster in 'A Note on the Text,' Charles Dickens, *Bleak House*, ed. Norman Page (1971; repr., Harmondsworth: Penguin, 1980), 35. There is also an account in Slater, *Charles Dickens*, 340–62.

[59]   'A Detective Police Party,' *HW*, 27 July and 10 August 1850, 409–14; 457–60; 'Three Detective Anecdotes,' *HW*, 14 September 1850, 577–80. Field was named in 'On Duty with Inspector Field,' *HW*, 14 June 1851, 265–70.

[60]   *HW*, 27 April 1850, 109–13.

character' of Bucket,[61] and its topicality was surely styled on the periodical discourse which had developed in *Household Words* by the time of the magazine's third year of publication. J. Hillis Miller identifies in *Bleak House* 'a complex fabric of recurrences'[62] which also characterizes both serial writing in parts and the containment of that serial within a periodical miscellany.

At the overlap between Dickens as editor and Dickens as author, there are parallels between *Bleak House* and the group authorship of the periodical which Dickens was editing at the time and in which he was representing a named female narrator. Although *Cranford* was unattributed for the first readers of the periodical, Mary Smith was named as narrator within the pieces which came to make up the serial as a whole. The two initial instalments of *Cranford* appeared during the early stages of the composition of *Bleak House*, a further two at the time of the first instalment of Dickens's part-work in March 1852 and the final three in January and April/May 1853. The two serials are mapped onto each other in Appendix 3. Mary Smith was the semi-fictional Gaskell figure who acted as narrator or editor of *Cranford* set against the other anonymized article writers or correspondents of *Household Words*. In *Bleak House*, Dickens presented the dual narrators of his novel who were an anonymous omniscient narrator and Esther Summerson, a woman both renamed and unnamed by her illegitimacy.

Dickens's double narrative was criticised at the time of the novel's original serialization.[63] The *Atlas* described the double narrative as making the 'web' of the novel too wide.[64] George Brimley wrote in *The Spectator*: 'Such a girl would not write her own memoirs, and certainly would not bore one with her goodness'. Brimley famously continued that Esther should 'confine herself to superintending the jam-pots at Bleak House'.[65] More recently, Phillip Collins has declared 'the Esther experiment … a failure' and the debate on the impact of the female narrator continues.[66] Alison Case suggests that Esther's contribution was not intended to

[61]   John Butt and Kathleen Tillotson, *Dickens at Work* (1957; repr., London: Methuen, 1982), 179; 196.

[62]   J. Hillis Miller, 'Interpretation in *Bleak House*,' in *Bleak House*, ed. Jeremy Tambling (Basingstoke: Macmillan, 1998), 33.

[63]   See Brahma Chaudhuri, 'Dickens's Serial Structure in *Bleak House*,' *The Dickensian* 86, no. 2 (1990): 67–84.

[64]   3 April 1852, 219; quoted in Chaudhuri, 69.

[65]   *The Spectator*, 24 September 1853, 924.

[66]   Philip Collins, *A Critical Commentary on 'Bleak House'* (London: Macmillan, 1971), 33. See also Lance Schachterle, '*Bleak House* as a Serial Novel,' *Dickens Studies Annual* 1 (1970), 212–24; Virginia Blain, 'Double Vision and the Double Standard in *Bleak House*: A Feminist Perspective,' *Literature and History* 11 (1985): 31–46; Lynette Felzer, '"Delightfully Irregular": Esther's Nascent *écriture féminine* in *Bleak House*', *Victorian Newsletter* 85 (Spring 1994): 13–20; Richard Gravil, 'The Androgyny of Bleak House,' in *Master Narratives: Tellers and Telling in the English Novel*, ed. Richard Gravil (Aldershot: Ashgate, 2001), 123–37 and Robert Tracy, 'Reading and Misreading *Bleak House*,' *Dickens Quarterly* 20, no. 3 (2003): 166–71. Gravil supplies a summary of the criticism (189, note 6).

represent 'mimetic consistency', identifying instead a 'gendered literary code' for the narrative.[67] That code may also be that of the periodical with its discourse of factual experience recounted under a thin veil of fiction taking a journalistic stance on the abuses of the day. Using this reading, there are identifiable parallels between the autobiographical viewpoint supplied by Esther, contextualized by the omniscient narrative of the part-work and the detached observation (with some agency in the plot) of Mary Smith whose narrative directly abutted articles appearing in *Household Words*. The two women each supplied a narrative in the past tense set against the omniscient present tense of the surrounding material although Mary's narrative was less exposed and more widely diffused. Her role as narrator was balanced out by the other first-person narrators of *Household Word* articles, creating that miscellany which is periodical discourse.[68]

In *Bleak House*, the two narrators each narrate half the novel's chapters and the double viewpoint can be seen as similar to that of periodical writers narrating within the framework of the magazine. This might also be compared with the technique of the Christmas numbers of *Household Words* which grouped other authors within an expanded frame. The instalments of *Bleak House* were themselves patterned by their identifiable narrative viewpoint with a maximum of four successive chapters being narrated from one perspective. For five of the instalments the anonymous omniscient viewpoint only was used[69] whilst it was only for instalment number 12 of the novel published in February 1853 that Esther was the sole narrator. This instalment concerned the revelation of her parentage when she meets Lady Dedlock at Chesney Wold and was also close in timeframe to the double episode of *Cranford* in January 1853 entitled 'The Great Cranford Panic', when Gaskell's occasional serial returned after a break of eight months. The omniscient chapters of *Bleak House* were individually named but ten of Esther's chapters were simply entitled 'Esther's Narrative' which suggests another internal serialized pattern created by the female narrator across instalments. The last chapter, 'The Close of Esther's Narrative', was designated in the style of headings used within the periodical when Collins began to use his alternate narrators in *The Woman in White* and later *The Moonstone*. In addition, the ending of *Bleak House* gives a sense of the continuing relationship which would be possible even after a serialized novel was completed within a periodical. Chapter 67 offered closure and 'dull repose' for the Chesney Wold characters but Esther concluded Chapter 68 with the open sentence 'even supposing –'. Her last words – and the fact that

---

[67]   Alison Case, 'Gender and History in Narrative Theory: The Problem of Perspective Distance in *David Copperfield* and *Bleak House*,' in *A Companion to Narrative Theory*, ed. James Phelan and Peter J. Rabinowitz (Oxford: Blackwell, 2005), 314; 313.

[68]   See also Keith Easley, 'Dickens and Bakhtin: Authoring in *Bleak House*,' *Dickens Studies Annual* 34 (2004), 185–232. The interaction between *Cranford* and the rest of *Household Words* is discussed in more detail in Chapters 4 and 5.

[69]   The third person instalments are 7 and 9 (September and November 1852) and 13, 15 and 17 (March, May and July 1853); see Appendix 3.

she was allowed them – deprioritized the importance of the omniscient narrator who had shared the narrative and should, given his omniscience, have prevailed. Lynette Felzer points out that '[t]he suspended hierarchy of the arrested sentence' created an 'open ambiguous anti-ending' to the novel. [70] This would have reflected the style of a periodical aiming to retain the reader's interest and contact when the serial was concluded. The serial patterns of narrative and group authorship are thus vital to the impact of both the part work and the periodical. [71]

Authorship and Branding

The authors of the core texts relied on the attribution or pseudonym constructed out of prior authorship, and this continued into their later careers. The influence of authorial branding will be traced here looking forward to its function in their subsequent publications.

Dinah Craik appears to have been satisfied with the pseudo-anonymity which her "name" provided since she used it for the rest of her life. Craik was described at her death as a 'widely known' though not 'public personage' [72] which suggests that this disguise was a designedly thin one giving 'the author of *John Halifax, Gentleman*' the authority to act in public whilst ostensibly remaining a private person. In 1866, an article in the *British Quarterly Review* responded to the character of Miss Gwilt in Collins's *Armadale* which had appeared alongside *Wives and Daughters* in the *Cornhill*. The article drew attention to the 'John Halifax, Gentleman' tag pointing out that this was not a mark of anonymity but an indication of the style and character to be expected of the writing: 'Other writers are cleverer, more impassioned, more brilliant, but we turn from their eloquent words to her tales of simple goodness with a sense of rest and relief.' [73] Strahan and Macleod found in Craik a match for their own project of maintaining the religious tone of *Good Words*. This relationship continued even after both editor and publisher were no longer associated with the magazine. Craik's novel *The Woman's Kingdom* appeared in *Good Words* in 1868 as did *Young Mrs. Jardine* in 1879. Two short novels for adolescents appeared in the periodical in the 1870s: *My Mother and I: A Girl's Love-Story* in 1874 and *The Laurel Bush* in 1876. Amongst other articles one of her last was 'Genius: Its Aberrations and Its Responsibilities' in *Good Words* whilst 'For Better for Worse' appeared in another periodical originally founded by Strahan. [74]

---

[70] Feltzer, 19; 18.

[71] See the discussions of serialization by Gerald Giles Grubb, 'Dickens' Pattern of Weekly Serialization,' *ELH* 9, (1942): 141–56 and Schachterle, '*Bleak House* as a Serial Novel'.

[72] [Margaret Oliphant], 'Mrs Craik,' *Macmillan's Magazine* 57 (December 1887): 82.

[73] 'The Author of John Halifax,' *British Quarterly Review* 57 (1866): 32; 33.

[74] 'Genius: Its Aberrations and Its Responsibilities,' *GW* 26 (1885): 229–32; 'For Better for Worse,' *Contemporary Review* 51 (1887): 570–76.

Anthony Trollope used his location and his composition method as branding. In addition to the echoes of factual narration discussed above, he appeared in his own narrative within *Framley Parsonage*, as if he were himself an inhabitant of Barsetshire. He called Frank Gresham's father 'an old friend of mine'.[75] Describing Griselda Grantly as 'somewhat statuesque in her loveliness', he added, '[T]o me she always seemed as though she wanted fullness of lip'. On the next page, however, this focus changed to the metafictional when he observed that the truth is 'a virtue for which a novelist does not receive very much commendation'.[76] The narrative was thus replicating the style of the surrounding articles to move in and out of group authorship, reflecting on composition and oscillating between novel and periodical.

This participation in group authorship could subsequently, however, distort the effect of the novel reprinted as a book where such features caused Henry James to complain after Trollope's death that he 'did not write for posterity; he wrote for the day, the moment'.[77] Reacting to the *Autobiography*, James described his fellow author's methods as both industrial and 'deliberately inartistic'.[78] The position of a serial effectively being written before the reader's very eyes would add to this sense of non-artistry although James was also commenting on the set-piece narration and direct addresses by the author which were a feature of Trollope's novels even before *Framley Parsonage*. The examples of group authorship with Thackeray and Sala demonstrate, however, that this supposed unreality emerged from the serial's technique in mirroring the articles with which it first appeared. Trollope happily reiterated his authorial branding as a writer of serials and he used his 'habit of industry' as a marker of his own authorship when he shaped his posterity through his *Autobiography.*[79]

In the case of Wilkie Collins, his prior authorship established him as a writer of sensation fiction which was itself a subset of periodical serialization. His four major novels of the 1860s helped to define the features of the genre discussed by reviewers such as Margaret Oliphant in *Blackwood's Edinburgh Magazine* and Henry Mansel in the *Quarterly Review*. These critics emphasized the role of serialization in the definition and transmission of the sensation genre pointing to the forward movement and anticipation of the next week's episode as a feature of sensation reading which thus exacerbated the gap between consumption and anticipation. In her first review on the subject, Oliphant highlighted '[t]he violent stimulant of weekly publication, with its necessity for frequent and rapid

---

[75]   *CM* 2, 308.

[76]   *CM* 1, 461; 462.

[77]   Henry James, *Century Magazine* n.s. 4 (July 1883); repr., in *The Barsetshire Novels*, ed. Tony Bareham (London: Macmillan, 1983), 65.

[78]   James in Bareham (ed.), 62.

[79]   Trollope, *Autobiography*, 121. See also Sarah Gilead, 'Trollope's *Autobiography*: The Strategies of Self-Production,' *Modern Language Quarterly* 47 (1986): 272–90.

recurrence of piquant situation and startling incident'.[80] Henry Mansel implicated readers in the spread of this diseased appetite when he accused them of demanding novels in forms such as the periodical, the volume in the circulating library and the 'railway novel'.[81] Susan David Bernstein discusses sensation in the context of Victorian anthropological interest in the primitive and in appetites stimulated by increased consumerism fuelled in part by the acquisition and presentation of such serial reading.[82] In the context of Dickens's *All the Year Round* Oliphant found, however, that Collins performed the task of serialization with 'delicate care and laborious reticence'.[83]

In terms of his own progression as an author, Collins returned to *All the Year Round* after writing *Armadale* for the *Cornhill* and this resulted in the serialization of *The Moonstone* in 1868. *Cassell's* then courted him in the wake of that success although he wrote to his mother as early as 6 January 1867 that he intended to 'open communications with the penny journals'.[84] The publishers of *Cassell's Magazine* sought to change the standing of their periodical by offering more well-known authors and Collins became part of the penny weekly's experiment to redefine its fictional content whilst maintaining the overall appeal to lower middle-class respectability. Having been employed as a staff writer for both *All the Year Round* and *Household Words*, Collins broke with Dickens again and heard of his friend's death just as he was putting the finishing touches to *Man and Wife* on 9 June 1870.[85]

On Collins's side, this move to *Cassell's Magazine* could be seen as a downward step in his career deleterious to the Collins brand but it was also a part of his quest for 'an entirely new public'.[86] Collins began his three-year collaboration with Cassell's in 1869 and *Man and Wife* was serialized between 20 November 1869 and 30 July 1870. Despite the new public and publication, the novel reused the plot device of the manipulation of marriage conventions notable in all four of Collins's blockbuster novels of the 1860s and even before that, in his earlier *Basil*.[87] Critics of the time focused on Collins's prior authorship by discussing his

---

    [80] [Margaret Oliphant], 'Sensation Novels,' *Blackwood's Edinburgh Magazine* 91 (1862): 569.

    [81] [Henry Mansel], 'Sensation Novels,' *Quarterly Review* 113 (1863): 484–6. See Nicholas Daly, 'Railway Novels: Sensation Fiction and the Modernization of the Senses,' *ELH* 66, (1999): 461–87.

    [82] Susan David Bernstein, 'Dirty Reading: Sensation Fiction, Women, and Primitivism', *Criticism* 36 (1994): 235–6.

    [83] [Oliphant], 'Sensation Novels,' 568.

    [84] Wilkie Collins to Harriet Collins, 6 January 1867, Collins, *The Public Face*, vol. 2, 59.

    [85] Wilkie Collins to Charles Ward, 9 June 1870, Collins, *The Public Face*, vol. 2, 192.

    [86] Wilkie Collins to Harriet Collins, 6 January 1867.

    [87] *Basil* appeared, in volume form only, in 1852. See Graham Law, 'The Serial Publication in Britain of the Novels of Wilkie Collins,' http://www.f.waseda.jp/glaw/arts/wcsp.pdf.

repeated choice of alternative narrative devices such as those used in *The Woman in White*, *Armadale* and *The Moonstone*. *Man and Wife* included the diary of Hester Dethridge and the *Saturday Review* produced the 'inevitable journal' review of the volume edition of *Poor Miss Finch*.[88] In the early 1870s then, Collins moved into new markets at a time when the periodical press was looking for extended audiences but still he could not escape that 'one everlasting cry'.

Gaskell's brand developed somewhat differently albeit also within the sphere of both Dickens and the *Cornhill*. After the volume edition of *Cranford* appeared in 1853, her next novel *North and South* was serialized also in *Household Words* in 1854–55. Dickens had been named as the author of the serial *Hard Times* between April and August 1854 immediately before this but *North and South* was attributed rather to 'the author of Mary Barton' each week. Although Gaskell's novel was not in first station as Dickens's had been, the industrial settings of Gaskell's two novels would have provided a good reason to invoke this prior authorship. The attribution of *North and South* began Dickens's practice of attributing the longer fictional serials using prior authorship which continued into *All the Year Round*. In terms of Gaskell's own authorship and its deployment by magazine editors, her next serialized novel *Wives and Daughters* appeared unattributed some ten years later in *Cornhill Magazine* between August 1864 and January 1866. This serialization partly overlapped Collins's *Armadale* and in this way three of the core authors continued their branded careers within the pages of the *Cornhill*. After being moved to an interior station in the magazine in November 1864, *Wives and Daughters* reassumed the lead station in the magazine in July 1865. This was because Collins's novel proved controversial when it was narrated through the journal of a female murderer and adulteress.[89] Marie Warmbold has identified in *Wives and Daughters* 'a Trollopian theme'[90] suggesting the serial effect of Trollope's influence on the *Cornhill* or at least his influence on the magazine's readers then and now. The magazine was looking to the effect of its premier author and the safety of the domestic to rescue its reputation and circulation figures, and in terms of Gaskell's prior authorship, *Wives and Daughters* completed the long-running if occasional Cranford/Duncombe/Hanbury series by using the village setting of Hollingford.

Warmbold also suggests that the monthly magazine provided 'a less demanding format' for Gaskell.[91] This may be true for her later novel but the exploration of *Household Words* will suggest that serialization and embedding in the weekly magazine was a significant factor in the creation of *Cranford*.[92] Even in the last

---

[88]   *Saturday Review*, 2 March 1872, 282–3; see above.

[89]   This interface is discussed in Catherine Delafield, *Women's Diaries as Narrative in the Nineteenth-Century Novel* (Farnham: Ashgate, 2009), 113–14.

[90]   Marie E. Warmbold, 'Elizabeth Gaskell in *Cornhill* Country,' *Victorian Periodicals Review* 33 (2000): 143.

[91]   Warmbold, 148.

[92]   See Chapters 4 and 5.

year of Gaskell's life, there was an echo of the much earlier sketch 'Mr Harrison's Confessions' in the title of Chapter 60 of *Wives and Daughters* – 'Roger Hamley's Confession' – which was presented in the *Cornhill* as the last chapter Gaskell ever wrote. When *Wives and Daughters* was concluded in the *Cornhill*, the editor Frederick Greenwood had to explain and write about her projected ending which she could not write herself because of her sudden death on 12 November 1865. Circumstance thus created the necessity for the novel to be absorbed further into the group authorship of the periodical. At the same time, however, Gaskell was finally named as Gaskell in Greenwood's postscript to the unfinished text.

The *British Quarterly Review* article from 1866 commended Gaskell for keeping women at the forefront, whilst criticizing sensation novelists such as Collins and Mary Elizabeth Braddon for seeing providence in no one but the 'detective police' and for representing in their characters 'an incarnation of every evil'.[93] Reviewers were thus using branding – which Craik, Gaskell, Collins and their publishers wished to perpetuate – as a point of differentiation between authors. Dickens welcomed Collins back to *All the Year Round* as 'the author of "The Woman in White"' and saw him leave again as 'Wilkie Collins' whilst George Smith's negotiations for a sequel to *Framley Parsonage* gave the *Cornhill* a new adjective, 'Trollopian'. There was a register of authorial voices created by the writer's named persona within the group authorship of the periodical. Authorship of a novel serialized within a periodical thus comprised many 'thresholds of interpretation' which acted as textual guarantors from the narrator of the novel through to the named or unnamed author, the illustrator, editor and publisher. The authors constructed for the consumption of periodical readers were given their context by the editors and publishers of the periodical, those collaborators who policed the code of discourse and underwrote the novel before, after and during its appearance as a serial.

---

[93]   'The Author of John Halifax,' 38; 34.

Chapter 3
Serialization and the Periodical Editor

The editor is clearly a vital force in the collaborative and competitive discourse of the periodical and thus of the serial it contains. If according to John Cassell he is 'to unite amusement with instruction',[1] the editor, in collaboration with the publisher, must encode his periodical according to its target market. This chapter discusses the ways in which editorial influence affected the positioning of the serial as part of this broader collaboration. It assesses the role of the periodical editor in conditioning the audience and in contextualizing the serial to maintain readership and profitability. Editorship will be considered by investigating the impact and role of the periodical publisher, the characterization of the editor, the pattern of the periodical series and the overall representation of editorial choices within that series.

The nineteenth-century periodical was published as part of a series which existed to provide access to reading within a controlled space, controlled both by the financial sponsorship of the publisher and the editorial choices which marked the style and register of that periodical. The serialized novel appeared within this space but as part of a marketing plan to sell fiction and to promote the repeat purchase of the periodical. Where the novelist was responsible for the serial, the editor was responsible for the series. The series has been described as 'a distinct form of control'[2] and the editor or publisher of a periodical was an identifiable and 'distinct' controller who was responsible for the borders and thresholds of the contributing parts. He (or in some cases they) appeared to have the final say in the competitive economy of the periodical as a text. Working inwards from the outer borders of the serial where it was bounded by the periodical, this chapter begins by assessing the impact and role of the publisher where this can be derived from the periodical. In parallel with the category of authorship, the chapter considers the characterization of the editor and his contribution to the character of the periodical. By providing an overarching discourse the editor/publisher set up the schema of the periodical series and it is argued that this created and reinforced the intertextual patterning of the novel serialized within a periodical.

---

[1]   'To the Reader,' *CIFP*, 31 December 1853, 1.

[2]   Norman. N. Feltes, *Modes of Publication of Victorian Novels* (Chicago: University of Chicago Press, 1986), 10.

The Role of the Publisher

The periodical publisher had commercial imperatives which shaped the series under his financial control. Periodical titles evolved within the growth process of publishing houses and adopted varying roles within the economic model of their sponsors. When the serials represented in this discussion appeared, the publishers were operating at varying stages in what might now be seen as the development cycle of periodical production. Bradbury and Evans were both publishers of and shareholders in *Household Words* but Dickens later asserted greater control over *All the Year Round* by owning 75 percent of it himself with the other 25 percent owned by his assistant Wills. *Cornhill Magazine* was a long-planned project from the established publishing house of Smith Elder, which was able to attract contributions from well-known writers through its existing catalogue. By contrast, Alexander Strahan, publisher of *Good Words* was a rising and ambitious publisher looking to break into the English (as opposed to the Scottish) market. Finally, the firm of Cassell's was re-launching its title as *Cassell's Magazine* from the basis of the temperance organization originally founded in the 1850s, but the managing partners Petter and Galpin were printers who had turned publishers because of their stronger business position.

The publishers of *Household Words*, Bradbury and Evans, had also been printers for Dickens's earlier publishers, Chapman and Hall. They (Bradbury and Evans) were the publishers of *Punch* from December 1842 and also Dickens's publishers from 1 June 1844. They were thus associated with the serialization of Dickens's novels as part works.[3] *All the Year Round* was then later printed by Chapman and Hall with Dickens and Wills acting as their own publishers. In this sense, the role of the publisher in Dickens's two periodicals was to a high degree subordinated to the role of the editor in the perception of the reader. This position is reflected in the balance of the discussion which follows here which considers ways in which publishers shaped the magazine series in which the serialized novels appeared. Dickens's role as editor/publisher is considered in the further section on editorial character. The initial discussion, therefore, focuses on George Smith as publisher of the *Cornhill*, Strahan as publisher of *Good Words* and Petter and Galpin as publishers of *Cassell's Magazine*. The magazines they produced were known (or became known) for a certain tone and style, and the names and perceived roles of the publishers were part of the context for the serialized novels. This section therefore addresses ways in which these publishers appeared on the page by focusing on the issues of tone, attribution and cross-selling which affected the three magazines during the appearance of three of the core texts: *Framley Parsonage*, *Mistress and Maid* and *Poor Miss Finch*.

---

[3]   These part works were: *Oliver Twist* (January to October 1846), *Dombey and Son* (October 1846 to April 1848), *David Copperfield* (May 1849 to November 1850), *Bleak House* (March 1852 to September 1853) and *Little Dorrit* (December 1855 to June 1857).

At the launch of *Cornhill Magazine*, it is clear that the pursuit of a competitive edge using an aggressive marketing strategy was tempered by caution in the approach to matters of politics and religion. Smith explained in his unpublished 'Recollections' that 'a novel by Thackeray was essential to my scheme' although at first he reasoned that Thackeray did not have 'the business qualities which go to make a good editor.'[4] He distinguished between his own role as publisher and that of his editor, perceiving that his energy would be able to compensate for Thackeray's lack of business acumen at the same time as ensuring Thackeray's contributions as an author. In 1901, Smith recalled his reasoning: 'Why should not Mr Thackeray edit the magazine, you yourself doing what is necessary to supplement any want of business qualifications on his part?'[5] Writing forty years after the event, Smith was reflecting back the esteem in which Thackeray was held after his premature death. Smith considered that 'any writer would be proud to contribute to a periodical under his editorship', and Jennifer Glynn, Smith's biographer observes, 'Together they assembled a wonderful collection of talent'.[6] Under his editor's signature, the publisher announced in the advertisement letter for the *Cornhill* in November 1859 that 'there is hardly any subject we don't want to hear about, from lettered and instructed men who are competent to speak on it,' indicating here the tone he sought to capture once he had employed Thackeray. In addition, however, the editor and publisher had their eye on the family audience, and the advertisement explained that '[at]t our social table we shall suppose the ladies and children always present' along with 'clergymen of various denominations to say grace in their turn'.[7]

The consciousness of this 'social table' advertised by Smith was highlighted by the actions of the publisher in 1860 when treating John Ruskin's economic sermons 'Unto this Last'. These were articles which appeared during the first year of the *Cornhill*'s publication and were thus part of the context for *Framley Parsonage* as a serial. Ruskin was already part of the publishing setup at Smith Elder which had among many other works produced his *Modern Painters* (1843–56), *Seven Lamps of Architecture* (1849) and *Stones of Venice* (1851–53). It was clearly in Smith's interests to support and promote his own author, and an article by Ruskin entitled 'Sir Joshua and Holbein' appeared unattributed in the magazine in March 1860. When 'Unto this Last' started to appear in August 1860, however, Smith/ Thackeray dropped the *Cornhill* convention of anonymity because of the backlash against them in the press. Only four 'Unto this Last' essays were published in the magazine (between August and November 1860) and the initials 'J.R.' were

---

4   George Smith, 'Our Birth and Parentage,' *CM* n. s. 10 (1901): 4. Smith's article drew on his 'Recollections of a Long and Busy Life' which is in the Smith Elder Archives in the National Library of Scotland.

5   Smith, 5.

6   Smith, 5; Jennifer Glynn, *Prince of Publishers: A Biography of the Great Victorian Publisher George Smith* (London: Allison and Busby, 1986), 124.

7   Quoted in Smith, 7.

added at the foot of the last page of each instalment. Ruskin's own father wrote to the publisher John Murray on 9 October 1860 of 'the utter unfitness of these Papers for a magazine'. He also observed at the time that 'the Editor would not be answerable for opinions so opposed to Malthus and the Times and the City of Manchester', and that this was why the management of the *Cornhill* printed the articles with an attribution.[8] Ruskin was allowed twice as much space for the final essay in order to conclude his arguments when Thackeray and Smith had to bring the series to a close and, having announced that J.S. Mill and Riccardo were in error, the essayist insisted that 'The real science of political economy ... is that which teaches nations to desire and labour for the things that lead to life'.[9]

The actions taken by Smith/Thackeray of attribution and truncation reflect the concerns of the publisher that the periodical itself should offer consistency within its miscellany. Ruskin had to be identified or separately designated in order to indemnify the publisher from accusations which might harm circulation within the targeted family audience: an audience who might be presumed to be reading other publications which were commenting on Ruskin's essays and who would also be buying books from the publishing house as well as reading *Framley Parsonage* month by month. Glynn suggests that there were also sensitivities over the criticism of Eton in the 'Paterfamilias' articles at the time which influenced the treatment of Ruskin's essays.[10] In the 1910 Jubilee issue of the *Cornhill*, former editor E.T. Cook observed about this incident that '[t]he conductor of any popular magazine or other "organ of public opinion" may well be a little ahead of his public, but he cannot afford to be too much ahead.'[11] In taking this visible action on the page, Smith was considering the wider context and influencing the placement of *Framley Parsonage* and the other *Cornhill* serials, fictional and non-fictional.

In *Good Words*, Alexander Strahan's religious policies clearly informed the tone adopted by the periodical on topics of the day. Strahan modelled himself on Charles Knight, the innovative publisher of the *Penny Magazine*.[12] He coined the title of the magazine and persuaded Macleod to use it, and the name 'Strahan & Co' adorned the title page. The value of the name of the publisher and its associations meant that even when Strahan himself was forced into bankruptcy in

---

[8]   Quoted in Glynn, 103.

[9]   John Ruskin, 'Unto this Last,' *CM* 2 (1860): 547.

[10]   Glynn, 103. An article by 'Jacob Omnium' (Matthew Higgins), Smith's future collaborator on the *Pall Mall Gazette* appeared in May 1860 entitled 'Paterfamilias to the Editor of the "Cornhill Magazine,"' *CM* 1 (1860): 608–15.The 'Second Letter' appeared in December 1860, leading out the whole issue (*CM* 2 (1860): 641–9) as did the 'Third Letter' in March 1861 (*CM* 3 (1860): 257–69).Glynn suggests that the *Cornhill* thus came to be perceived as a champion of public school reform (128).

[11]   E.T. Cook, 'The Jubilee of the *Cornhill*,' *CM* 28 (1910): 14. Cook also edited the works of Ruskin (1903–12).

[12]   Patricia Thomas Srebrnik, *Alexander Strahan: Victorian Publisher* (Ann Arbor: University of Michigan Press, 1986), 33.

early 1872, his creditors insisted on the rights to that name until September 1874.[13] Thackeray's clergymen saying grace were more at the forefront of Strahan's strategy but it is still possible to trace the Scotsman's commercial imperative and the cross-publicizing of his wares within the magazine during the serialization of *Mistress and Maid*.

In January and February 1862 two extracts from *Vesper*, first published in 1861 appeared in *Good Words*. The writer, the Swiss Countess de Gasparin, was identified only as the 'author of "The Near and Heavenly Horizons"'.[14] The Countess had founded a nursing school in Lausanne in 1859, demonstrating that nursing could be a profession outside of a religious order, an action relating broadly to the proposals made by Craik about women's roles. The Countess's two separate works *Les Horizons Prochains* and *Les Horizons Celestes* had appeared in 1859 but the English translation was published by Strahan as *The Near and Heavenly Horizons* in 1861. This reference to prior authorship in the periodical number was part of the pragmatic objectives of the publisher to market other titles he was publishing. The practice continued during the serialization of *Mistress and Maid*. 'The Crimson Flower' by the Countess appeared in May with the same proclaimed authorship, accompanied by an illustration of a young girl in despair by J.D. Watson immediately after 'Old Maids and Young Maids', and another piece about Egypt entitled 'The East' appeared in July.[15]

There were other close-knit references to female authors which helped to promote works published by Strahan. 'A Cast in the Waggon' a two-part short story by Sarah Tytler 'author of "Papers for Thoughtful Girls"' appeared in *Good Words* in March and April 1862 in part to promote the *Papers for Thoughtful Girls* which Strahan published that year. The completely anonymous fictional novella 'Memoirs of an Unknown Life' was published by Strahan after it had appeared as a six-part serial in 1861 and the resulting by-line of the 'Unknown Author of "Memoirs of an Unknown Life"' reappeared for the article 'Old Maids and Young Maids' in May. In this article, the 'Unknown Author' then referred to Tytler's *Papers* along with 'The Afternoon of Life' and 'My Life: what shall I do with it?'[16] Tytler was the alternative penname of the Scottish novelist Henrietta Keddie who usually separated her output between fiction (as Keddie) and religious-based fact (as Tytler).The 'Unknown Author' was practising the same non-naming approach as Dinah Craik and remained unnamed in spite of Strahan's specific naming strategy in the second and third years of the publication of *Good Words*.[17] The use of prior authorship as attribution was thus both a marketing tool for the publisher and a mark of respectability for the author. The use of named clergymen

---

13   The debts and rights are discussed in Srebrnik, 119–20.
14   'Vesper,' *GW* 3 (1862): 9–13; 81–8.
15   *GW* 3, 302–6; 399–403.
16   *GW* 3, 299.
17   See Srebrnik, 40.

and respectably veiled but known female authors fitted both the tone and the commercial stance which Strahan was adopting.

The publishers Cassell, Petter and Galpin re-launched *Cassell's Illustrated Family Paper* as *Cassell's Magazine* in 1867, and in 1869, they sought increased circulation for the *Magazine* by securing the services of Wilkie Collins. The historian of Cassell's writes that Collins 'might have been expected to do the magazine credit, but ... presumed to hold views about the integrity of [his] art'.[18] As a publishing house, Cassell's used the magazine to promote the original founder's 'amusement with instruction' and so to cross-sell other products such as factual serials and improving literature. Their approach to meeting the challenges of the magazine market going into the 1870s can be illustrated by their recorded relationship with Collins and the impact of the periodical on the appearance of his serialized novels.

Because of his status as an established writer, Collins was quite prepared to quibble in negotiating terms for *Poor Miss Finch*. His control over the content of his work would later generate a terse public argument with Arthur Locker during the subsequent serialization of *The Law and the Lady* in *The Graphic* in 1875.[19] His letters to Cassell's in 1871 indicate his commercial stance along with an eye towards his potential inability to meet deadlines. Cassell's had in his words been offered 'first refusal' of his 'next work of fiction',[20] and he effectively offered them a respite from their problematical relationship with Charles Reade whose serial *A Terrible Temptation* was attracting adverse publicity for the *Magazine*. Collins appeared to be goading the publishers into offering a higher rate than was at first proposed by pointing out that it was not the number of instalments for which he should be paid – like a wholesaler – rather that he was 'selling ... an *Idea*', his intellectual property. He insisted: 'I voluntarily abridge for the sake of the literary result. The suppression which diminishes the number of my weekly parts, involves quite as much mental work as the prolixity which might enlarge them.'[21]

Collins was prioritizing authorship over editorship and this led to a power struggle which can be traced in the context of the serialization of *Poor Miss Finch* and before. On 17 August 1869 Collins wrote to Galpin, the commercial partner, about his contract for the earlier serial *Man and Wife*: 'I remind you that mine is the only hand which holds the threads of the story, and mine are the only eyes which see it as one complete whole – while others merely see it as a succession

---

[18]   Simon Nowell-Smith, *The House of Cassell 1848–1958* (London: Cassell, 1958), 121.

[19]   The impact on that serial is discussed in Catherine Delafield, 'Text in Context: *The Law and the Lady* and *The Graphic*,' in *From Compositors to Collectors: Essays on Book-Trade History*, ed. Matthew Day and John Hicks (London: British Library, 2012), 133–53.

[20]   Wilkie Collins to Cassell, Petter and Galpin, 14 January 1871, Collins, *The Public Face*, vol. 2, 231.

[21]   Wilkie Collins to Cassell, Petter and Galpin, 2 February 1871, Collins, *The Public Face*, vol. 2, 235.

of parts.'[22] He later co-operated by removing at the proof stage a 'damn it' from *Man and Wife* but he also insisted in a letter addressed to 'Cassell, Petter and Galpin', the company as a body 'that this concession may not be construed into a precedent'. As an experienced writer of serialized novels he took a lofty stance which is worth quoting in full. He continued:

> Readers who object to expletives in books are – as to my experience – readers who object to a great many other things in books, which they are too stupid to understand. It is quite possible that your peculiar constituency may take exception to things to come in my story, which are essential to the development of character, or which are connected with a much higher and larger moral point of view than they are capable of taking themselves. In these cases, I am afraid you will find me deaf to all remonstrances.[23]

Collins's letters nonetheless demonstrate that he was keen to write for this publisher's 'constituency' which had been in formation since 1853. As discussed in Chapter 2, Collins wrote to his mother after he had finished *Armadale* for the *Cornhill* that he would 'make a new start, with a new public', the readers of the penny journals.[24] Collins's contract forbade 'the slightest alteration' to his text and in this the author insisted to Galpin, 'I am only claiming the privilege which has already been accorded to me by Mr Dickens in "All the Year Round" and by the Proprietors of The Cornhill Magazine'.[25]

Cassell's side of this correspondence is not extant but they were apparently keen to exploit their new attraction and so ostensibly complied. The printing works was destroyed in the Blitz in 1941 along with any copies, and this absence of any replies to Collins produces a curiously one-sided argument. On the other hand, the publishers controlled the *Magazine* as a series and there is evidence which demonstrates that the publishers' control was firmly reasserted over the text of *Poor Miss Finch* as both serial and novel. Firstly, Cassell's were able to use the final sanction of print to ensure that their mission as a family paper was fulfilled despite Collins's contractual control of the novel itself. As the immediate result of Collins's seeking to address this 'peculiar constituency', the *Athenaeum* would note 'the sanctifying influence of *Cassell's Magazine*' on the novel and sneer at the impact of its 'edification by weekly instalments'.[26] In addition Cassell's enhanced

---

[22] Wilkie Collins to Thomas D. Galpin, 17 August 1869, Collins, *The Public Face*, vol. 2, 147.

[23] Wilkie Collins to Cassell, Petter and Galpin, 25 September 1869, Collins, *The Public Face*, vol. 2, 152.

[24] Wilkie Collins to Harriet Collins, 6 January 1867, Collins, *The Public Face*, vol. 2, 59. *Cassell's Illustrated Family Paper* was founded in 1853.

[25] Wilkie Collins to Thomas D. Galpin, 17 August 1869, Collins, *The Public Face*, vol. 2, 147.

[26] [D.E. Williams], *The Athenaeum*, 17 February 1872, 202–3; repr., in *Wilkie Collins: The Critical Heritage*, ed. Norman Page (London: Routledge and Kegan Paul, 1974), 191; 192.

the commercial arrangement reached over Collins's 'voluntary abridgment' of the serial by the sharp practice of producing *Poor Miss Finch* in a single volume reprint of the *Magazine* produced once the serial was completed.[27] This version originally outsold the volume edition contracted to George Bentley and concluded the working relationship between novelist and publisher. In these ways, the appearance and resonances both of *Man and Wife* and of *Poor Miss Finch* in the *Magazine* were finally re-presented through the 'larger point of view' of editorial choice and publisher positioning.

In 1870, the *Athenaeum* commented on a group of publishers who were 'especially concerned with the literature of the people' and have '*grown* into their present position' with a wide readership. Along with Low, Nelson, Warne and Routledge, the reviewer cited Strahan and Cassell, concluding that 'they are not so much men as systems'.[28] The name, reputation or perceived 'system' of the publisher occupied a place in the readers' perception and the resulting intertextual commentary might be both coincidental and commercial. Publishers shaped a series simply through their financial backing but were also investing in a carefully positioned and marketable product. The publishers were systems in so much as they acted as named but anonymous channels to market for the serials under discussion. These channels, however, were never neutral in providing the context for the serial's growth from issue to issue, and the spaces in which the novels were originally situated reflect their placement within the series as well. The novels emerged as a result of commercial imperatives within the financial production model of the publisher, and through different types of collaboration ranging from the co-operation between Smith Elder and Trollope to the confrontation of Cassell's with Collins.

The Characterization of the Editor

Laurel Brake and Julie Codell have observed that nineteenth-century periodicals 'consist of individuals' contributions patched together and fitted, very practically, to the space, readership, and politics of the structure of a single periodical issue.'[29] Most periodicals had an overarching editor, and it was the editor or editor/publisher who established a pattern into which the serials were 'fitted'. This section considers how the editor was personified within the periodical and how the character of the editor functioned within the series. There were varying approaches to the deployment of an editor in the magazines under discussion. After John Cassell's death, the editorship of *Cassell's Magazine* was largely an administrative role behind the scenes with a few exceptions discussed below. Thackeray was chosen

---

27   This is discussed in Chapter 6.

28   'Literature of the People,' *The Athenaeum*, 1 January 1870, 14.

29   Laurel Brake and Julie Codell, 'Encountering the Press,' in *Encounters in the Victorian Press*, ed. Laurel Brake and Julie Codell (Basingstoke: Palgrave Macmillan, 2004), 1.

for the *Cornhill* in response to his existing reputation although he was not Smith's first choice[30] and struggled with some of his responsibilities. Strahan completed much of the editorial task for *Good Words* himself although Norman Macleod was vital to the tone of the periodical with his Evangelical and royal connections although Macleod appears to have intervened more after the personal attack on him in the Evangelical press in 1863.[31] In addition to these male editors of the core periodicals, there were, of course, female editors of family magazines such as Mary Elizabeth Braddon (*Temple Bar* and *Belgravia*), Ellen Wood (*Argosy*) and Florence Marryat (*London Society*).[32] Focus on the five serialized novels has directed discussion in this study to five male-edited magazines and the gender impact of the female editor would also benefit from further research. With specific reference to sensation fiction, Beth Palmer concludes that Braddon, Wood and Marryat 'utilized the transgressive and porous space of the periodical press to their advantage'.[33]

The choice of editor (or apparent editor) was part of the ongoing message of the periodicals series. Amongst the five magazines under discussion, Charles Dickens was clearly named as editor of *Household Words* and *All the Year Round*. When *Household Words* was launched in 1850, he was already experienced in periodical publication and had developed as an author from the pseudonymous 'Boz' to being the named author of *Dombey and Son* and of *David Copperfield*. Norman Macleod was named as editor from the fifth issue of *Good Words* in February 1860[34] and had already edited both a Scottish religious periodical and Strahan's short-lived *Christian Guest*. *Cornhill Magazine* was edited by the known but unnamed Thackeray, unnamed in the environment of the monthly periodical but very well known to be the *Cornhill*'s editor in the wider press and clearly identifiable from his own contributions. The editor of *Cassell's Magazine* changed often and was unnamed to maintain the continuity of the series which had been launched in the 1850s and then re-launched twice in the 1860s but always under the 'Cassell's' banner. Within these magazines, an editor's contribution was not always specifically identified as such within the 'competitive economy' of the periodical issue. Dickens addressed his periodical audience directly as editor and was named as author of his fiction serials but also contributed unattributed journalistic articles. Thackeray was unnamed as a fiction author but used his 'Roundabout Papers' to address the *Cornhill* readership and to create the register of the periodical as a whole. Macleod provided a monthly editorial which largely

---

30   Smith had initially approached Thomas Hughes, author of *Tom Brown's Schooldays*; see Spencer L. Eddy, *The Founding of the 'Cornhill Magazine'* (Muncie, Indiana: Ball State University, 1970), 9–11.

31   See Srebrnik, 42; 55–61.

32   See Beth Palmer, *Women's Authorship and Editorship in Victorian Culture: Sensational Strategies* (Oxford: Oxford University Press, 2011), 1–8.

33   Palmer, 184.

34   *Good Words* appeared weekly for the first year of its publication.

reinforced the religious tone of *Good Words* whilst the ever-changing editor of *Cassell's Magazine* was usually invisible against the backdrop of the named but deceased founder of the original temperance organization.

Letters from Dickens to his assistant editor W.H. Wills demonstrate that he aimed to be the overall arbiter of *Household Words* despite his frequent absences. In 1850, for instance, Wills was forced to respond when Dickens objected to one of his decisions and this indicates the way in which the function of Dickens's name within the periodical was impressed upon his staff. Wills wrote on 12 July, 'I am exceedingly jealous of anything appearing which might have the remotest tendency to damage the name which appears at the top of each page; and which is responsible for every word printed below it.'[35] Wills who was described by Dickens's first biographer John Forster as 'discharging [his] duties with amiable patience and ability for twenty years',[36] became bolder in the second year of publication, protesting in October 1851 that 'Elegance of Fancy cannot be thrown broadcast over such an acreage of letter press' that is 'twenty-four pages of print published fifty-two times a year'.[37] Wills tempered this by acknowledging 'the latitude of confidence' given him but requested 'the systematic benefit of another judgment before publication.'[38] The 'Fancy' to which Wills was referring in 1851 itself referred back to Dickens's first 'Preliminary Word', the self-styled 'faltering lines' which opened *Household Words* on 30 March 1850.[39] Like '[t]he adventurer in the old fairy story', the writer finds himself urged to 'Go on!' and '[t]o show to all, that in all familiar things, ... there is Romance enough, if we will find it out'.[40] The editor, who was not unknown to his new public, planned to write of the past and the present, of joys and sorrows, home and abroad adding with carefully judged humility: 'We have considered what an ambition it is to be admitted into many homes with affection and confidence ... to be associated with the harmless laughter and the gentle tears of many hearths.'[41]

The transition from *Household Words* to *All the Year Round* nine years later in 1859 was a significant border or marker where Dickens again addressed his readership directly. Forster described *All the Year Round* as 'a substitute for the older series'[42] in order to gloss over the circumstances of the launch which took

---

[35]   W.H. Wills to Charles Dickens, 12 July 1850, R.C. Lehmann, *Charles Dickens as Editor* (London: Smith Elder, 1912), 30–31.

[36]   John Forster, *The Life of Charles Dickens*, 2 vols (London: Chapman and Hall, n. d.), vol. 2, 48. Forster who worked on *Household Words* himself and owned a one-eighth share (as Wills did) recommended Wills for the post (Forster, 48).

[37]   W.H. Wills to Charles Dickens, 17 October 1851, Lehmann, 74.

[38]   Lehmann, 75.

[39]   'A Preliminary Word,' *HW*, 30 March 1850, 1.

[40]   'A Preliminary Word,' 1; 2.

[41]   'A Preliminary Word,' 1.

[42]   Forster, 48. Forster alluded to the terms of the personal and commercial separation in his biography when he commented on Dickens's initially injudicious choice of title for the new periodical: *Household Harmony* (Forster, vol. 2,164).

place after Dickens broke away from Bradbury and Evans over the publicity surrounding his separation from his wife Catherine. Dickens used the printed appearance of the periodical to stress this moment, and the resulting paratext had an influence over both series and serial. Having presented *Household Words* in columns for nearly nine years, the editor wrote across those columns to advertise the new periodical, quite literally disrupting the reader's customary pattern.[43] This was notable at the 'Address' which opened the last number on 28 May 1859 and 'A Last Household Word' which closed it. The opening 'Address' restated the prospectus of the new magazine already being published elsewhere with Dickens insisting that 'Nine years of HOUSEHOLD WORDS, are the best practical assurance that can be offered to the public, of the spirit and objects of ALL THE YEAR ROUND'.[44] He advertised this similarity by thus differentiating the periodical titles from the main text of the 'Address'. In all but name the periodicals were pronounced to be identical, employing the same staff, and they actually appeared side by side for five weeks from 30 April after which *All the Year Round* used its new amalgamated title. On 28 May the last contractually required issue of *Household Words* appeared and Dickens could thus announce in this last number that the circulation of the new magazine was already three times that of its predecessor. Dickens exerted his editorial authority with the same sense of series control not only across columns but by referring once again to the first number of *Household Words* from1850: 'The first page of the first of these Nineteen Volumes, was devoted to a Preliminary Word from the writer by whom they were projected, under whose constant supervision they have been produced, and whose name has been (as his pen and himself have been), inseparable from the Publication ever since.' A separately spaced sentence was added for dramatic effect: 'The last page of the last of these Nineteen Volumes, is closed by the same hand', and the very last 'household words' are 'THE END OF THE NINETEENTH VOLUME, AND OF THE SERIES'.[45]

The editor had both to draw a line under the periodical and to ensure its continuity, a continuity supplied in his own person both as editor and as author. This physical and typographical closure occurred in the last issue of the 'older series' which allowed *All the Year Round* to begin in dramatic fashion with the unadorned opening lines of *A Tale of Two Cities*: 'It was the best of times, it was the worst of times.' These opening lines gained added weight because of their position within the periodical at the boundary between the two periodical series. The responsibility of being editor impelled Dickens to give the lines an even more emphatic value which was also external to their context within the novel. Their intertextual function is even greater as part of *All the Year Round* in the history of publishing, and it cannot be coincidental that the novel itself concerned substitution

---

[43] 'Address,' *HW*, 28 May 1859, 601; 'A Last Household Word,' *HW*, 28 May 1859, 620.

[44] 'Address.'

[45] 'A Last Household Word.'

and resurrection. By the end of the serial, *Household Words* has sacrificed itself for *All the Year Round* as Sydney Carton sacrificed himself for Charles Darnay.

On the inside cover of the first issue of *Cornhill Magazine*, Thackeray described himself as 'a Conductor of a Concert, in which I trust many skilful performers will take part'.[46] His use of the term 'conductor' might be seen as a challenge to the presentation of the role of editor in Dickens's periodicals. Since Dickens was the only named contributor and designated himself 'inseparable from the Publication', it was often believed that he was the author of all contributions to the periodicals under his editorship, and commentators have suggested that he shaped other contributions so that they conformed to an overall 'Dickensy' style.[47] Thackeray and Smith, however, were aiming to encourage new contributors and to "orchestrate" their publication as the output of an amiable group of equals. Thackeray in his turn wanted the magazine to 'bear my *cachet* … and be a man-of-the-world magazine' although each contributor had the power of veto over content.[48] When Thackeray welcomed Trollope to the periodical, he described novels as 'wares' and novelists as pastry cooks. Thackeray wrote, 'the public love the tarts (luckily for us) and we must bake and sell them'.[49] In this letter, it was implied that the educational factual articles and serials made up the 'bread and cheese'. Thackeray was thus appealing as 'a man of the world' to Trollope and Trollope himself was keen to promote and commemorate this environment and atmosphere in later quoting from the letter in his *Autobiography*. In 1859, Thackeray at once acclaimed Trollope as a 'Co-operator in our New Magazine'.[50]

Thackeray was known to be the editor of the *Cornhill* and was permitted to exercise his character in the conversational 'Roundabout Papers', his 'rambling papers'[51] as he called them. Through these he could also react to topical events such as his 'Week's Holiday' (where he cannot escape the postman) or 'Round about the Christmas Tree'.[52] Despite the success of the magazine, Thackeray was keen to play down the role of editor with the aim of maintaining a gentlemanly

---

[46]   Quoted in Robert A. Colby, 'Goose Quill and Blue Pencil: The Victorian Novelist as Editor,' in *Innovators and Preachers: the Role of the Editor in Victorian England*, ed. Joel H. Wiener (Westport, CT: Greenwood Press, 1985), 203.

[47]   This is discussed by John Drew, *Dickens the Journalist* (London: Palgrave Macmillan, 2003), 115.

[48]   W.M. Thackeray to George Smith, 7 September 1859, *Letters and Private Papers of W.M. Thackeray*, ed. Gordon Ray (Oxford: Oxford University Press, 1946), vol. 4, 149; Glynn, 123–4.

[49]   W.M. Thackeray to Anthony Trollope, 28 October 1859, Trollope, *Autobiography*, 137.

[50]   Trollope, *Autobiography*, 137.

[51]   [W.M. Thackeray], 'Roundabout Papers No. 9: On a Joke I Once Heard from the Late Thomas Hood,' *CM* 2 (1860): 752.

[52]   [W.M. Thackeray], 'A Roundabout Journey: Notes of a Week's Holiday,' *CM* 2 (1860): 623–40; 'Roundabout Papers No. 10: Round About the Christmas Tree,' *CM* 3 (1861): 250–56.

status for his contributors, those 'co-operators' or '*raconteurs*'. He could self-referentially mention the orange-covered magazine in which his material appeared[53] and, despite the anonymity of the serialized novel, name Trollope as '*Raconteur en chef*'.[54] In this last paper, which appeared at the end of the first year of publication, he wrote about the ongoing impact of his own role and also of Smith's as publisher. In 'Thorns in Cushions' he suggested some of the issues which affected him as editor: that 'it is not the fire of adverse critics which afflicts or frightens the editorial bosom'[55] but rather the letters appealing for publication to support widows and orphans. He had also come to recognise the letters which began with flattery but were 'snakes' to which he exclaimed: 'Away, reptile, to the waste-paper basket, and thence to the flames!'[56] These were the thorns in the cushion of the 'editorial chair' and because of these letters he hated the postman whom he could not escape on holiday.[57] He bemoaned his lot as a 'public man' when it appeared that being editor had caused him to be more exposed as an author to correction over issues within his fiction as, for instance, over criticism of his representation of ballet dancers in his serial *Lovel the Widower*.[58]

Within his editorial 'Papers', however, he also openly supported Smith as a private man. In 'On Screens in Dining Rooms' he defended his publisher from a *Saturday Review* comment which described Smith as 'totally unread'.[59] The reviewer was Edmund Yates who had been expelled from the Garrick Club in 1858 following complaints by Thackeray. Quoting from the *New York Herald*, the reviewer added of Smith that 'his business has been to sell books, not read them'.[60] Thackeray criticised this 'Mr. Nameless' who had written disparagingly of the publisher and insisted that Smith's dinners were private and so should be beyond the scope of such criticism in the press.[61] Given the known role of Smith's monthly dinners in promoting the *Cornhill* and encouraging contributions, this was on the one hand disingenuous but on the other a smoke screen over the commercial arrangements which supported the publication of the magazine. The *Cornhill* was given this aura of apparent ease of production with Thackeray the harassed editor and 'man of the world' co-ordinating a few friends in the publication of a monthly periodical – but with a circulation of 70,000.

---

[53] [W.M. Thackeray], 'Roundabout Papers No. 6: On Screens in Dining Rooms,' *CM* 2 (1860): 253 and 'Roundabout Papers No. 8: De Juventute,' *CM*, 2 (1860): 501.

[54] [Thackeray], 'On a Joke I Once Heard,' 760.

[55] [W.M. Thackeray], 'Roundabout Papers No. 5: Thorns in Cushions,' *CM* 2 (1860): 125.

[56] [Thackeray], 'Thorns in Cushions,' 127.

[57] [Thackeray], 'Thorns in Cushions,' 125; 126.

[58] [Thackeray], 'Thorns in Cushions,' 127; 128.

[59] [Thackeray], 'On Screens in Dining Rooms,' 255.

[60] Quoted in Glynn, 131.

[61] [Thackeray], 'On Screens in Dining Rooms,' 256.

Thackeray relinquished the editorship in April 1862, blaming the hardship of saying "no" to potential contributors which he described in 'Thorns in Cushions'. The joint influence of the two launching collaborators can be measured by the judgement that Smith remained the magazine's 'guiding spirit' until Leslie Stephen took up the editorship and reinvigorated the magazine in 1871.[62] G.H. Lewes was on the editorial board and acted as consulting editor from May 1862 and Smith seems to have saved money by employing him on a retainer and paying Frederick Greenwood considerably less than he had paid Thackeray.[63] The style of editorship, however, continued to benefit from the mythological status of Thackeray albeit in a rather different context from that of the equally mythologized John Cassell described below.

Norman Macleod saw editorship as a duty in parallel with his parochial duties, describing it in his journal on 3 June 1861 as '[a] peculiar department of my ministerial work to which I have been "called"'.[64] In this, he also distinguished his role as an author within the periodical, explaining: 'I cannot, therefore, write stories merely as a literary man, to give amusement, or as works of art only, but must always keep before me the one end of leading souls to know and love God.'[65] In August 1861, he wrote to his friend John Ludlow: 'so long as I have Good Words there shall be "preaching" in it, direct or indirect, and no shame, or sham, about it. This, along with my secularity, will keep it, so far, distinct from other periodicals.'[66] Strahan, of course, saw this distinctiveness as providing a competitive edge which he could ally with the use of the illustrated serial as a selling device for *Good Words*. The serial allowed *Good Words* to compete with *Cornhill Magazine* at the boundary between the middle-class and lower middle-class literate public. The other distinction on which Strahan was able to capitalize was that of Macleod's role as 'one of Her Majesty's Chaplains for Scotland'. Macleod was appointed Chaplain to the Queen in 1857 and recorded instances of meeting his royal patron regularly in his journals and letters. On 9 September 1861, he wrote: 'After dinner I had a most interesting conversation, for about half-an-hour, with the Prince Consort, and a good long one with the Queen.'[67] On 8 May 1862, Macleod described meeting his 'afflicted Sovereign face to face' as 'a sister in humanity' five months after Albert's death.[68] John Wellwood notes that after Macleod's death two stained glass windows at Crathie church were given

---

[62]   Glynn, 137; 138–9.

[63]   Glynn, 138.

[64]   Quoted in Donald Macleod, *Memoir of Norman Macleod* (London: Daldy, Isbister and Co., 1876), 2:110.

[65]   Macleod, *Memoir*, 2:110.

[66]   Macleod, *Memoir*, 2:113.

[67]   Macleod, *Memoir*, 2:116.

[68]   Macleod, *Memoir*, 2:122.

by the Queen in memory of her chaplain[69] and Strahan exploited the title of 'Her Majesty's Chaplain' in magazine issues, collected volumes and reprints in book form.

Strahan had launched his short-lived *Christian Guest: A Family Magazine for Leisure Hours and Sundays* in February 1859 with Macleod as 'Reviser'.[70] Macleod himself had been editor of the *Edinburgh Christian Magazine* since 1849 and his biographer Wellwood describes this as 'a miniature plan or first sketch of Good Words'.[71] What Macleod termed his 'secularity' put him on a collision course, however, with more traditionalist views within the Evangelical church. The early prospectuses for *Good Words* promised 'good words only from week to week'.[72] The provision of 'healthy recreation'[73] which Macleod proposed in his closing statement to *Good Words* for December 1860 promoted reading outside the scriptures and the title of *Christian Guest* was an indicator of how the publisher and editor tried to put religious-based material into the market for reading 'all the week'.[74] Macleod's editorials conveyed religious – even pious – messages and his personal contributions were of the same order. His best-selling work, *Reminiscences of a Highland Parish* appeared in *Good Words* in 1863 after Craik's serial was concluded. 'Wee Davie' had appeared from February 1861, drawing religious lessons from the death of a small boy, and *The Old Lieutenant and his Son* serialized from April to December 1861 was written in a similar vein and was extended over nine months as a substitute for the delayed *Mistress and Maid*. Even Wellwood complained that 'The Old Lieutenant began in Good Words before he knew it was to be a story, and continued without sight of an end, is disjointed in the narrative, and loaded with extraneous matter.'[75] Macleod confided in his journal on 3 June 1861 that other churchmen did not always appreciate his aims: 'Many good people don't understand the purpose of Good Words, and so it sometimes shocks or scratches them.' Macleod's brother, Donald Macleod was, of course, editor of *Good Words* after Norman's death and also responsible for publicizing these private papers in 1897. He would thus wish to exonerate the magazine from the accusation of putting inappropriate reading matter between its covers for 'Sunday reading'.

The editorial style of *Cassell's Illustrated Family Paper*, predecessor to *Cassell's Magazine*, allowed for direct addresses to the reader of the periodical as part of its educational role. Cassell described himself as 'mine host' in the launch issue on

---

[69]   John Wellwood, *Norman Macleod* (Edinburgh: Oliphant, Anderson and Ferrier 1897), 141.

[70]   The last issue appeared in December 1859 (Srebrnik, 36–7).

[71]   Wellwood, 85.

[72]   [Macleod], 'We wish you a Good New Year!' *GW* 1 (1860): 1.

[73]   [Macleod], 'Note by the Editor', *GW* 1 (1860): 796.

[74]   Macleod's concluding words in 1860 reiterated that *Good Words* was a 'Periodical for *all the week*' ('Note by the Editor').

[75]   Wellwood, 93

31 December 1853.[76] In relaunching the *Paper* four years later as a quarto rather than a folio, he proclaimed it 'healthy, sound, first-rate and at the same time cheap literature.'[77] E.S. Dallas wrote in 1859 that 'John Cassells (sic) has a soul greater than his inches' referring to Cassell's mission to provide coffee and cheap books 'to regenerate the world'.[78] This was an allusion to Cassell's origins in the grocery trade. Dallas described Cassell's publications as 'not without merit. They do not pretend to be of a very high order, but at least they are the genuine berry, with but a slight admixture of chicory'.[79] Dallas found the *Illustrated Family Paper* 'in some respects well done' and 'the most mentoring of the penny serials'.[80] Cassell had, however, sold this name to his partners when he was declared bankrupt in 1855 and had effectively been their employee ever since. On 21 January 1865 Cassell signed his name to a prospectus entitled 'Something for Everybody' during his returning stint as editor. He died aged only 48 on 2 April 1865 and then had to be re-invoked within the *Paper* to preserve the religious, temperance and 'mentoring' educational mission which was part of the value acquired by Petter and Galpin when Cassell sold out to them.

It can be demonstrated from his obituary in the *Paper* that Cassell's name retained power within the periodical as a means of associating the company with a range of other significant publications including the *Illustrated Family Bible*, a part work which began to be published in 1859. A picture of John Cassell was bound into the volume edition of the *Paper* for 1865–66 with the greeting 'Yours Truly, John Cassell' as if the deceased editor were in direct communication with his readers. He was the subject of a memorial article on 20 May in which the continuing use of his name was actually ascribed to the involvement of his wife. The author of the article claimed that 'The honoured name of Cassell will still belong to the firm, for Mrs Cassell, who so devotedly entered into her husband's views, and sustained him in his good objects, will continue to retain an interest in the business.'[81] The obituary writer went on to bemoan Cassell's death 'in manhood's prime' and praised his labours on behalf of the working man: 'While striving himself to climb the moral and social steep, he let down at every step a strong arm to those beneath, and gave many a lusty "Excelsior" cheer to encourage them on.'[82] Cassell was firmly positioned both typographically and ideologically in the context of his own magazine. This so-called 'Memoir' of a 'fellow-labourer' appeared as the third column on a page otherwise devoted to 'The School of Self-Culture' where 'Our Schoolmaster' answered 'questions of general interest'

---

[76]   *CIFP*, 31 December 1853, 1.

[77]   *CIFP*, 5 December 1857, 391.

[78]   [E.S. Dallas], 'Popular Literature – Prize Essays,' *Blackwood's Edinburgh Magazine* 86 (1859): 686.

[79]   [Dallas], 'Popular Literature – Prize Essays,' 686.

[80]   [Dallas], 'Popular Literature – Prize Essays,' 686.

[81]   'John Cassell,' *CIFP*, 20 May 1865, 263.

[82]   'John Cassell,' 262.

from the *Paper*'s correspondents.[83] A deferred 'lecture on the English Language' made way for the 'Memoir' and the resulting advice column created by the 'Schoolmaster' effectively reminded readers of Cassell's style of editorship and his approach to his educational objectives. In addition, an interjection from the unnamed 'Editor of the "Family Paper"' was positioned between the title of the article and its commencement using a different typeface at the head of the third column to introduce the tribute: 'In introducing this Memoir of our lamented friend and fellow-labourer, we think it well to state that it is from the pen of a minister of religion who has long known him and appreciated his labours'.[84] This had the collective effect of binding the deceased editor more closely into the continuing series.

The latter parts of this 1865 'Memoir' read like an overview of the Cassell, Petter and Galpin catalogue in spite of the current editor's reassurance that it was a personal account of the man himself. The associations of the name of Cassell were perpetuated in the *Paper* and acted as a marker of moral and therefore, commercial value. The reminder to the reader that Cassell's 'energies overflowed' was code for the bankruptcy he endured after overreaching himself financially, since, despite their 'sympathising',[85] Petter and Galpin were indeed his creditors. His literal and stylized image within the periodical occupied a place somewhere between editor and publisher.

Looking forward to the context of *Poor Miss Finch*, the *Family Paper* had seven editors in the eighteen months between Cassell's death and the launch of *Cassell's Magazine* in 1867.[86] The *Magazine* then had four editors in its seven years of publication under the overall supervision of George William Petter, the editorial partner at Cassell, Petter and Galpin. These were William Moy Thomas (1867–68), John Lovell (1868–69), Hugh Reginald Haweis (1869–70) and George Manville Fenn (1870–74). In many ways the periodical became more formal as *Cassell's Magazine* than it was under John Cassell's editorship. It would have been difficult to maintain a consistent tone without the editorial continuity of a Dickens or the ongoing sympathetic partnership of Smith/Thackeray and Strahan/Macleod. The new prospectus for *Cassell's Magazine* on 9 March 1867 announced an array of contributors or 'eminent names' including 'G.M. Fenn' who would later become editor himself. '[William] Moy Thomas' was also listed and he was the first editor from April 1867 to March 1868. The publishers were '[r]elying with confidence ... upon the able editorship of the gentleman whose services they have been fortunate enough to secure'[87] but they clearly tried out a large number of editors before the next re-launch under another revised title, *Cassell's Family Magazine* in 1874.

---

83 'John Cassell,' 262.
84 'John Cassell,' 262.
85 'John Cassell,' 263.
86 See Nowell-Smith, 75–7.
87 *CassM*, 9 March 1867, 448.

Following the serialization of Collins's two novels, Henry George Bonavia Hunt was long-term editor of the *Family Magazine* from 1874 to 1896.

The regularity of these changes at *Cassell's Magazine* coinciding with a new financial year each April suggests that the moves were made under contractual terms, since Petter retained overall editorial control within the company. This is clearly a different model from that adopted by either of Dickens's periodicals. *Good Words* and the *Cornhill* operated with some degree of personal reciprocity between editor and publisher and within a longer time frame than the year which Petter and Galpin imposed on their first three editors. Macleod and Thackeray were personally identified with their magazines; Cassell's no longer had a named living editor but preserved his image for sound commercial reasons.

The Editor/Publisher and the Pattern of the Periodical Series

The direct addresses which appeared in the periodicals not only represented the editor in character and set the style of the periodical. They also indicated or signalled changes of direction, and the editor thus set up and perpetuated the pattern of the series in which the serial then appeared. This section considers the ways in which the editor was deployed to suggest such a pattern for the reader and to guide reading across time periods which encompassed both a serial and the ongoing appearance of the magazine series.

As discussed above, Dickens did not use *All the Year Round*'s first issues to make his aims clear other than by writing a serial himself. It was at the end of *A Tale of Two Cities* and immediately before the first chapters of the serialization of *The Woman in White* on 26 November 1859 that he made his editorial statement about the objectives of the periodical now under his direct control. His embedded prospectus stated that: 'it is our hope and aim, while we work hard at every other department of our journal, to produce, in this one, some sustained works of imagination that may become a part of English Literature.'[88] Although the pattern of fiction was established, this standard proved difficult to maintain as was demonstrated by crucial interfaces between the fictional serials. The first two instalments of *A Day's Ride* by Charles Lever, the serial which would succeed Collins's hit, appeared with the last two of *The Woman in White* on 18 and 25 August 1860. After fifteen instalments, however, *Great Expectations* was brought in from 1 December 1860 to revive the magazine's fortunes, and *A Day's Ride* was relegated to a place inside the magazine until it concluded on 23 March 1861. The appearance of *Great Expectations* as a weekly serial was thus significant as a textual representation of Dickens's ongoing responsibilities for the sales of the magazine series. The tenth instalment of *A Day's Ride* was published on 27 October 1860 with Lever's serial still taking the lead. In the final column of this issue, however, appeared the first advertisement announcing that 'In No. 84 of

---

[88]   *AYR*, 26 November 1859, 95.

ALL THE YEAR ROUND, TO BE PUBLISHED ON SATURDAY, DECEMBER THE FIRST, [w]ill be commenced GREAT EXPECTATIONS, BY CHARLES DICKENS, A NEW SERIAL STORY'.[89] This 'new work' would 'continue' for eight months. In No. 83 on 24 November the trailer once again stressed the place this serial would occupy in the lives of the magazine's readers; it was 'To be continued from week to week until completed in August'.[90]

The experience of holding the public's attention and occupying a place within their lives became more pragmatic than the 'Fancy' described in *Household Words*. The time frame of expectation for a serial became an important threshold within *All the Year Round*. At the end of *Great Expectations*, Dickens announced not only the succeeding serial but also the one after that. He once again used the opportunity to advertise across columns: 'OUR readers already know that the next number of this Journal will contain the first portion of a new romance by SIR EDWARD BULWER LYTTON, which will be continued from week to week for six months. On its completion, it will be succeeded by a new serial story by MR. WILKIE COLLINS, to be continued from week to week for nine months.'[91] Novels still unwritten were presented to be interwoven into readers' and potential purchasers' lives for well over a year in advance. Material improvements in production were also highlighted when Dickens announced that the repeal of the Paper Duty would allow the magazine's paper quality to be improved to 'enhance the mechanical clearness and legibility of these pages'. A somewhat ponderous announcement attempted to distinguish the periodical from others whose fiction was less likely to become a part of English Literature: 'Of the Literature to which we have a new encouragement to devote them [the pages], it becomes us to say no more than that we believe it would have been simply impossible, when paper was taxed, to make the present announcement'.[92] In fact, the promise of quality and continuity of output was vital. Earlier magazines including *Cassell's Illustrated Family Paper* had sometimes just stopped serializing a piece of fiction leaving readers without an ending,[93] and the *British Quarterly Review* had claimed in 1859 that '[t]he whole of this kind of work … may be executed by a pair of scissors, with an incredibly small amount of intelligence to guide them'.[94]

Within the first series of *All the Year Round*, *The Moonstone* was in many ways the culmination of the fiction-leading project proposed by Dickens for the periodical. After it was concluded Dickens appeared to draw another line under

---

[89] *AYR*, 27 October 1860, 72. This was repeated for the three following issues (96, 120 and 144).

[90] *AYR*, 24 November 1860, 168.

[91] *AYR*, 3 August 1861, 437. The serials were Bulwer Lytton's *A Strange Story* and Collins's *No Name*.

[92] *AYR*, 3 August 1861, 437.

[93] *The Arctic Crusoe: a Tale of the Polar Seas* by Percy St John, the first serial in *CIFP*, suffered this fate in 1854.

[94] 'Cheap Literature,' *British Quarterly Review*, 29 April 1859, 330–31.

his output with a re-launch at the end of 1868 which changed and updated the layout of *All the Year Round*. This new series had a more elaborate title heading although the hierarchy of naming and framing was largely maintained. The series was also published in a new size to distinguish it, for those collecting the volume editions, from the preceding twenty volumes. The editorial process marked this new boundary. Following the final instalment of *The Moonstone* on 8 August 1868, the two-part 'Autobiography of a Small Boy' ended abruptly on 22 August and was succeeded by *Hester's History* in thirteen parts. This 'new serial tale' was designed to conclude not just the twentieth volume of *All the Year Round* but the whole of the first series. The author was the Irish novelist Rosa Mulholland, and Dickens stressed in advertising at the end of the first instalment of the 'tale' on 29 August that it would 'be continued from week to week until completed in the present volume'.[95] Dickens then re-launched the periodical on 5 December having trailed his intentions as an opening announcement. Like the opening and closing announcements for *Household Words*, the text of his new prospectus was prioritized over the text of *Hester's History* on both 19 and 26 September.[96] The announcement was reprinted as a postscript with the usual further advertising of Dickens's farewell reading tours and this clearly undermined the finality of the very last serial, the three-part short story 'The Abbot's Pool' which ended on 28 November with a closing 'Amen' from the words of the Lord's Prayer.[97] Editorship was thus prioritized over authorship despite the pious closure which the end of the serialized short story had presented. The apparent smoothness of the transition was hampered, however, by suspicions circulating at the time that Dickens was no longer the editor, and he was forced on 5 December to deny the contents of 'a very unjustifiable paragraph [which] has appeared in some newspapers.' He headed his own paragraph 'TO THE PUBLIC' and described the rumours as 'wilfully or negligently untrue, if any respect be due to the explicit terms of my repeatedly-published announcement of the present New Series under my own hand. CHARLES DICKENS.'[98]

The balance between authorship and editorship was clearly a delicate one in terms both of Dickens's own contributions to *All the Year Round* and of his treatment of the works of others in the wider interests of the series under his control. Although *Cornhill Magazine* was also edited by a novelist, the tone of that periodical was rather different and Thackeray's involvement can be described more briefly. As editor, he also indicated a pattern to readers using less obvious devices which also marked the volume of the periodical. For instance in the Roundabout Paper 'On Some Late Great Victories' in June 1860, he described the contribution as 'this last article of our first volume', reminding readers of the availability of the six-monthly collected *Cornhill*. The June issue had opened with

95   *AYR*, 29 August 1868, 288.
96   *AYR*, 19 September 1868, 337; 29 September 1868, 361.
97   *AYR*, 28 November 1868, 596.
98   *AYR*, 5 December 1868, 1.

'London the Stronghold of England' by Francis Fowke, and Thackeray continued the military theme by describing the issues of the magazine as 'the six great, complete, prodigious and undeniable victories achieved by the corps which the editor of the CORNHILL MAGAZINE has the honour to command'.[99] He insisted that the magazine had 'a hundred thousand buyers' and therefore a million readers. His contributors were denoted 'volunteers' although these grand statements were undermined by a rather tetchy footnote from 'ED. *C.H.M.*'. The note continued the theme of the 'Thorns in Cushions' Paper about the impossibility of supplying a personal response to all 'candidates', and Thackeray interrupted the flow of his own speech in the character of 'Imperator' by claiming that '[t]he average of contributions has been for the last two months 100 a-week'.[100] The sweeping procession to the 'Hill of Corn' concluded, however, with a description of the market in which the *Cornhill* flourished: 'Crowned with flowers the captains enter the temple, the other magazines walking modestly behind them.'[101]

Six months later a 'Paper' once again marked the end of a volume by describing the *Cornhill* voyage on which Trollope, who was named in the article, had performed his duty of '*Raconteur*'. Thackeray indicated that in the following year he himself would be supplying a more substantial novel than *Lovel the Widower* which had concluded back in June, and he grandly welcomed the launch of a magazine under the 'command' of one of his 'esteemed companions' despite the fact that this new title might challenge the circulation figures quoted six months previously. He was alluding to *Temple Bar* which was launched in late 1861 and edited by George Sala, the author of 'William Hogarth' which had been serialized in the *Cornhill* from February to October 1860. 'At home,' Thackeray claimed, 'and over our immense dominions, there are markets enough for our wares.'[102] This was glancing back to the earlier commercial ventures of Smith Elder as suppliers to the Empire, the success of which had allowed them to move into publishing.[103]

Where Thackeray wrote at these significant boundaries as a comic 'Imperator', Macleod treated his editorship of *Good Words* as if it were an extension to his pulpit. His 'secularity' letter to John Ludlow quoted above emphasized the periodical's preaching 'direct or indirect'.[104] Despite his vow at the end of Volume 1 to 'retire behind the scenes',[105] Macleod was represented as an all-pervasive influence on his periodical. Just as Dickens advertised his conductorship on every page of *Household Words* and *All the Year Round*, so from the fifth issue in

---

[99] [Francis Fowke], 'London the Stronghold of England,' *CM* 1 (1860): 641–51; [W.M. Thackeray], 'Roundabout Papers no. 4: On Some Late Great Victories,' *CM* 1 (1860) 758.

[100] [Thackeray], 'On Some Late Great Victories,' 759.

[101] [Thackeray], 'On Some Late Great Victories,' 760.

[102] [Thackeray], 'On a Joke I Once Heard,' 760.

[103] See Glynn, 19.

[104] Quoted in Macleod, *Memoir*, 2:113.

[105] [Macleod], 'Note by the Editor.'

February 1860 onwards each page of *Good Words* was headed: 'Edited by Norman Macleod D.D.' The front page of the volume editions of *Good Words* continued to emphasize Macleod's position with the additional authority of the running proverb from which the name of the periodical derived. The quotation 'Good Words are worth much and cost little' is from another priest and writer, George Herbert.[106] Macleod's status as editor was balanced by his status as clergyman and the name and godliness of an individual became the threshold or border of the periodical reading experience.

Macleod's sermonizing was itself a pattern within the periodical which used an unremitting sense of dailiness as part of its religious appeal. His fiction which appeared in serial form also had the quality of a sermon and as editor, Macleod provided the opening article for nine issues in 1862 under such titles as 'A Word in Season', 'Moments in Life', 'What if Christianity is not True?', 'Sunday', 'Missions in the Nineteenth Century' and 'Four Difficulties Solved in Jesus Christ'.[107] His tone was that of the clergyman seeking access to readers' lives with that mix of the secular and religious which he had proposed in December 1860, at the end of the first year of the publication of *Good Words*. In Macleod's absence in November and December 1862 his place was taken by the Irish Presbyterian minister William Fleming Stevenson who contributed 'On the Biography of Certain Hymns' and then 'On Vagabonds', [108] and this rhythm of religious introduction was disrupted only in June as part of Strahan's cross-selling process for the respectability of his star novelist. As discussed in Chapter 2, the only non clergyman to write a leader in 1862 was 'the Author of "John Halifax, Gentleman"' with her 'Five Shillings' Worth of the Great World's Fair'[109] although in August, Macleod solved the riddle of this absence by writing in the Thackeray mode his 'Rambling Notes on a Ramble to North Italy' and then in September 'A Peep at the Netherlands and Holland'.[110] The role of clergymen in the production of *Good Words* was thus a significant feature of its appeal and of its rhythm as a periodical. As a sixteen-page weekly for its first year, readers could find in it 'Good Words for Every Day in the Year' dated and ready for their consumption. Macleod explained at the end of 1860 that '[t]he faithful exhibition of Evangelical truth shall go hand-in-hand with every department of a healthy literature' and he advertised a series for 1861 entitled 'Our Sunday Evenings: A Series of Papers for Family Reading' written by a range of

---

[106] From *Jacula Prudentum* (1651), a collection of proverbs.

[107] *GW* 3, 1–3; 65–8; 129–31; 193–7; 257–62; 385–9.

[108] *GW* 3, 641–5; 705–11.

[109] [Dinah Craik], 'Five Shillings' Worth of the Great World's Fair,' *GW* 3 (1862): 321–7.

[110] *GW* 3 (1862): 449–54; 513–9. The interaction between editor and collaborators is discussed further in Catherine Delafield, 'Marketing Celebrity: Norman Macleod, Dinah Mulock Craik, and John Everett Millais in Alexander Strahan's *Good Words*,' *Victorian Periodicals Review* 46 (2013): 255–78.

named clergymen including himself.[111] In 1862, this continued with 'At Home in the Scriptures: A Series of Family Readings for Sunday Evenings' by Rev. W. Arnot. *Good Words* could thus reinforce its position by reflecting the pattern of the Christian year within the framework of a clergyman editor associated with royalty and with high educational standards.

The periodical itself might be presented as if it were a clergyman visiting the reader's own home but it is notable that the pattern would cause Macleod and his editorship to fall foul of other Evangelicals within a few years of proclaiming '[t]he faithful exhibition of Evangelical truth'. In April and May 1863, Macleod became the target of a series of six articles in the Evangelical *Record*. A different pattern of guided reading emerged when it was traced by the writer of these articles, identified subsequently as the Scottish Presbyterian minister Thomas Alexander, who complained that Evangelical names introduced other less acceptable authors 'on their wings'.[112] It was argued that the combined contents of *Good Words* as it was arranged could not be regarded as wholesome or suitable for reading within a Christian household. *Good Words* was accused of introducing sensation writers with their 'diseased appetite' and this with particular reference to Trollope whose serious story 'The Widow's Mite' had appeared in January 1863, very much tailored to the style of a religious periodical.[113] *The Leisure Hour* was pronounced to be more suitable for the Sabbath because of its 'weekday reading with a religious tone'.[114] Alexander identified a new threshold created by the pattern which Macleod had established: 'That the light, loose, unsound article in its attractive sparkling and showy dress, will be pondered as well as read, is all but certain', he observed; 'that the sound Evangel will be either read or pondered is not so certain.'[115] Despite this adverse publicity the periodical's sales figures were not harmed since Strahan could claim a circulation of 70,000 in 1863, comparable with that of the *Cornhill*.[116]

While *Good Words* found the religious year a convenient and appropriate rhythm to follow, *Cassell's Magazine* moved away from some of the patterning devices employed by its precursor, *Cassell's Illustrated Family Paper*. The advice column, letters and chess problems no longer appeared and the columns for women provided by the Matron, Fanny Fern and Penelope Jot were also silently dropped.[117] The recurring pattern was supplied rather by the fiction serial which came to greater prominence within the *Magazine*. The editorial absence created by

---

[111] [Macleod], 'Note by the Editor.'

[112] [Thomas Alexander], '"Good Words": The Theology of the Editor and Some of Its Contributors Reprinted from the "Record" Newspaper' (London: Record Office, 1863), 6.

[113] [Alexander], 59; 'The Widow's Mite,' *GW* 4 (1863): 33–43.

[114] [Alexander], 15.

[115] [Alexander], 6.

[116] See Srebrnik, 46.

[117] A list of the articles by Fern and Jot appears in E.M. Palmegiano, 'Women and British Periodicals 1832–1867: A Bibliography,' *Victorian Periodicals Newsletter* 9 (1976): 33.

the death of John Cassell was occasionally filled by a randomly occurring series termed the editor's 'Carte Blanche', and a contribution by the editor Haweis on 15 January 1870 argued with those who claimed that 'magazine reading is bad for the mind.' This was a bold rhetorical device in the same issue as the ninth instalment of *Man and Wife* but Collins's serial had already boosted sales of the magazine to 70,000 a week. Haweis could, therefore, afford to quote from his detractors by drawing attention to that recurring pattern when he observed that 'novel reading is frivolous and magazines usually begin with an instalment of a novel.' [118] Haweis continued in the same vein to discuss the miscellany presented by the periodical and was even happy to allude to criticism of his own magazine's production values:

> critics claim that 'the essays and sketches – which are sometimes irreverently called "padding" – are not solid enough for those hard intellects which revolt at anything a degree softer than nails; then the poems are trash; and finally, the pictures are often badly drawn, worse cut, and worst of all printed!'

With an eye on the successful product which was then boosting sales, however, Haweis riposted that: 'The magazine is the favourite form for popular literature; and those who consider it a bad form must remember that the greatest writers of the age have adopted it.' He was alluding here to Dickens who had recently died but this also meant that he could draw particular attention to his own star writer. '[N]or are we aware', he continued tortuously, 'that Mr. Wilkie Collins writes with less genius in magazines than elsewhere.' [119] This was also rather disingenuous since all Collins's novels from *The Dead Secret* (1857) onwards were serialized in periodicals but once again the serial was seen within the context of the series where it was the editor's responsibility to view the content as a whole.

Haweis, a clergyman who was known as a theatrical preacher, finally ridiculed himself as editor in this piece by offering to write 'a special word … about novel reading' concluding that 'this is so important a subject that it requires a "Carte-Blanche" all to itself, conceived and executed in our most ponderous and didactic style.' [120] This follow-up article was never published, however, and Haweis was soon supplanted by Petter's administrative musical chairs, leaving the pattern of fiction in place. Under Manville Fenn, editor from April 1870, the direct address to the reader disappeared just as the letters page had done from the earlier *Paper*. As discussed above, the management of Cassell's as final arbiter later became less convinced about the value of Collins's contribution to the magazine's image.

The context for the serialization of novels within periodicals was dictated by editorial choice. The religious and pious messages of *Good Words* and to some extent *Cassell's Magazine* were in contrast with the elements of learned discussion in *Cornhill Magazine* and the earlier social journalism of *Household Words*.

---

[118] 'On Reading Magazines,' *CassM*, 15 January 1870, 140.
[119] 'On Reading Magazines.'
[120] 'On Reading Magazines.'

Macleod routinely opened and framed each issue within a religious pattern based on the calendar whilst Thackeray usually closed an issue with his recapitulation in the 'Roundabout Papers' which offered a genial invitation to read again next month. Dickens assumed that his 'conductorship' was the border which framed all periodical material whilst Cassell's used the opposite extreme of administrative anonymity capped by the name of the deceased founder. Editors created the style and register of the periodical in which the serial appeared and manifestations of editorial character set the tone. The *Cornhill* promoted the idea of 'co-operation' as editorial policy, contributors working together within the borders set by the magazine whilst *Household Words* and *All the Year Round* were 'conducted'. Evidence shows that Wills edited, Smith edited and Strahan edited but they were not the named controllers of the text. Dickens, Thackeray, Macleod and Cassell had epitextual associations for readers and their characters were projected within the periodicals they edited. The editor and publisher thus provided for the periodical the peritexts[121] or thresholds for reading which were indicated both by signposts of intent at key moments in the development of the periodical as well as by the regular borders set up between the issues themselves. The editors supplied both regular content and markers of direction such as Dickens's 'Preliminary Word' of 30 March 1850 or Macleod's *Good Words* advertorial at the end of 1860. In terms of signposts or prospectuses, *All the Year Round* fulfilled its mission to produce and prioritize fiction whilst the *Cornhill* adopted a less regular pattern of subject matter and used a register of conversational discussion interwoven with its serials and the factual pieces which Thackeray described to Trollope as 'the getting out of novel spinning, and back into the world'.[122]

Editorial contributions guided reading and helped to market the educational impact of the magazines. The editors also discussed the role of fiction in their own characters as indicated above. The effect of the serial read in its original context is dependent on the control of the series in which it appeared, and this effect was also influenced by the material in which the serial was embedded within the outer borders of the periodical. It is possible then to distinguish between editorial borders and the adjoining authorial boundaries of the serialized novel supplied by the novelist. These authorial boundaries divided the novel into instalments and created an interface between the serial and other periodical matter which does not exist in later editions of the novel. The boundaries were redrawn by the volume edition of the novel and restated in a new context by the volume edition of the periodical, and this is considered in more detail as the afterlife of the serial in Chapter 6. Chapter 4 will consider how the periodicals themselves created the discourse which acted as a boundary or threshold for serialized fiction.

---

[121] Gérard Genette, *Paratexts: Thresholds of Interpretation* (1987; repr., trans. Jane E. Lewin, Cambridge: Cambridge University Press, 1997), 16. He discusses the publisher's peritext for a published book.

[122] W.M. Thackeray to Anthony Trollope, 28 October 1859, Trollope, *Autobiography*, 137.

Chapter 4
The Periodical and the Serialized Novel

The novels which provide exemplars of the serial in the mid-Victorian period appeared in five magazines. This chapter assesses the periodicals which serialized the core novels and reviews the contributory aspects of their layout, discourse and rationale for existence. Dickens's journals and *Cornhill Magazine* have been treated in a number of studies, and for this reason, the bulk of the discussion within the chapter addresses *Cassell's Magazine* and *Good Words* which are less widely represented in scholarly debate. The relationship of these family magazines to each other and to the market for print in the mid nineteenth century is also discussed. The digitization of Dickens's periodicals in *Dickens Journals Online* has made it possible to read and reference the surrounding matter in *Household Words*, and the chapter begins by demonstrating how periodical content acted upon the evolution of *Cranford*. There then follows an examination of the presentation of fiction in *All the Year Round*, *Cornhill Magazine* and *Good Words*. These magazines were founded with fiction in mind and are addressed to an already conditioned audience. Finally the evolution of *Cassell's Magazine* is traced, demonstrating how Cassell's periodicals followed a trajectory which marks the transition of the penny journal into a vehicle for fiction by established novelists.

Household Words

As a new periodical emerging from Dickens's experiences as a journalist himself, *Household Words* had both to differentiate itself in the market and to provide a familiar experience for new readers. Sub editor, William Henry Wills had worked on *Chambers's Edinburgh Journal* as well as with Dickens on the *Daily News*. Dickens wrote to him before the first number of *Household Words* appeared insisting that there should be no obvious similarities between their new periodical and these other publications: 'There is nothing I am so desirous to avoid, than imitation.'[1] Lorna Huett has observed, however, that Dickens's periodicals had a certain imitative 'hybridity'. She suggests that he modelled the printing practices of *Household Words* on cheap magazines such as the *London Journal* and *Penny Magazine* but that the overall size of the magazine created the added *gravitas* of a highbrow monthly review so that the bound volume might find its place in

---

[1]   Charles Dickens to W.H. Wills, 11 February 1850, in R.C. Lehmann, *Charles Dickens as Editor* (London: Smith Elder, 1912), 22.

a library beside the *Reviews*.[2] *Cornhill Magazine* would later also challenge the ideologies of the periodical form in its adoption of both the fiction content of the penny weeklies and the weightier discussion of the monthlies, and *Good Words* and *Cassell's Magazine* imitated this pattern in the 1860s and 1870s with a clearly expressed religious agenda. Huett claims that '*Household Words* took on the base aspect of the penny press in order to rehabilitate the weekly serialisation of fiction from within.'[3] As we shall see below, however, the fictional material evolved itself to take on some elements of the format and style of the periodical.

The Cranford sketches which retrospectively became instalments were always designed to abut the mixture of social journalism and sentimental poetry with which they first appeared. Catherine Waters has described the 'multi-authorship (subsumed in the branding of a corporate voice)' which characterized *Household Words*,[4] and Gaskell's novel was part of a collection of articles made smoothly into a group under the title of *Household Words*. This makes *Cranford* a different entity from that of a novel commissioned for an allocated space like Gaskell's later *North and South* and Collins's *The Dead Secret* in *Household Words*, different also from those serialized novels which appeared in *All the Year Round* and *Cornhill Magazine* from the outset. Readers of these novels were led to expect and anticipate the next instalment as well as the completion of the whole within an advertised timeframe.

Elizabeth Gaskell was familiar with the way in which *Household Words* operated by the time she contributed the first Cranford pieces. The first instalment of her short story 'Lizzie Leigh' was published in the first number of *Household Words* on 30 March 1850, advertised as appearing 'in four chapters'.[5] This was a story broken into planned parts and set in the past – as *Cranford* was – in 1836. The instalment followed on from Dickens's expansive 'Preliminary Word' which concluded 'go on cheerily' and quoted extensively from Duke Senior's 'Sermons in stones' speech in *As You Like It*. This address provided not only a statement of intent but a vital buffer between the proposed 'elegance of fancy' and the gloomy opening of Gaskell's short story, effectively the first sentence of a brand new periodical, which then ran: 'WHEN Death is present in a household on a Christmas Day, the very contrast between the time as it now is, and the day as it has often been, gives a poignancy to sorrow, – a more utter blankness to the

---

²   Lorna Huett, 'Among the Unknown Public: *Household Words, All the Year Round* and the Mass-Market Weekly Periodical in the mid Nineteenth Century,' *Victorian Periodicals Review* 38 (2005): 78–9.

³   Huett, 79.

⁴   Catherine Waters, *Commodity Culture in Dickens's Household Words: The Social Life of Goods* (Aldershot: Ashgate, 2008), 20.

⁵   *HW*, 30 March 1850, 2.

desolation.'[6] Subsequent instalments of 'Lizzie Leigh' were moved to the third station on 6 April and to the sixth on 13 April.[7]

Eighteen months later 'Our Society at Cranford' also occupied the opening station of *Household Words* beginning, on 13 December 1851, 'IN the first place, Cranford is in possession of the Amazons.'[8] These act as opening lines not only for the first Cranford piece but also for the number of *Household Words* the periodical as well as for the future, but as yet unplanned, novel. In this sketch, Gaskell was confident enough to draw attention to the new reading practices of the mid nineteenth century when Deborah Jenkyns and Captain Brown compared Dr Johnson's *The Rambler* with more modern publications including *Hoods Own*. Gaskell had, of course, intended to refer to *The Pickwick Papers* as a contemporary comparison in 1840s Cranford but Dickens substituted the reference. Mary Smith pointed out in parenthesis that this work was 'then publishing in parts' whilst Miss Jenkyns riposted, 'I consider it vulgar, and below the dignity of literature, to publish in numbers.'[9] In the context of a periodical edited by Dickens whose name appeared on the very page this is wonderfully self-referential, an element which will subsequently be lost when the novel is read in volume form even with the *Pickwick* reference restored.

Many of the occasional pieces in *Household Words* were published, like 'Lizzie Leigh' and 'Our Society at Cranford', in first station on their first appearance but subsequently relocated. Tracing the station of articles in *Household Words* reflects the impact of the pattern created by each weekly number and the conditioning implied for the reader of the text. Dickens's *A Child's History of England* appeared in first station on 25 January 1851[10] but then subsequently always appeared as the last article, setting a pattern for the items in this station being his own. 'The Roving Englishman' commenced in second station on 29 November 1851[11] but often appeared in last station, suggesting it was popular enough to stand in for what might have then been anticipated by readers to be a Dickens article. 'A Digger's Diary' opened the number on 29 January 1853[12] but was subsequently moved to the inside pages once its irregularity belied its title. It was concluded after only four instalments once the writer Richard Horne – or rather Horne's narrator – had reached Melbourne. The context within each issue is also instructive. As with his first 'Fancy' Dickens provided a buffer once again when he opened the 6 April 1850 issue with his sickeningly sentimental 'A Child's Dream of a Star' before Horne's three-part 'True Story of a Coal Fire' was projected to appear 'in three chapters'. The two subsequent 'chapters' were moved further inside the

---

[6]   *HW*, 30 March 1850, 2.
[7]   *HW*, 6 April 1850, 32–35 and 13 April 1850, 60–65.
[8]   *HW*, 13 December 1851, 265.
[9]   *HW*, 13 December 1851, 268.
[10] *HW*, 25 January 1851, 409–12.
[11] *HW*, 29 November 1851, 409–12.
[12] *HW*, 29 January 1853, 457–62.

two succeeding numbers with the second chapter closing the number.[13] Again, Harriet Martineau's 'The Sickness and Health of the People of Bleaburn' began in first station on 25 May 1850 but its three other parts were buried within the periodical before the vague but combative ending on 15 June that '[t]here was such a Mary Pickard; and what she did for a Yorkshire village in a season of fever is TRUE.'[14] Charles Knight's 'Illustrations of Cheapness' appeared at different stations but the final part, 'The Steel Pen' number five in the series, migrated to first station on 7 September 1850.[15] Dickens's own 'From the Raven in the Happy Family' filled in fifth on 11 May 1850 but moved to first station for two subsequent appearances.[16] Thus, for example, on 8 June 1850, Dickens's 'Raven' led off a weak number of the periodical which included 'Illustrations of Cheapness: Tea' and the third instalment of 'The Sickness and Health of the People of Bleaburn'. Martineau's contribution wavered as its divisions were manipulated to fill the number with an apparent mis-division when 'Part III' was announced three pages into the instalment.[17] Dickens's preferences as editor become apparent from a brief exploration of these emerging series within the early numbers, demonstrating also the formation of the context for *Cranford*.

Dickens referred to the need for a strong lead-off piece in his letters to Wills. On 29 December 1852, for instance, he worried about a 'good first article' but ignored 'The Great Cranford Panic'.[18] It may be that the two men were concerned about timescales for the completion of Gaskell's contribution 'in two chapters'.[19] In the event, Sala's 'My Man. A Sum' appeared in first station on 8 January 1853 with the 'The Great Cranford Panic' third. Its completion apparently assured, the second part of Gaskell's story appeared in second station on 15 January following on from Henry Morley's 'Scholastic'.[20] Gaskell completed a sequence of four appearances around this time with 'Cumberland Sheep-Shearers' on 22 January. She had contributed 'The Old Nurse's Story' to the Christmas number on 25 December and it was when Dickens was writing to her about the proofs of this story that he added the terse postscript 'Cranford???' which now betrays the

[13] *HW*, 6 April 1850, 26-32; 13 April 1850, 68–72; 20 April 1850, 90–96.

[14] [Harriet Martineau], 'The Sickness and Health of the People of Bleaburn,' *HW*, 15 June (1850), 283–8; 288.

[15] [Charles Knight], 'Illustrations of Cheapness: The Steel Pen,' *HW*, 7 September 1850, 533–5.

[16] [Charles Dickens], 'From the Raven in the Happy Family,' *HW*, 11 May 1850, 156–8; 8 June 1850, 241–3; 24 August 1850, 505–7.

[17] *HW*, 8 June (1850), 256–61; 259.

[18] Charles Dickens to W.H. Wills, 29 December 1852, Dickens, *Letters*, vol. 4, 843.

[19] *HW*, 8 January 1853, 390.

[20] [George Augustus Sala], 'My Man. A Sum,' *HW*, 8 January 1853, 385–88; [Henry Morley], 'Scholastic,' *HW*, 15 January 1853, 409–13.

delays in the submission of the 'Panic'.[21] Although these pieces were unattributed, Gaskell's authorship might be traced by the hyper-attentive reader to establish an alternative segmentation from the corporate voice of the periodical. Gaskell's short story 'Morton Hall' was part of a group of contributions around Christmas 1853 and was set in a village five miles from the town of Drumble which stands for Manchester in *Cranford*.[22] 'Morton Hall' used a female narrator as *Cranford* did and in its second part employed some of the social comedy of *Cranford* as well as the later family-saga style of *My Lady Ludlow*. In a reverse reference, the first chapter of 'The Great Cranford Panic' cross-referenced a great old house in Cumberland two weeks before the sheep-shearer article although Gaskell would surely have preferred to remain unknown when a typesetting error in the article on 22 January quoted 'Eunice's father' instead of 'Emma's' on the subject of gruel.[23]

In addition to the management of the lead items in *Household Words*, readers became accustomed to the idea that an article might be recalled in subsequent numbers as the Cranford sketches were. Alongside the second instalment of *Cranford*, 'A Love Affair at Cranford' on 3 January 1852, appeared an article entitled 'What *I* Call Sensible Legislation' in which 'a Scotchman' observed that *Household Words* had 'reached the mature figure of ninety'.[24] The first and ostensibly only instalment of *Cranford* had appeared in the first station of that 90th number on 13 December 1851. On 3 January the 'Scotchman' explained that he read 'back numbers of newspapers and journals as a habit, in order that I may form an opinion on the topics debated in them, after all effervescence has gone off.' He summarized the experience of reading issue number 21 of *Household Words*, 'wading ... through articles on Railways, Water-supply, Education, Lieutenant Waghorn, and such matters, which you seem to think extremely worthy of attention'.[25] He gave, apparently inadvertently, a summary of the published context in which *Cranford* was being read, effectively writing an unheralded second instalment of 'Comic Leaves from the Statute Book', the fifth article on 17 August 1850 which had offered 'mirth provocatives of the Statutes at Large'.[26] The approach by the 'Scotchman' was itself comic at the writer's expense at the same time as giving the readership of *Household Words* a direction on their own role in

---

[21]   [Elizabeth Gaskell], 'Cumberland Sheep-Shearers,' *HW*, 22 January 1853, 445–51; 'The Old Nurse's Story,' *HW*, 25 December 1852, 583–92; Charles Dickens to Elizabeth Gaskell, 1 December 1852, Dickens, *Letters* vol. 4, 812. A full list of Gaskell's contributions is in Appendix 4.

[22]   [Elizabeth Gaskell], 'Morton Hall,' *HW*, 19 November 1853, 265–72 and 26 November 1853, 293–302.

[23]   *HW*, 8 January 1853, 395; *HW*, 22 January 1853, 451.

[24]   [James Knox], 'What *I* Call Sensible Legislation,' *HW*, 3 January 1852, 341–44; 341.

[25]   [Knox], 341.

[26]   [William Weir & W.H. Wills], 'Comic Leaves from the Statute Book,' *HW*, 17 August 1850, 502–504; 504.

the process of periodical reading. This 'older' and wiser correspondent, created for the periodical by Edinburgh publisher James Knox, called for 'a judicious supervision of the press' and insisted that: 'Our ancestors were saved, by the care of their rulers, from all trouble on this score. Their reading was selected for them by their Government, as a child's books are chosen carefully by a judicious father.'[27] This reflects the influence of Dickens the editor, supervising both the periodical and the serialized articles during this time.

In addition to this recollection and patterning, a retrospective order was also imposed on periodical material by the indexes to the volumes of *Household Words* which were organized by key words to guide readers and buyers. Indexes to the volume editions grouped Gaskell's pieces under 'Cranford, Our Society at', 'Cranford, Memory at' and so on, already suggesting the way in which the sketches might ultimately become a whole. In Volume 4, however, they appeared under 'Cranford' and then in alphabetical order of title so that instalment two was listed first and instalment one last.[28] Editorial policy and filing was thus prioritized over narrative sequence. There are single entries in Volumes 5 and 6 but Volume 7 more helpfully lists the last three sketches chronologically in order of publication.[29] This process resulted in subtle re-writing to give prominence to chosen themes. In Volume 6 the two-part 'Great Cranford Panic' became 'Cranford, the Great Panic in.'[30] This was a regularly used process for highlighting another layer of collective authorship, for instance on the theme of Australia. Apart from an absence of Australian articles in Volume 2, there are between two and ten articles indexed under Australia in the first eight volumes of *Household Words*, a total of 32 in less than four years.

The gaps and chronological discrepancies in the unfolding *Cranford* were not dissimilar from those represented in other occasional pieces in *Household Words* of the time such as 'The Roving Englishman' by Eustace Grenville-Murray or 'A Digger's Diary. IN OCCASIONAL CHAPTERS' by Horne, who was formerly a staff writer for *Household Words*. The 'Digger' was reclassified under 'Australian' for the purposes of the indexes and Murray's pieces were listed as 'Roving Englishman, The' even though the first two pieces were actually entitled 'A Roving Englishman' before becoming an established feature. Appendix 4 demonstrates some of the patterns emerging from *Household Words* grouped around the 'occasional chapters' of *Cranford*, together with the recurring appearance of the theme of Australia and the 'roving' subjects covered in Grenville-Murray's material. Gaskell's other contributions are also listed in chronological sequence demonstrating how the individual authors were subsumed into the periodical number and so created that patterning of reappearances which merged fact with fiction.

---

27 [Knox], 341.
28 *HW* 4 (1851–52): ix.
29 *HW* 7 (1853): ix.
30 *HW* 6 (1852–53): ix.

The 'Roving Englishman' began publication on 29 November 1851 and appeared at irregular intervals until March 1856. '*A* Roving Englishman' became '*The* Roving Englishman' for the third episode (my italics) in the same number as 'A Love Affair at Cranford' on 3 January 1852. Anne Lohrli and *Dickens Journals Online* have identified Grenville-Murray as the author of earlier pieces[31] but the 'Englishman' was given a consistent identity through attribution and ongoing authorship although Murray himself also wrote other unattributed 'Chips' and articles throughout. Like *Cranford*, 'The Roving Englishman' became a serial in retrospect. In the twenty-fifth instalment on 24 December 1853, the 'Englishman' even provided a retrospective rationale for his series:

> I do not know whether such little sketches of far away life and manners as I paint so poorly may please you; but at any rate they are fresh from nature, and I hope no word ever creeps into them to make any man the worse. If, therefore, in passing an idle half hour with the Roving Englishman, you should now and then acquire a better knowledge of other nations than you had before, it will not be time misspent; for I honestly believe that most of the wars and ill feeling between nations, arise from not knowing each other better.[32]

A week later the next offering in the New Year's Eve number began rather strangely 'The Greek Lent is over, and it is Easter at Constantinople'[33] although this was much like one of Mary Smith's linking passages. It concluded with 'A Defence of Fleas' and broke off abruptly as if this were an attempt to fill the page, jarring with that grand plan laid out only the week before.

'A Digger's Diary' appeared only four times and was then quietly abandoned. It also used an internal narrator for apparently real events. Although it fitted with the theme of Empire which had emerged, the supply of articles did not prove reliable within the periodical's weekly scheme. Despite the fact that Horne used an intradiegetic fictional narrator for the 'Diary', continuity was established by identifying the author through prior authorship as an 'old contributor'. For the first instalment on 29 January 1853, a note was printed below the title: '[This is really a pleasant narration from actual experience. It is written by an old contributor to these pages, and reaches us in portions as it is sent from Australia.]'[34] The reintroduction of the familiar narrator was again comparable with the integration of Mary Smith within the periodical, not just within the novel. This reassurance also had the tone of fiction itself in its protestation, a style later used by Wilkie Collins for his documentary narratives in both *The Woman in White* and *The Moonstone*.

---

[31] Anne Lohrli, '*Household Words*' *A Weekly Journal 1850–1859 Conducted by Charles Dickens* (Toronto: University of Toronto Press, 1973).

[32] [Eustace Grenville-Murray], 'The Roving Englishman: A Greek Feast,' *HW*, 24 December 1853, 396–7.

[33] [Eustace Grenville-Murray], 'The Roving Englishman: Greek Easter at Constantinople,' *HW*, 31 December 1853, 415.

[34] *HW*, 29 January 1853, 457.

Household Words has thus been described as operating on 'the borderline between reportage and fiction'.[35] The contributions of the 'Englishman' and the 'Digger' were designed to be educational but also used partially fictionalized narrators on the model of *The Pickwick Papers* and of material in *Chambers's Edinburgh Journal*. Catherine Waters has identified from this 'the fluidity of the boundary between informational and imaginative writing'[36] and within *Household Words* this is where the instalments of *Cranford* were operating. The serialized novel unfolding to a plan was yet to come in this periodical with *Hard Times* commencing on 1 April 1854. It was in 1859 that Dickens used his new periodical *All the Year Round* to put fiction and the habit of serialization into first station.

All the Year Round, *Cornhill Magazine* and *Good Words*

These popular fiction-bearing periodicals were all launched within a seven-month period between April 1859 and January 1860. Their similarities and differences are discussed below but the aim of this section is to highlight the frames into which the core novels were placed for the serial reader. *All the Year Round* and *Cornhill Magazine* emerged with clear prospectuses which were both fulfilled and redefined by the authors of the serials within. *Good Words* evolved to meet the challenge of these other family magazines, its fiction carefully contextualized in an avowedly religious periodical.

The rhythms and patterns of *All the Year Round* cohered around fiction as the dominant form in the new periodical where Dickens aimed to produce 'some sustained works of imagination that may become part of English literature.'[37] The context for this pivotal statement balanced between the final instalment of *A Tale of Two Cities* and the first instalment of *The Woman in White*, gave added weight to his plan. Lessons had undoubtedly been learned from the periodical serialization of *Hard Times*, *North and South* and *The Dead Secret* in *Household Words* which impacted on decisions made about fiction in the 'new series'. The experience of both serial and periodical publication and the maturing competitive market for family magazines influenced the fiction being produced and the authors who were employed to produce it. Fiction and the ongoing serial was usually chosen to lead off a number of *All the Year Round* but this had to be adapted at critical points of changeover and of flagging sales such as happened between Charles Lever's *A Day's Ride* and *Great Expectations*. *A Day's Ride* was moved inside the numbers of *All the Year Round* from 1 December 1860 when *Great Expectations* opened. Dickens's novel remained in first station throughout its serialization and Lever's novel continued as an anomalous second fictional serial in fourth, fifth or final

---

    [35]   David Parker, 'Dickens, Edward Said and Australia,' in *Down Under with Dickens: Papers Selected from the International Dickens Conference Melbourne 2004, ed. Alan* Dilnot (The Dickens Fellowship: Melbourne, 2006), 35.

    [36]   Waters, 16.

    [37]   *AYR*, 26 November 1859, 95.

station until its conclusion on 23 March 1861. In this way Dickens's own periodical serials as an author were themselves contingent, influenced in their timing, format and length by periodical sales.

Lessons learned about the serialization of fiction were also put into practice by other periodicals. Bradbury and Evans founded *Once a Week* to replace *Household Words* when the latter title was absorbed into *All the Year Round*. *Once a Week* differentiated itself from Dickens's new periodical through its use of illustration. It was a weekly magazine which cost three pence, as opposed to *All the Year Round* at two pence, and first appeared in July 1859. Two other magazines which targeted the family market using fiction and illustration would also debut in the next six months. Although very different from one another, *Cornhill Magazine* and *Good Words* were competing for a partially overlapping readership. The *Cornhill* used its sense of a coterie audience to increase the importance of belonging whilst *Good Words* appealed to religious feeling and the rewards of learning in a controlled space.

The choice of Thackeray as editor of *Cornhill Magazine* indicated to observers the likely role of fiction and illustration within the new periodical. Thackeray wrote to G.H. Lewes that the title was meant to suggest 'a sound of jollity and abundance'[38] although it had the dual purpose of advertising the location of the publishing house. Leonard Huxley, writing a history of Smith Elder in the early twentieth century also observed that being talked about was 'the best advertisement of all'.[39] On 9 March 1861, *The Economist* described the *Cornhill* as 'a kind of "Chambers' Journal" for the higher classes of society'.[40] This suggests the types of benchmarks available in the early 1860s. *Chambers's Edinburgh Journal* had been in existence since 1832 with its mixture of education and entertainment although it too had begun serializing fiction during the 1850s. This also demonstrates how magazines were pitted against one another and were both categorized and afforded status by such comparisons. Barbara Quinn Schmidt points out that *Cornhill Magazine* was aimed at middle class readers with leisure time who were seeking a better quality of life through the knowledge and information being imparted.[41] Alvar Ellegård observes that fiction came to dominate the magazine's content but Andrew Maunder identifies a 'shrewd mixture of ingredients'.[42] On 3 March 1860, after the third number had appeared, Trollope described the *Cornhill* as 'an established

---

[38] Quoted in Leonard Huxley, *The House of Smith Elder* (London: Privately Printed, 1923), 95.

[39] Huxley, 91.

[40] Quoted in Alvar Ellegård, *The Readership of the Periodical Press in Mid-Victorian Britain* (Göteburg: Göteburg Universitet, 1957), 33.

[41] Barbara Q. Schmidt, 'The *Cornhill Magazine*: Celebrating Success,' *Victorian Periodicals Review* 32 (1999): 202.

[42] Ellegård, 33; Andrew Maunder, '"Discourses of Distinction": The Reception of the *Cornhill Magazine* 1859–60', *Victorian Periodicals Review* 32 (1999): 242.

literary property'.[43] He clearly had a vested interest in the ongoing success of the periodical and in allying himself with its editor and publisher, but circulation figures and contemporary impact certainly supported his statement. Maunder has more recently looked back to its 'mythic status as a cultural signifier'[44] which was created not only by Smith and Thackeray but by the interaction between Trollope's fiction and the educational content. This was the combination dubbed 'tarts' and 'bread and cheese' by Thackeray.[45] More pragmatically the cost of the magazine at a shilling a month compared very favourably with the cost of acquiring a three-volume novel at 31s 6d since the novel was accompanied by the other serials and commentaries as well as the entertaining 'rambling papers'. *Cornhill Magazine* was also less than half the price of *Macmillan's Magazine* which had first appeared two months earlier and cost 2s 6d.

A number of the *Cornhill* was 128 pages long with text printed in a single column so that it read like a book. *All the Year Round* was weekly and un-illustrated and read more like a newspaper in columns. Dickens clearly expected his readership to transfer their loyalties to his new periodical by retaining some of its appearance and characteristics, and by naming the incorporation with *Household Words* on the title page. The statement 'with which is incorporated "Household Words"' appeared on the masthead of every number. It has been noted that links with the American printing process meant that *All the Year Round* could not be as topical as *Household Words* had been and that its subject matter was adjusted accordingly.[46] John Drew notes that there are fewer articles on emigration, education and industry and more on foreign topics and on science. *Good Words* was also printed in two columns beginning as a 16-page weekly in January 1860 before becoming a monthly from January 1861. Its illustrations which began to appear in February 1860 ran across columns which interrupted the text and created a hybrid feel between book and newspaper but it would have read more like a magazine because of its 64-page format.

Within these formats, *All the Year Round* and *Cornhill Magazine* used authorship and anonymity in different ways to suggest a wholeness and continuity. Dickens's portrayal of himself as a conductor in his periodical conjured up the image of an orchestra or soloists brought into a harmonious whole by the actions of the editor/publisher. Thackeray used alternative terminology, and when Smith had agreed on Trollope's contribution of *Framley Parsonage* to the *Cornhill*, Thackeray wrote speedily to acclaim him as a 'Co-operator in our New Magazine'.[47] This reflected that 'man of the world' tone for which they strove and Thackeray often

[43]   Anthony Trollope to George Smith, 3 March 1860, Trollope, *Letters*, vol. 1, 98.

[44]   Maunder, 239.

[45]   W.M. Thackeray to Anthony Trollope, 28 October 1859, Trollope, *Letters*, vol. 1, 91.

[46]   John Drew, *Dictionary of Nineteenth-Century Journalism* (London: Academia Press and the British Library, 2009); quoted in *DJO*, http://www.djo.org.uk/indexes/journals/all-the-year-round.html.

[47]   W.M. Thackeray to Anthony Trollope, 28 October 1859, Trollope, *Letters*, vol. 1, 91.

acknowledged his other 'co-operators' within the pages of the *Cornhill*. He would use illustrations to differentiate their contributions and to link those contributions across different numbers of the magazine. As a weekly, *All the Year Round* was sparsely decorated and the appearance of single authorship (by Dickens) was encouraged by the flow and framing of the text.

Good Words operated on a different model because of its naming strategy. The appearance of the periodical with Macleod's name as the ongoing strapline in a similar manner to that of Dickens appeared imitative but Strahan also chose to name his contributors within that controlled space. In spite of the religious tone of the message in *Good Words*, repeat purchase was still its goal. Macleod introduced the first issue in January 1860 by proposing a contract:

> Before ... entering further in our literary labours, and commencing an intercourse of thought which may possibly be continued for many years, we ask our readers to unite with us in expressing the honest prayer before God that "good words", and good words only, may be published from week to week.[48]

This contract reflected the 'synchronic or inner relations'[49] of the magazine's ideology. It associated the concept of work or 'labour' with that of literature and proposed, if humbly, a relationship which would extend over subsequent numbers of the magazine. As editor, Macleod was asking for the prayers of his unseen congregation but he also seemed to suggest that the reader had a role to play in apprehending the periodical's contents in the right context.

The first issue of *Good Words* sold 32,000 copies in January 1860 compared with the much-vaunted 120,000 sold of the first issue of *Cornhill Magazine*.[50] This comparison would gain more validity once *Good Words* became a monthly publication from January 1861 onwards, having been published weekly for fifty weeks in 1860. Its appearance coinciding broadly with the disappearance of *Household Words* as an independent title marked a point of differentiation and continuation which suggested that 'household words' could now be 'good words' too. On the inside cover of the first number, Macleod made the allusion himself when he pointed out that 'the "good words" of Christ have become as "household words" in our Christian homes'.[51] Strahan's *Christian Guest: A Family Magazine for Leisure Hours and Sundays* which was predecessor to *Good Words* ceased publication. The more general title of the new periodical moved the target audience boundary out once more from simply Sunday reading. By January 1862, the reported circulation of *Good Words* was 70,000, broadly comparable with the

---

[48]   'We Wish You a Good New Year!' *GW* 1 (1860): 1.

[49]   Andrew Maunder, '"Monitoring the Middle-Classes": Intertextuality and Ideology in Trollope's *Framley Parsonage* and the *Cornhill Magazine* 1859–60', *Victorian Periodicals Review* 33 (2000): 53.

[50]   Patricia Srebrnik, *Alexander Strahan: Victorian Publisher* (Ann Arbor: University of Michigan Press, 1986), 39.

[51]   Quoted in Srebrnik, 38.

Cornhill, and *The Bookseller* commented on 26 September 1861 that 'of religious magazines, the only one that is progressing is *Good Words* which appears to devour all others'.[52]

Macleod's biographer Wellwood sums up the intentions behind *Good Words* which were 'to represent various schools of Christian thought, and make a point of human interest and scientific instruction'. Wellwood describes the magazine as 'the mirror of the editor's mind, full of spirituality, yet taking in with relish the outer world'[53] although this mirror was created firstly by the framing mechanism of Macleod's name and secondly by the editorial decision-making of Strahan, the publisher. Patricia Srebrnik observes that Strahan took on the 'bulk of the editorial work' so that he was 'in large part conductor' of *Good Words*.[54] It has also been suggested that Strahan consciously amalgamated audiences across classes, borders (meaning England and Scotland) and churches.[55] Wellwood claims that Macleod 'had his eye on the intelligent mechanic, whom the evangelical prints repelled' and this offers some insight into the range of targeted readers, readers of sermons and of fiction although it must be noted that the price of 6d a month did put *Good Words* out of reach for the working-class reader.[56] Wellwood surmises that 'in the narratives (not to say novels) many a maiden aunt, who thought fiction in general of the devil, snatched a fearful joy'.[57] At the point of overlap with competing serials in the monthly *Cornhill* and weekly *All the Year Round*, *Good Words* was differentiated by its overtly religious content. It was also differentiated from *All the Year Round* by the accompanying illustrations and this section concludes with an overview of this aspect of *Good Words* as a periodical.

The first illustration in *Good Words* appeared on the first page of the fifth weekly number in February 1860. Strahan advertised 'Illustrations from Scripture' by 'J.B.' who, in fact contributed only four illustrations in 1860 including this first one of 'The Story of the Ethiopian and Philip'.[58] The established monthly pattern of the periodical as discussed in Chapter 3 was of an opening address and closing scripture study, a pattern which evolved during the first year of publication. The first novel serialized in *Good Words* was *Lady Somerville's Maidens* by an unidentified author in 24 parts beginning from the sixth number in February 1860. It was illustrated intermittently by five in-house artists, James Archer contributing five illustrations, Keeley Halswelle four, Clark Stanton and Hughes Taylor two, and William Orchardson one. The stuttering start was highlighted by

52   Quoted in Srebrnik, 46.

53   John Wellwood, *Norman Macleod* (Edinburgh: Oliphant, Anderson and Ferrier 1897), 88.

54   Srebrnik 42; 1.

55   Srebrnik, 2.

56   Wellwood, 88; Srebrnik, 39.

57   Wellwood, 88.

58   See *GW* 1 (1860): iv; 65. The majority of this volume is available at http://www.electricscotland.com/history/goodwords/index.htm.

the inconsistencies of the illustrators and continued within the text itself which overflowed the boundaries of the numbers of the periodical.[59] The main pattern of the periodical in its first year was supplied by the weekly 'Good Words for Every Day in the Year' which concluded every number. The other serials included the seven-part 'A Summer Study of Ferns', the six-part 'Aspects of Indian Life During the Rebellion' and the occasional 'Lessons for Young Men' and 'Journey by Sinai to Syria'. By 1862, during the serialization of *Mistress and Maid*, the structure was more regular and was capitalizing on Macleod's apparent editorial control. John Everett Millais provided twelve illustrations for *Mistress and Maid* in 1862 at the same time as he was illustrating Trollope's *Orley Farm*, published in monthly parts between March 1861 and October 1862. The most celebrated collaboration between Millais and Strahan/Macleod was yet to come in his later illustrations to *The Parables of Our Lord* which appeared in *Good Words* in 1863 and in volume form in 1864.

Unlike the separate single-page images of the *Cornhill*, the illustrations in *Good Words* interrupted the text of the novel on each opening page. Visual impact for the serial was paramount but this placement meant that an illustration was not always embedded in the text to which it referred. Like those in the *Cornhill,* the illustrations for the novels were proleptic in that they might depict a scene from any part of the instalment which followed. As with his clergymen contributors, Strahan's naming policy towards his illustrators was distinctive since he was attempting to gain commercial leverage from their celebrity and associations. In the volume edition of the periodical, for instance, the illustrators were given joint billing on the title page of *Good Words for 1862* with Millais listed first, followed by five other names including Holman Hunt, John Tenniel and Frederick Walker.[60] In 1862, in addition to the twelve illustrations for *Mistress and Maid*, Millais also illustrated the poems 'Olaf' and 'Highland Flora'.[61] It is ironic that Strahan made no capital out of two of the illustrations from 1862 which would now be recognised as highly characteristic of their artists: 'King Sigurd' by Edward Burne Jones and 'Until Her Death' by Frederick Sandys.[62] Like Jones and Sandys, Hunt, Tenniel and Walker supplied only one illustration each in 1862[63] but because of their relative lack of public recognition there was no reference to the former two artists on the title page. Jones was about to become well known in William Morris's company

---

[59]   After the longest section of the serial (Part I), the parts were misaligned within the allotted space of their weekly numbers, overlapping as follows: Parts II and III (*GW* 1 (1860*)*: 427), III and IV (491) and V and VI (635).

[60]   *GW* 3 (1862): iv.

[61]   'Olaf,' *GW* 3 (1862): 25; 'Highland Flora,' *GW* 3 (1862): 393.

[62]   'King Sigurd,' *GW* 3 (1862): 248; 'Until Her Death,' *GW* 3 (1862): 312.

[63]   These illustrations are Hunt's biblical 'Go and Come' in January immediately opposite the first illustration and instalment of *Mistress and Maid* (*GW* 3 (1862): 32); Tenniel's 'The Battle of Gilboa' in February (89) and Walker's 'Out Among the Wild Flowers' in November (657).

as a result of the 1862 Great International Exhibition described by Craik in the June issue of *Good Words*, and Sandys had produced for the periodical one of his most celebrated works as the incidental accompaniment to Craik's filler poem. In their case, it was the artists who were gaining celebrity from their appearance in the periodical.[64]

Although Strahan's primary interest in illustrations was in their power to educate and instruct with a religious tone, he was not immune to the marketing power of a celebrity illustrator. Simon Cooke describes *Good Words* as a 'visual display in which imagery is cleverly used to complement its dour articles and sombre poems.'[65] This would appear to suggest that Millais's illustrations are not 'failed paintings' but rather successful art within a failed text and this will be further explored in the re-reading of *Mistress and Maid* as a serial in Chapter 5.

Cassell's Magazine

When *Poor Miss Finch* began to be serialized in 1871, the publishing house of Cassell, Petter and Galpin was several removes from its original foundation as a temperance organisation, and the legacy of the original company had an impact on the reception of the novel. On 1 July 1848 the first issue of John Cassell's journal the *Standard of Freedom* was subtitled a 'Family Paper' and in 1850 his serials or part works of books and histories started to appear. The young John Cassell had memorably announced to a temperance meeting: 'Give the people mental food and they will not thirst after the abominable drink which is poisoning them.'[66] His *Cassell's Illustrated Family Paper* ran weekly at the price of one penny and in several forms between December 1853 and March 1867. It was re-launched in 1867 as *Cassell's Magazine*, which serialized Wilkie Collins's *Man and Wife* from November 1869 to July 1870 and *Poor Miss Finch* from September 1871 to February 1872.

Cassell's Illustrated Family Paper performed a range of interrelated functions within the market for family periodicals. It firstly promoted the educational and temperance aims of Cassell who believed that working people required their 'mental food'. Within the competitive environment created by journals such as the *Penny Magazine*, *London Journal* and *Reynolds Miscellany* founded in the 1830s and 1840s, the *Paper* also pursued its commercial aims by being illustrated using new techniques with varying degrees of success. In addition, at the time of its launch it fulfilled the legal aim of circumventing stamp duty by avoiding news and comment as a 'paper'. The prominence of the word 'family' in the title is also significant following on from the *Standard of Freedom*. The *Paper* was a conservative, general interest, illustrated family miscellany intended for Sunday

---

[64] See Simon Cooke, *Illustrated Periodicals of the 1860s: Contexts and Collaborations* (London: British Library, 2010), 179–81.

[65] Cooke, 67.

[66] Simon Nowell-Smith, *The House of Cassell 1848–1958* (London: Cassell, 1958), 9.

reading at home and designed, according to its first number, to 'unite amusement with instruction' with the editor as 'mine host' supplying 'a bill of fare to all who do him honour by their company'.[67] In this launch issue, Cassell proposed to provide 'faithful pictures of far-distant lands … so that in imagination we may live with those who lived before us, and inhabit countries we never saw'. He emphasised the role of the illustrated periodical in the home with its 'pen and pencil pictures for the family circle': 'The young will not be overlooked … neither will the ladies be forgotten – needlework and the newest fashions will come in for a share of attention.'[68] In the claim that Fiction 'will open her richest stores of fancy', fiction itself was designated female and nine months later Cassell announced that the services of Mrs Burbury[69] had been engaged for the serial *French Hay; or Lost and Found: a Tale of English Village Life.* The editor had no doubt that the work of the female author would 'find a ready welcome in the homes of thousands, appealing as it does to our everyday business, and the ordinary interests of common life'.[70]

The headpiece of the *Paper* was designed by John Gilbert, a long-term contributor to the *Illustrated London News* who has been described as one of 'the originators of pictorial journalism'.[71] Using this framing device, each number pictured the family, led by papa, reading together as a reflection of 'the ordinary interests of common life'. In accordance with the magazine's first principles, the central family group was depicted with the sciences in the form of a globe, a microscope and some test tubes, and with the arts through an easel and a sculpture. This headpiece of the reading family survived in various formats until January 1865. Over time, a real dog replaced the original toy one and a cricket bat was incorporated into the design. Latterly, the children also became more grown-up and more studious in their attention, clearly indicating the *Paper*'s original and ongoing target market. Fiction had an educative role or was at least seen as the way in which readers could be drawn to educational material although Mary Hamer suggests that *Cassell's Illustrated Family Paper* and *Chambers's Edinburgh Journal* 'admitted [fiction as] a concession to human weakness'.[72] Graham Law points out that the *Paper* was one of the popular fiction weeklies which reached a wider mass audience through its lower price but was not as respected as *All*

67   *CIFP*, 31 December 1853, 1.

68   *CIFP*, 31 December 1853, 1.

69   *CIFP*, 31 December 1853, 1. Edwina Hicks Burbury was advertised in *CIFP* as the author of *Florence Sackville* (1853) which was a novel admired by Charlotte Brontë (Catherine Malone, 'Burbury , Edwina Jane (1818/19–1870),' in *Oxford Dictionary of National Biography*, http://www.oxforddnb.com/view/article/40415).

70   *CIFP*, 30 September 1854, 335.

71   Lisa Small, 'Gilbert, Sir John (1817–1897)', *Oxford Dictionary of National Biography*, http://www.oxforddnb.com/view/article/10693. Gilbert is identified as the original designer by Patricia Anderson, *The Printed Image and the Transformation of Popular Culture 1790–1860* (Oxford: Clarendon Press, 1991), 95.

72   Mary Hamer, *Writing by Numbers: Trollope's Serial Fiction* (Cambridge: Cambridge University Press, 1987), 28.

the Year Round and *Once a Week* because of its 'crude and ill-written' stories.[73] The *Paper* was a penny weekly unlike the twopenny *Household Words*; the later *Cassell's Magazine* also cost a penny with *All the Year Round* twopence and *Once a Week* threepence. For comparison, during 1860, *Good Words* appeared weekly at 1½d but was later sixpence monthly. In 1859, the *British Quarterly Review* listed the *Family Paper* with seven other magazines in the article entitled 'Cheap Literature' which concluded, 'We do not expect high scholarship in our penny instructors and entertainers'.[74] Overall the writer in the *British Quarterly* found the *Paper* both misguided and 'well-intended', conceding that, aside from the melodramatic fiction catering 'to a low and ignorant taste', the *Paper* 'aimed at being instructive and educational in other departments.'[75] The *Paper* thus helped to reinforce the perception of the serial reading public as working class, and Cassell's audience remained upper working- and lower middle-class throughout its publishing history.

At the end of 1857, Cassell as editor announced the change from folio to quarto format by reiterating the latter's 'more elegant and book-like appearance' at the same time as reminding 'the country' that 'nothing can contribute more readily and efficiently to a people's progress than a healthy, sound, first-rate and at the same time cheap literature.'[76] The letters page on 12 December 1857 advised the correspondent 'YOUNG PRETENDER' on 'wholesome' reading since '[m]any of the works of the writers of the last century make us wonder how their books could have been admitted into the libraries of men with wives and daughters.'[77] In the same issue, the 'Matron' offered a weekly column of 'plain, practical familiar directions as to all branches of domestic economy',[78] and there were 'Hopes and Helps for the Young' along with the continuing chess problems and filler poems. The structure and anticipated follow-on parts of the *Paper*'s contents suggest its place as a periodical publication in the lives of its family readers. The seasonal issues and reference to current events and cross-references to reports from other sources gave this sense of an embedded record presenting the immediate one-off miscellany of the weekly number within overarching factual series covering personal topics, domestic advice and embroidery patterns. In a letter of 1858 Cassell explained that he was reconsidering the type of 'mental food' to be served when he wrote that 'novels [are] appropriate vehicles in the conveyance of useful lessons ... thus advancing the Moral and intellectual welfare of the People at large.'[79] The fictional serials included in the *Paper*, however, were very much the output of

---

[73]   Graham Law, 'The Serial Publication in Britain of the Novels of Wilkie Collins', http://www.f.waseda.jp/glaw/arts/wcsp.pdf: 10.

[74]   'Cheap Literature,' *British Quarterly Review* 29 (1859): 313.

[75]   'Cheap Literature,' 337; 339; 337.

[76]   *CIFP*, 5 December 1857, 391.

[77]   *CIFP*, 12 December 1857, 32.

[78]   *CIFP*, 12 December 1857, 7.

[79]   Letter to Lord Brougham, 27 September 1858; quoted in Anderson, 120.

popular pot-boiling novelists such as John Frederick Smith and Percy B. St John. Like Mrs Burbury's, their serials acquired descriptive subtitles such as Smith's *The Soldier of Fortune: a Tale of War* and St John's *The Arctic Crusoe: a Tale of the Polar Seas*. In the new series from 1857, two 'continuous tales' or serials were promised including Smith's very long-running *Smiles and Tears: A Tale of our Times* and *The Substance and the Shadow* which followed it in 1858. The *British Quarterly Review* article accused Smith of 'much button-holding in [his] narratives', and it was suggested that *The Substance and Shadow* contained 'plot enough for half-a-dozen ordinary novels, hurried on with breathless expedition.'[80] In 1871, *Poor Miss Finch* too acquired the descriptive sub-title 'A Domestic Story' and this overt packaging for family consumption was a formula which extended into the layout of the magazine at all stages of its evolution.

The fictional serial in *Cassell's Illustrated Family Paper* in the 1850s and 1860s was thus part of a vehicle for educational material and advice. Launching the quarto version on 5 December 1857, the *Paper* congratulated itself on 'the sterling value' of its 'substance ... [which] far surpasses all its competitors of the cheap periodical press'. The editorial table which headed the back page claimed that 'CASSELL'S ILLUSTRATED FAMILY PAPER–New Series challenges comparison in its literary and artistic departments with any of its *illustrated* contemporaries'.[81] The *Paper* was making its appeal to a clear segment of a market which was about to be expanded considerably with the launch of *All the Year Round*, *Once a Week* and *Macmillan's Magazine* in 1859, and of *Cornhill Magazine*, *Good Words* and *Temple Bar* in 1860. These were periodicals aimed at a mainstream middle-class audience but Cassell's market was also targeted by *Once a Week* in the mid 1870s when the latter was owned and edited by George Manville Fenn, by then a former editor of *Cassell's Magazine*.[82] In March 1867, Cassell's announced a changed format designed to compete with these other magazines which were serializing novels. A new prospectus was supplied for the rechristened *Cassell's Magazine* announcing that 'Fiction of powerful interest will form the prominent feature of its pages but with this will be associated Popular Articles on Topics of the Day, Striking Narratives, Biographical Memoirs, and Papers on Special Subjects'.[83] The *Magazine* changed some of the regular features which had been part of Cassell's original scheme including the advice column, letters page and chess puzzle. Women's guidance from 'the Matron' and the special 'Advice to the Young' were also withdrawn and it has been suggested that 'after 1860 the *Paper* devoted itself increasingly to purely escapist amusement, to the exclusion of more

[80] 'Cheap Literature,' 335; 336.

[81] *CIFP*, 5 December 1857, 16.

[82] See Stephen Elwell, 'Editors and Social Change: A Case Study of *Once a Week* (1859–80), in *Innovators and Preachers: the Role of the Editor in Victorian England*, ed. Joel H. Wiener (Westport: Greenwood, 1985), 35–9.

[83] *CIFP*, 5 December 1857, p. 16.

informative but less saleable material'.[84] It was after 1874 when the *Magazine* became *Cassell's Family Magazine* that the fiction serials were supplemented once again by regular series such as 'Chit Chat on Dress', 'Women Who Work' and the 'How To' column.

At the same time, the new columnists in *Cassell's Magazine* who wrote as both named and anonymous contributors were also targeting a more informed readership using a revised approach to the advice column to educate the reader through direct address. The *Magazine* strove to differentiate the working class observations of 'Mrs Brown's Budget' from the more sophisticated 'Mrs Malachite's Maxims' with her 'few plain truths about dress, parties and servants'.[85] In the first 'Maxim', there was even a joke at the expense of the popular advice of Mrs. Beeton as well as that of Sarah Stickney Ellis, an older commentator on etiquette. The columnist observed: 'I will write and publish maxims for my own sex, just as that excellent teacher of youth and deportment Mrs Ellis did in her work "The Wives, Mothers, Daughters, Aunts and Female Cousins of England"'.[86] Both 'Brown' and 'Malachite' are short-lived columns in the environment of the *Magazine* but it is notable that the editor was now able to use the services of named female contributors such as Frances Power Cobbe and Eliza Lynn Linton in place of the anonymized 'Fanny Fern' from the *Paper*.[87] Enhanced production values together with the ability to adapt layout and attract the eye were developed in the magazine's later illustrations, and illustrators such as William Hughes and Mary Ellen Edwards also formed part of the continuity and community of the periodical in series.

At another level of serial patterning, the monthly collected issue and annual volume edition were significant factors of *Cassell's* place in the market. Despite the absence of the word 'family' from the title of the new magazine, the publishers continued to recommend themselves to readers within the family circle, believing that *Cassell's Magazine* 'will be warmly welcomed as a cheerful companion for every family fireside' and will build into a 'handsome volume' with 'permanent value' at the end of the year.[88] The original prospectus drew attention to the idea of the daily or weekly value of the magazine within the home as well as its collective value as a bound work which could be reviewed for the purposes of record. The periodical was acting as a form of advice manual with a place in a community of information through which the reader could achieve social and educational goals which were appropriate to the 'family fireside'. As discussed in Chapter 6, the

---

84   Anderson, 89.

85   *CassM*, 9 March 1867, 7.

86   *CassM*, 9 March 1867, 8. Mrs Malachite was referring to Sarah Stickney Ellis's much reprinted publications, *The Women of England* (1839), *The Daughters of England* (1842), *The Wives of England* (1843) and *The Mothers of England* (1843).

87   See, for instance, 'Fanny Fern', 'Lady Doctors,' *CIFP*, 5 December 1857, 390 which concluded that the columnist did not 'believe in' them.

88   *CIFP*, 9 March 1867, 448.

appearance of *Poor Miss Finch* in volume form thus brought sensation material into the home under Cassell's authorised and domestic covers, at the same time as giving the publishing house the commercial advantage of publishing a novel as if it were a regular part work from their educational list.

Simon Nowell-Smith observes in his history of Cassell's that '[t]he success of a popular magazine rested upon the avoidance of trouble.'[89] *Cassell's Magazine* could not afford to alienate its family audience and its reputation suffered from the association with Wilkie Collins's novels. The pattern within the periodical demonstrates the importance attached to the role of a family magazine as a 'fireside companion' and 'welcome guest'. Cassell's ultimately abandoned the plan of employing mainstream novelists to expand its readership. In *Cassell's Family Magazine* they returned to that family audience gained through their reputation for providing education and healthy literature, safe for the newly literate to read. A frame had already been set by the periodical's original popularity and style as *Cassell's Illustrated Family Paper*, and the period of association with Collins clearly illustrates how a novel and periodical might suffer from aggravated competition in a space where the two are also dependent as texts. The serial was written and presented within the boundary of the periodical. This chapter has established the rationale for the frames into which those serialized core novels were fitted. The next and central chapter revisits the novels in context in order to explore the unending and unfinished Victorian serial contained within its original boundaries and thresholds.

---

[89] Nowell-Smith, 121.

Chapter 5
The Serialized Novel

This chapter explores the original context for the serialized novel within the mid-Victorian family magazine. Re-placed within the periodical, the material text of the novel as serial can be viewed at its specific cultural moment. According to Margaret Beetham and Kay Boardman, 'The serial was one of the commercial, rhetorical and structural strategies to involve the reader',[1] and the chapter considers how such strategies were deployed through the five core novels. Each of the novels is discussed to identify the effect of intertextuality within the periodical miscellany and to assess the serial's format and contribution to the periodical. Richard Altick describes the 'coloration' of the serial within the periodical as being created by 'the physically proximate content of nonfiction'[2] and the localized impact of the serialization of the novel is analysed against other texts and in the context of accompanying illustrations. Andrew Maunder suggests that magazines presented 'a world of competing as well as complementary discourses'[3] and the discussion here assesses the ways in which the text of the novel was both competing and complementary within the discourse of the periodical.

This chapter makes the most specific links between serial and magazine. For each serial there is a dedicated section which considers the relationship with or development of the register of the periodical in which it was embedded. Each section also explores the intertextual commentary created by the serial's interaction with other material and in particular, where appropriate, the impact of illustration within the magazine. It will be demonstrated that even complementary serials used elements of competition as part of their rhetoric for existence within the periodical's discourse.

Cranford in *Household Words*

In the first number of *Household Words* the editor offered in his 'Preliminary Word' to accompany the train traveller in the modern present 'thankful for the privilege of living in this summer-dawn of time'. He also added that 'Our Household Words will not be echoes of the present time alone, but of the past too'. Elizabeth Gaskell's

---

[1] Margaret Beetham and Kay Boardman, *Victorian Women's Magazines* (Manchester: Manchester University Press, 2001), 4.

[2] Richard D. Altick, *The Presence of the Present: Topics of the Day in the Victorian Novel* (Columbus: Ohio State University Press, 1991), 67.

[3] Andrew Maunder, '"Monitoring the Middle-Classes": Intertextuality and Ideology in Trollope's *Framley Parsonage* and the *Cornhill Magazine* 1859–60,' *Victorian Periodicals Review* 33 (2000): 45.

Cranford sketches were set in a completed past which occupied an intertextual place within the issues of a periodical constructed out of the discussion of the present. Within these individual closed numbers, the sketches were additionally set apart by the repetition and indexing of the town's title; despite the lack of attribution, the name of the town itself flagged up the continuity of authorship across 55 weeks of periodical publication.

In addition to the discussion of Gaskell's authorship and Dickens's editorship, Chapter 4 has contextualized the tone and style of *Household Words* using the evolution of *Cranford* as a means to explore the reading content of the periodical during its early years of publication. This has established that the register of the periodical was created in part by *Cranford*'s interaction with the recurring topics of journalism in *Household Words* at the fluid boundary between fact and fiction. The section which follows here can now interrogate the serial in context by considering how the sketches would have been consumed within the numbers of the periodical. As we have seen, *Cranford* unfolded in nine parts at irregular intervals between 13 December 1851 and 21 May 1853 before its publication as a single volume in June 1853. As discussed below, its serial intentions became clearer in the later instalments but during the appearance of the original sketches, Gaskell's novella in serial form interacted with a range of other material including Dickens's *A Child's History of England* and a number of non-fictional articles which echoed other fiction including the novels *Oliver Twist* (1838) and *Nicholas Nickleby* (1839).[4] The patterns of references to seafaring, to empire and to emigration contextualized Peter Jenkyns's disappearance and reappearance in *Cranford*. The final instalment entitled 'A Happy Return to Cranford' then appeared on 21 May 1853 in the same issue as Henry Morley's 'Our Last Parochial War' which provided a parallel and darker commentary on the culture of another small town, the semi-fictional Cess-cum-Poulton.

As a serial, *Cranford* evolved on an incidental basis and became a novel in retrospect. Gaskell protested to John Ruskin in 1865, the year of her death: 'The beginning of Cranford was one paper in Household Words – and I never meant to write more; so killed poor Captain Brown – very much against my will.'[5] It can be demonstrated that the continuation of *Cranford* was stimulated by editor-demand and control. Dickens as editor was proactive in the presentation of the sketches and wrote on 21 December 1851 to tell Gaskell that he had called the second of her pieces 'A Love Affair at Cranford'.[6] Gaskell later told John Forster on 3 May 1853 during a disagreement with Chapman and Hall about the first collected edition: 'I did not know what "Friends in Need" was, at first; you know the HW people always make titles for me.'[7] As sub-editor, Wills was clearly aware

---

[4]   See also Chapter 2 for a discussion of the relationship with *Bleak House* (1852–53).

[5]   Elizabeth Gaskell to John Ruskin, 24 February 1865, Gaskell, *Further Letters*, 269.

[6]   Elizabeth Gaskell to John Forster, 3 May 1853, Gaskell, *Further Letters*, 87.

[7]   Charles Dickens to Elizabeth Gaskell, 21 December 1851, Dickens, *Letters*, vol. 4, 558.

that the word 'Cranford' was needed in the title to establish a pattern within the 'occasional' series and to gain retrospective control for the volume index. Despite the fact that the rhythm of the regular serial had not yet been developed, it was not, as we have seen, uncommon for occasional articles to evolve into collected works as the Cranford sketches did. Its process of evolution based on customer demand makes *Cranford* anomalous as an example of a serialized novel; it was not broken into parts from a planned whole. It was, however, a text whose reception and composition were influenced by its periodical context, and the intertextual relationships of the episodes are features of the serial's accumulation into a full-length narrative.

The collected edition of *Cranford* is discussed in more detail in Chapter 6 but the amendments made for its first publication demonstrate some of the significance of the original consumption of the serialized version.[8] Alan Shelston observes that the volume edition developed 'a coherence of its own out of the original episodes'.[9] In the first instalment, the absence of men among the 'Amazons' was described and after the deaths of Captain Brown and Miss Jenkyns, the reader was told dramatically 'Cranford is Man-less now', a line which provided significant closure.[10] With the introduction of Signor Brunoni, Mr Holbrook and Mr Hoggins in the later unplanned sketches, this line was removed for the volume edition. The second instalment in *Household Words* then began with Mary Smith's connective text about the 'love affair': 'I am tempted to relate it, as having interested me in a quiet sort of way, and as being the latest intelligence of Our Society at Cranford',[11] a sentence which was also removed from the volume. In addition the 'shadow of a love affair' in Chapter 3 of the volume edition was originally 'the love affair I am coming to: – gradually, not in a hurry, for we are never in a hurry in Cranford'.[12] As the sketches were not expected to recur at the original time of publication, these touches and repetition were used to remind readers of the periodical version of their engagement with the evolving stories.

A new pattern was signalled, however, when 'The Great Cranford Panic' was advertised as two chapters. These 'chapters' appeared in successive weeks unlike the other two previous pairs of episodes which had appeared unheralded on 13 December 1851/3 January 1852 and 13 March 1852/3 April 1852. In the 'Panic' Mary Smith was given the opportunity to introduce the story by explaining her absence from the pages of *Household Words*: 'Soon after the events of which I gave an account in my last paper, I was summoned home by my father's illness; and for a time I forgot, in anxiety about him, to wonder how my dear friends at

8   The variants are listed in Elizabeth Gaskell, *Cranford*, ed. Alan Shelston, vol. 3, *The Works of Elizabeth Gaskell*, ed. Joanne Shattock. 10 vols. (London: Pickering and Chatto, 2005), 361–8.

9   Shelston (ed.), xv.

10   *HW*, 13 December 1851, 274.

11   *HW*, 3 January 1852, 349.

12   *HW*, 3 January 1852, 350.

Cranford were getting on'.[13] This passage remained in the volume edition although it contributed to time scheme irregularities in the collection. One of these is already evident for the volume reader at the end of the second chapter when Miss Jenkyns and the young Flora Gordon, daughter of Jessie Brown become contemporaries; in *Household Words*, Miss Jenkyns was dead by the time of the second instalment. Other related items were, of course, smoothed over for the volume. The Gordons were the Campbells in the first instalment and became the Gordons in 'A Happy Return to Cranford' but were the Gordons throughout the volume edition. In fact, in 'The Great Cranford Panic' Gordon's was a local shop frequented by Miss Pole.[14] The newly projected pattern for the two-part piece translated more readily into *Cranford* the novel through Mary's thread at the end of the second 'Panic' chapter where she announced her plan to make enquiries about the 'Aga Jenkyns' mentioned by Signor Brunoni's wife.[15] There was then, however, a further three-month gap in *Household Words* until the last group of sketches[16] which offered more links back to the original 'Memory at Cranford' from 1852. During this period, Gaskell was in the midst of writing *Ruth*[17] but it is clear that a collection of 'Cranford' was by now being planned although the author claimed disingenuously at the time to be detached from this. In the May 1853 letter to John Forster, she wrote: 'I seldom see the Household Words and I do not even remember if I have written six or seven Cranford papers ... and I do not know how large a vol it would make.'[18]

The context and resonances of the material framework within which the *Cranford* narrative was originally published are thus highly relevant to its development into a full-length narrative. A re-creation of its intertextual impact within the pages of *Household Words* demonstrates the pattern of the reading experience in *Household Words* in 1852–53. The Cranford episodes would be regarded as 'occasional'. The only serial apparently ongoing was Dickens's own *A Child's History of England* which appeared at least once a month between 25 January 1851 and 10 December 1853, and was advertised on 18 January 1851 to be 'continued, at regular intervals, until the History is completed'.[19] It was only in 1854 that the consistency of a novel in weekly parts was established with *Hard Times* which commenced on 1 April that year followed by Gaskell's *North and South* from 2 September. The subject matter and discourse of other occasional series such as 'The Roving Englishman' and 'Digger's Diary' with their associated themes of travel and Australian emigration impacted on the first reception of

---

[13]   *HW*, 8 January 1853, 390.

[14]   *HW*, 8 January 1853, 390.

[15]   *HW*, 15 January 1853, 420.

[16]   2 April 1853, 7 May 1853 and 21 May 1853.

[17]   See Linda K. Hughes and Michael Lund, *Victorian Publishing and Mrs Gaskell's Work* (Charlottesville: University Press of Virginia, 1999), 85.

[18]   Gaskell, *Further Letters*, 87.

[19]   *HW*, 18 January 1851, 408.

the Cranford instalments. Gaskell's sketches were horizontally integrated into *Household Words* as 'factual fiction',[20] a phrase descriptive of the texts occurring at David Parker's 'borderline' and Catherine Waters's fluid 'boundary' discussed in Chapter 4. The sketches adopted the style of the periodical's social commentary and *Cranford* can therefore be evaluated as a serial and as a novel through that periodical context.

Re-read as a serial, *Cranford* began in the lead station on 13 December 1851 followed by articles on the Merchant Seaman's Fund, and on the sale of poisons and of pork insurance. There was also a poem called 'A Child's Prayer' and a final article entitled 'A Beginning and an End' about the christening of a princess and the funeral of a duchess. On 6 December 1851, the week before 'Our Society in Cranford', the lead article was a discussion of pawn-broking entitled 'My Uncle'. In the first of Gaskell's sketches, Jessie Brown shocked Miss Jenkyns by introducing into polite conversation 'my uncle, who has the best assortment of Shetland goods of anyone in Edinbro'.[21] The pattern of poetry, social journalism and domestic commentary was established and Gaskell's sketch fitted into it. The second instalment appeared two weeks later immediately following 'A Wassail for the New Year' by George Meredith so that 'Wassail to every soul, my lads,/ Wassail to every soul!'[22] immediately prefaced 'A Love Affair at Cranford'. In Mary Smith's introductory 'latest intelligence' sentence there was the deliberate echo of the title of the first designedly well-rounded instalment, and the sketch reflected both shared subject matter and the established periodical structure. This number of *Household Words* opened with 'Pearls from the East' on Hindu mythology which would resonate later with both the adventures of the second Brown family in India and the return of Peter Jenkyns in the periodical nearly two years later. The 'Antipodes' was a reference to New Zealand rather than the usual Australia, and the 'Sensible Legislation' article by the 'Scotchman' followed with its references back to other initially rounded material. A brief piece on the French pawnbroker as 'ma tante' even referred back to the lead article 'My Uncle' from four weeks before. There were 'Anecdotes of Monkeys' and 'the Roving Englishman' attended a masked ball in Vienna. The number closed, however, with a second piece by the 'Englishman' which consisted of a comic alphabet of personal advertisements, tracing 'the processes of courtship through the advertising columns' of an Austrian newspaper.[23] A sixty year-old widower is to marry: 'D, however, – Deborah, doubtless – sees the question popped'[24] and this was surely a humorous intertextual reference to Miss Jenkyns herself.

---

[20]   Jennifer Phegley, 'Clearing Away "The Briars and the Brambles": The Education and Professionalisation of the *Cornhill Magazine*'s Women Readers 1860–65,' *Victorian Periodicals Review* 33 (2000): 25.

[21]   *HW*, 13 December 1851, 268.

[22]   *HW*, 3 January 1852, 349.

[23]   'Advertisement', *HW*, 3 January 1852, 359.

[24]   'Advertisement.'

After two further months, the third sketch 'Memory at Cranford' appeared on 13 March 1852 once again following a poem. This time it was 'The Use of Flowers' beginning 'Sweet human flowers of passing loveliness/ Bloom a life's pathway with celestial splendour'[25] which in turn acted as the gateway to Miss Matey's sharing information about her past life with Mary. New Zealand was the subject of 'From a Settler's Wife' whilst Harriet Martineau wrote on 'Guns and Pistols', Dickens on 'Fine Arts in Australia' and Wills on 'A Sea Coroner', this last casting an ominous shadow on the potential fate of Peter Jenkyns. The number opened, however, with 'A Sleep to Startle Us' in which Dickens recounted a visit to a ragged school in tones which echoed both *Oliver Twist* and *Nicholas Nickleby*. The emphasis on suffering children continued on 3 April 1852 when 'Drooping Buds' on children's hospitals led out the number which also contained 'Visiting at Cranford'. Gaskell's sketch was positioned immediately before another sentimental poem called 'The Growth of Good' which provided a direct lead-in to the instalment: 'And thus in every human heart/ A germ of good is sown,/ Whose stirrings upward to the light/ Are seen by God alone.'[26]

After another nine months, 'The Great Cranford Panic. IN TWO CHAPTERS' on 8 January 1853 gave the first real sense of a serial unfolding although it was probable that the allocated word limit for the piece was exceeded and a division introduced to suit the pattern of the periodical. Mary Smith's absence was explained in the tone of Horne's 'Digger' made an occasional correspondent by the long voyage to Australia although, of course, she was only as far away as Drumble. With the introduction of the Brunonis and Mary's discovery of the existence of Aga Jenkyns, Morley's article on 'Silk from the Punjab' was timed well to appear immediately before the instalment. There was also an ongoing Australian article on whaling in Hobart and a historical article by Sala to lead off. Chapter 27 of *A Child's History* on Henry VIII concluded the number. 'Chapter the Second' of the 'Panic' on 15 January then appeared in a number dominated by Henry Morley who wrote about toys, malaria and education. In anticipation of the interest in a second part, Gaskell's instalment was moved forward into second station after Morley's 'Scholastic' in the character of 'Mr Green', a man who has read schoolteachers' advertisements in order to decide on his children's education. This offered more parallels with Dickens's novels and the tone of the article was carried through into the opening link between the two 'Panic' instalments: Miss Pole's interpretation of events and the 'fresh trait[s] of villany'[27] which appear with every repetition of her adventure.

The 'Panic' offered a serial indication in having a promised second chapter but Mary Smith's resolution at the end 'to make further inquiry'[28] was not, of course, immediately fulfilled since the next instalment did not appear for another three

---

25   *HW*, 13 March 1852, 588.
26   *HW*, 3 April 1852, 55.
27   *HW*, 15 January 1853, 413.
28   *HW*, 15 January 1853, 420.

months when 'Stopped Payment at Cranford' once more followed a sentimental poem on 2 April. 'The Feast of Life' provided a context for Miss Matey's situation since it concluded that life's 'dainties are turned into wormwood and gall,/ For the hearts that are heaving and ache.' The instalment then opened with Mary's connective question 'Was the "poor Peter" of Cranford the Aga Jenkyns of Chunderabaddad, or was he not?'[29] In this number, Sala's 'The Kingdom of Reconciled Impossibilities' appeared in second station where a surreal world of dreams and nightmares nonetheless set some of the scene for the Cranford pieces: 'a land of unfulfilled promises, of broken engagements, of trees for ever blossoming but never bearing fruit, ... of dramas never played out'. The world conjured by Gaskell and by the multiple knowledge areas of the *Household Words* writers was defined here, where '[e]verything in the kingdom is impossible. [new paragraph] Impossible, yet reconciled.'[30] Given the title of the Cranford instalment, this link was made more blatant by Sala's depiction of a potential nightmare incident: '[i]f we have a cheque to get cashed, the iron-ribbed shutters of the bank are always up when our cab drives to the door, and somebody near us always says, without being asked, "Stopped payment!"'[31] Twelve pages later, came the news that the Town and Country Bank 'had stopped payment. Miss Matey was ruined'.[32]

On 7 May 1853, Sala's 'Powder Dick and his Train,' described 'seamen-captains' and their 'pictorial and literary delineators', once again resurrecting pictures from *Dombey and Son*, as well as prefiguring Peter Jenkyns's impending return in the description of 'mahogany cheeks and sun-crimsoned foreheads and embrowned hands'.[33] Sala's description of 'The Life of Poor Jack' which concluded the number on 21 May picked up the pattern of returning seafarers, calling for the education of sailors from the point of view of a spokesman called Aholigal Cockle who proclaimed his position in society as landlord of The Tar Ashore.[34] This number of *Household Words* contained the last instalment of *Cranford* but the issue opened with 'Our Last Parochial War' through which Gaskell's town from a completed past was set up against the barely fictional Cess-cum-Poulton, a town very much in the present. The real town of Poulton-cum-Seacombe near Liverpool had been the subject of a public health inspection in 1851. Morley's introduction of a narrator from nearby Beadleville within the article was very similar to that of Gaskell's use of Mary Smith despite the more hard-hitting nature of the 'War' piece overall. The inhabitants of Cess-cum-Poulton have resisted any efforts at implementing the Public Health Act of 1848, 'the contest against the sanitary innovators being very violent'.[35] The facts about the real town were woven by

---

[29] *HW*, 2 April 1853, 108.
[30] *HW*, 2 April 1853, 104.
[31] *HW*, 2 April 1853, 103.
[32] *HW*, 2 April 1853, 115.
[33] *HW*, 7 May 1853, 240.
[34] *HW*, 21 May 1853, 286.
[35] *HW*, 21 May 1853, 268.

Morley into the satirical article which announced that '[t]he rotting away of the life in the Old Town of Cess-cum-Poulton is best expressed by the assurance that, on an average, each person there born, decays and dies eight and a half years sooner than he should.'[36] This discussion was more sinister in tone but nonetheless similar to that of the initial householder 'Amazons' in the first instalment of *Cranford*. 'We are not talking about reason; we are talking about rates,' explained Morley's internal narrator, Bumble-like: not death rates or birth rates but parochial rates.[37]

This nightmarish alternative to Cranford was perhaps the method by which Dickens's readers were being encouraged to say goodbye to the Gaskell sketches which appeared in collected, closed form a month later. Dickens wrote to Gaskell on 13 April 'You shall collect Cranford where you please'[38] but there is a danger in reading the volume edition of *Cranford* without its adumbrated context. Dorothy Collin, for instance, suggests that *Cranford* resists closure at the deaths of Captain Brown and Mr Holbrook[39] but the discussion here demonstrates that the serial was kept open and unending through editorial choice, and through its positioning within *Household Words* where a number was both open and closed. Martin Dodsworth announces that 'the later chapters of *Cranford* are an attempt to expiate the guilt of the Captain's death',[40] ignoring the commercial demands of the periodical and the cultivation of its readers by editor and author. Hilary Schor states that *Cranford* is 'an extended commentary on the ways women are taught to read cultural signs and a serious critique of the role of literature in shaping female readers',[41] and the role of periodical reading in this education should surely not be ignored.

This section has demonstrated how *Cranford* the serial read in context comes to occupy a place in the contemporary world of the periodical from which some critics believe it to be excluded. Tim Dolin's description of *Cranford* as 'an enclave within the larger narrative of history'[42] is also a description of the serial within *Household Words*. The links with the other material of the periodical indicate *Cranford*'s ability to be a microcosm of the miscellany it represents. Dolin suggests that magazines were a 'female miscellany' which 'textually instated

---

[36]   *HW*, 21 May 1853, 265.

[37]   *HW*, 21 May 1853, 269.

[38]   Charles Dickens to Elizabeth Gaskell, 13 April 1853, Dickens, *Letters*, vol. 5, 62.

[39]   Dorothy W. Collin, 'Strategies of Retrospection and Narrative Silence in *Cranford* and *Cousin Phillis*,' *Gaskell Studies Journal* 11 (1997): 28. See Margaret Beetham, 'Open and Closed: the Periodical as a Published Genre,' *Victorian Periodicals Review* 22 (1989): 96–100 and Lorna Huett, 'Commodity and Collectivity: *Cranford* and the Context of *Household Words*,' *Gaskell Studies Journal* 17 (2003): 34–49.

[40]   Martin Dodsworth, 'Women without Men at Cranford,' *Essays in Criticism* 17 (1963): 139.

[41]   Hilary M. Schor, 'Affairs of the Alphabet: Reading, Writing and Narrative in *Cranford*,' *Novel: A Forum on Fiction* 22 (1989): 288.

[42]   Tim Dolin, '*Cranford* and the Victorian Collection,' *Victorian Studies* 36 (1993): 194.

the ephemerality of the woman's collection'[43] without specifically recognising the place of the Cranford sketches within one of these very magazines. Thomas Recchio regards this as a 'rich' but not consistent context, seeing the narrative of *Cranford* in opposition to the 'journalistic world of *Household Words*' and harmonizing rather with complementary threads of subject matter such as the orient and domestic economy.[44]

It is clear, however, that fact and fiction complemented one other within the patterning of instalments and their surrounding subject matter. *Cranford* the serial was perceived in an intertextual relationship which also reflected the register and tone of the periodical. This created a pattern of publication across the numbers of the magazine which situates Gaskell's work within the context of periodical writing rather than novel writing.

Framley Parsonage in *Cornhill Magazine*

In his *Autobiography*, Anthony Trollope famously described serialization as a 'rushing mode of publication' adding that it was 'injurious to the work done'.[45] Although he claimed that he did not favour the 'hurried publication of incompleted work',[46] he was nonetheless driven to accept the invitation to contribute to *Cornhill Magazine* in 1859. George Smith initially turned down Trollope's offer of 'Tales of All Countries' and the Irish novel *Castle Richmond*, requesting instead 'a continuous story to extend through twenty four sheets of the Magazine, which would be equivalent to the bulk of an ordinary three volume novel'.[47] *Castle Richmond* was under contract to Chapman and Hall and was published by them in 1860. The individual *Tales of All Countries* appeared variously in *Cassell's Illustrated Family Paper*, *London Review*, *Public Opinion* and the *Illustrated London News* in late 1860 and 1861, and were published in two volumes also by Chapman and Hall in 1861 and 1863. The 'continuous story' supplied by Trollope for *Cornhill Magazine* was *Framley Parsonage*, the first number appearing only two months after the author's initial response to Smith.

This circumstance makes the success of the *Cornhill* on its first appearance all the more extraordinary. Thackeray wrote to Trollope on 28 October 1859: 'One of our chief objects in the Magazine is the getting out of novel spinning and back into the world'.[48] In terms of serialization or 'novel spinning' within the periodical, Trollope proved the ideal bridge despite some early problems with the instalment process, as evidenced by letters between the author and his publisher. Trollope

---

[43]   Dolin, 190.

[44]   Thomas Recchio, *Elizabeth Gaskell's 'Cranford': A Publishing History* (Farnham: Ashgate 2009), 49; 50.

[45]   Trollope, *Autobiography*, 139.

[46]   Trollope, *Autobiography*, 138.

[47]   George Smith to Anthony Trollope, 26 October 1859, Trollope, *Letters*, vol. 1, 90.

[48]   Trollope, *Autobiography*, 137.

was sent a specimen page against which to measure his contributions but an early instalment took up more than its allotted space. Trollope wrote to Smith, 'I have cut out a page – but it was as that you asked for hearts blood. And the fault must have been your own in giving me too long a page as a sample – I had all the words counted, so that I might give you exactly what I had undertaken to give & no more.'[49] George Smith's role as publisher clearly impacted on Trollope's as serialist, and David Skilton in his edition of *Framley Parsonage* suggests that some of the letters and requests were part of Trollope's endeavour to show himself an alert and serious author. For Smith, Trollope insisted, 'I have prided myself on completing my work exactly within the proposed dimensions',[50] and the survival of such letters in conjunction with his carefully crafted *Autobiography* reinforce his portrayal of himself as the businesslike producer of novels. This was a role which Henry James and other contemporary reviewers would later find distasteful when the novel-writing was separated from the periodical. Smith and Thackeray, however, lighted on the very author who could produce the fiction which would match their educational and commercial objectives. This beginning of a serial novelist's career illustrates clearly the dichotomy between the craft of novel-writing promoted by reviewers and the essentially commercial publisher's imperative which fed the market for reading in the nineteenth century.

Andrew Maunder describes Trollope's novel as 'part of the discursive package presented by the *Cornhill*'.[51] Patterns within the multi-stranded periodical were created through illustration as well as through the accompanying serials, factual series and poems. This section considers how the *Cornhill* used the serial during the appearance of *Framley Parsonage*, discussing firstly the launch issue, the editorial framework and register of the periodical and then the interaction of the intertwining serials. These elements are then re-combined for the reading of the serial through its illustrations, and the section thus identifies the significance of the boundaries and thresholds of the novel on its first appearance.

Trollope's serial provided the very opening words of *Cornhill Magazine* at the end of December 1859. There had been coverage elsewhere of the chosen editor and title of the periodical but to *Framley Parsonage* was given the responsibility of launching one of the landmark publications of the nineteenth century. The first instalment was not supported by an illustration and Trollope was bold enough to survey his chosen profession from a distance for his opening exposition of Mark Robarts: 'the first page or two of this narrative must be consumed in giving a catalogue of the good things which chance and conduct together had heaped upon this young man's head'.[52] This was in fact an apt description not just of the opening of the novel but of the opening of the periodical, and throughout the first number, there were other 'catalogues' indicating the 'good things' which the magazine

---

[49]   Anthony Trollope to George Smith, 25 November 1859, Trollope, *Letters*, vol. 1, 92.
[50]   Trollope, *Autobiography*, 119.
[51]   Maunder, '"Monitoring the Middle-Classes,"' 45.
[52]   *CM* 1 (1860): 1.

aimed to offer. Catherine Clive, simply designated 'V', effectively paralleled the new periodical with the new year when she wrote: 'Its leaves the turning hand await;/ Those fresh unopen'd leaves comprise/ Th'unread, but written words of Fate'.[53] For Trollope, those words were not only unread but unwritten too.

The first part of Trollope's serial was given pride of place but the editor was clearly a dominant force in setting up the magazine's rationale and register. Most significant, perhaps, was the presentation of the knowing type of novel-writing which would create the 'social table' and 'man of the world' tone for which editor and publisher were striving. This was re-emphasized by the accompanying material both from Thackeray himself and from other contributors. Thackeray's *Lovel the Widower* appeared in tandem with *Framley Parsonage* for the first six months of Trollope's serialization although *Lovel*'s instalments were about half the length of the main serial. Thackeray's novella was also illustrated from the start whereas the first *Framley Parsonage* illustration did not appear until the fourth instalment in April. As *Framley Parsonage* did, *Lovel* also took a meta-fictional stance at its commencement and Thackeray actually opened with the parallel rhetorical question: 'Who shall be the hero of this tale' adorned with a vignette capital 'W'.[54] Like Trollope, Thackeray reflected the artificiality of his narrative and of the serial itself when he listed some 'little mysteries' and then promptly solved them, claiming 'were I not above any such artifice, I might easily leave the reader to ponder for a month'.[55] The two serials thus complemented each other from the outset, and a diversion '[b]efore entering on the present narrative' was provided by the satirical treatment of the profession of editor. The narrator of *Lovel*, Mr Batchelor observed: 'I daresay I gave myself airs as editor ... and proposed to educate the public taste, to diffuse morality and sound literature throughout the nation, and to pocket a liberal salary in return for my services'.[56] These comments might seem innocuous and out of place in the pages of a novel but they were both daring and very much contextualized by their place in the first number of the newly launched periodical. In effect, the character of Thackeray was embedded in a Thackeray novel within a Thackeray periodical. To conclude that first number, Thackeray then spoke in his own character as editor using his first 'Roundabout Paper' to embed the fiction within the magazine.

This 'Paper' offered a further context for the serialization of Trollope's novel with Thackeray as editor explaining the role of fiction 'as that of providing 'jellies': 'Figs are sweet, but fictions are sweeter'.[57] He continued on the same theme reflecting in public the prospectus and private letters which preceded the launch of the magazine: 'Novels are sweets. All people with healthy literary appetites

---

53   'The First Morning of 1860,' *CM* 1 (1860): 123, ll. 38–40.
54   *CM* 1, 44.
55   *CM* 1, 58.
56   *CM* 1, 56.
57   *CM* 1,128; 126.

love them – almost all women;– a vast number of clever, hard-headed men.'[58] The 'Paper' explained that the *Cornhill* would supply that combination of 'wholesome roast and boiled' fact with the added reward of fiction which was so often the rationale of the nineteenth-century periodical. Thackeray offered the credentials of the authors he had elsewhere described as 'Co-operators' but without naming them. His 'fellow-travellers'– both readers and authors – were part of that coterie around the table. He continued the voyaging analogy at the same time as that of the mealtime with its jellies by describing the serials as 'two novels under two flags, the one that ancient ensign which has hung before the well-known booth of *Vanity Fair*; the other that fresh and handsome standard which has lately been hoisted on *Barchester Towers*.'[59] Trollope's reintroduction of the characters of his previous three Barchester novels was being endorsed. More broadly, the position of *Framley Parsonage* was clearly stated as 'fresh', both a part of and separate from the magazine in which it was being serialized.

After the first instalment, *Framley Parsonage* appeared in the first station of the *Cornhill* on only three other occasions. It alternated places with *Lovel the Widower* for the first six months as shown in Appendix 5. It appeared twice in second station in successive months in November and December 1860 when there was no other fiction to act as balance for the number. The serial instalment was thus always positioned as part of a considered whole consistent with the original concept of equality of contribution. In April 1861, Thackeray's *Philip* was brought into first station in order to carry the reader forward into the next volume ready for life after *Framley Parsonage*, and the narrator of *Philip* announced that he was 'a novelist who knows everything about his people.[60] *Philip* and the other articles would then continue to appear post-*Framley Parsonage* in order to structure the third volume of the *Cornhill* which concluded in June 1861. At the textual interface, Richard Doyle's 'Bird's Eye View of Society' including a lavishly illustrated fold-out section immediately following the last instalment of Trollope's serial.[61] This series of detailed crowd scenes then continued into volumes 4 and 5 of the *Cornhill* but that first 'Bird's Eye' illustration 'At Home' supplemented the ending of *Framley Parsonage* in April when the fictional couples were united during the fictional months of July, August, September and October. The apparent future then became the present where 'old Lady Lufton still reigns paramount in the parish' and dictates the choice of nursery at Framley Court.[62] Given the ongoing response of readers to the novel over sixteen months, Trollope was able to transform this scene into a place with which readers were familiar, as if these were real people being described 'at home'. The impression created was that Barsetshire as well as

---

[58]   *CM* 1, 127.

[59]   *CM* 1, 128.

[60]   *CM* 3 (1861): 401. *Philip* had started in first station in January. It subsequently occupied the third station in February and the second in March (see Appendix 5).

[61]   *CM* 3, 497.

[62]   *CM* 3, 496.

Cornhill Magazine lived on in an unending narrative, and, in fact, the next novel in the series, *The Small House at Allington* would begin in the *Cornhill* 18 months later in September 1862.

In addition to these fictional serials, there were other factual serials which established a reading pattern and also adopted the trademark *Cornhill* response to their own structure. The pattern of the periodical volume can be illustrated by tracing the structure and content of these interwoven serials including examples of their meta-narrative commentary. In June 1860 the last of the illustrated 'Studies in Animal Life' concluded: 'With this homily, dear reader may be closed our FIRST SERIES of Studies, to be resumed hereafter, let me hope, with as much willingness on your part as desire to interest you in mine'.[63] Whilst this was clearly planned to conclude the first volume of the *Cornhill*, George Sala's instalment of 'William Hogarth' in the same number seems not to have filled its allotted space and there was a blank half page where the author intended to make a break to 'sweep the stage, and sound the whistle for the curtain to draw up on the drama of The Rake's Progress'.[64] This number then concluded with the 'Roundabout Paper' which saluted the success of the first six months of the periodical as discussed in Chapter 3. Thus *Lovel the Widower* and 'Studies in Animal Life' concluded at the end of the volume while 'William Hogarth' continued by reaching out strongly to its next instalment. *Framley Parsonage*, having opened with an illustration, closed rather more innocuously with Mark Robarts attempting once again to sell his horse. The next volume for July–December 1860 then opened with the first instalment of a new factual serial, 'The Four Georges' by Thackeray himself which appeared in lead station on three of its four appearances. James Hinton writing his 'Physiological Riddles' later published in 1862 as *Life in Nature* addressed the 'common reader' that month and described his project as 'a future task', a serial.[65] In the second of his four parts on 'Why We Grow' he exclaimed in conclusion that 'space for the present fails, and possibly the reader thinks that he has had enough'.[66] In the same number Sala used an equally meta-narrative format when he rejoiced in the seventh instalment of 'William Hogarth' that 'another chapter remains to me wherein to depict my hero in his golden prime'.[67] This was a number which clearly needed such hooks to ensnare readers during the second six months of the periodical's publication.

In September, Trollope himself drew attention to the unfolding narrative and the expectation of readerly concentration by that hooked audience, trusting that his 'readers will all remember' a development from the July instalment.[68] After a low-key ending to this instalment of the novel, 'William Hogarth' was being strung

---

[63] *CM* 1, 690.
[64] *CM* 1, 735.
[65] *CM* 2 (1860): 21; 32.
[66] *CM* 2, 174.
[67] *CM* 2, 241.
[68] *CM* 2, 296.

out for its ninth 'Tail-piece' in October. The September episode archly betrayed Sala's reluctance to conclude when he insisted that '[o]f these [other works] I must treat, even on the threshold of the scene from which I must soon depart altogether'.[69] In October Sala then drew particular attention to the length of the final essay which took only twenty pages to cover nineteen years.[70] He referred back to the 'eighth stage of these travels in search of Hogarth' the previous month, and then to the length of the serial on 'the great Englishman who had been my theme in these pages during the last nine months'.[71] As he announced, 'I rise from the labour of sixty-seven happy nights',[72] the *Cornhill* readers moved immediately into the ninth instalment of *Framley Parsonage* and, since 'The Four Georges' had also concluded earlier on in the number, it was thus the novel that had to keep up the serial responsibilities of the *Cornhill* for the rest of the volume. The 'Roundabout Paper' for the month referred to the orange-covered periodical and its readers,[73] and Trollope too moved his characters around at Miss Dunstable's party, developing his plots rather as the editor had intertwined his serials. Trollope summarized Mrs Proudie's 'adverse criticism as Lady Lufton is waiting for us in the ante-room' and then returned to Miss Dunstable: 'We must go back to our hostess, whom we should not have left for so long a time, seeing that this chapter is written to show how well she could conduct herself in great emergencies'.[74] It can thus be demonstrated that Trollope exposed the structure of his own writing within the context of a periodical which was itself a vehicle forever questioning its structure in both editorials and in the other articles and serials of the interwoven pattern surrounding *Framley Parsonage*.

It was clear too that the serialization impacted on the text itself, and there were many ways in which Trollope exploited the serial format as he was learning it. In April 1860, for example, he opened the instalment by repeating the last line of the previous month: 'And now how was he to tell his wife?' This repetition drew attention to the gap in between for the reader with Trollope adding that this 'was the consideration heavy on Mark Robarts' mind when last we left him'.[75] Trollope often addressed his readers and he gave them a place in the serial's discourse in August 1860: 'I fear that my friend Sowerby does not, at present, stand high in the estimation of those who have come thus far in this narrative.'[76] He had already suggested that 'some of my readers may have sat at vestries' as Mark Robarts does and that, although 'people think that heroes in books should be so much better than heroes got up for the world's common wear and tear', Lord Lufton may not

  [69] *CM* 2, 369.
  [70] *CM* 2, 438.
  [71] *CM* 2, 439; 461.
  [72] *CM* 2, 461.
  [73] *CM* 2, 501.
  [74] *CM* 2, 471; 479.
  [75] *CM* 1, 449.
  [76] *CM* 2, 144.

be worthy of Lucy Robarts's love.[77] In December 1860, he delayed still further a long-awaited meeting between Lucy and Lady Lufton to add a complex layer of shared understanding in an address to his audience: 'In that little room we found ourselves once before – you and I, O reader; – but Lucy had never before visited that hallowed precinct'.[78] This suggests that the control required for his serial-writing assignment had influenced and inspired the narrative structure and content.[79] In the April 1861 number, Trollope entitled his last chapter 'How they were all Married, had Two Children, and lived Happy ever after' in a final pragmatic expression of the conscious novel-writing process. He described how his 'four couple of sighing loves' were 'all made happy', and once again exposed the fiction by insisting, 'I, as leader of the chorus, disdain to press you further with doubts as to the happiness of any of that quadrille'.[80] Some of these characters would, of course, reappear and be unhappy in the two further 'chronicles of Barsetshire'.[81] For the moment, the third volume of the *Cornhill* in which *Framley Parsonage* was concluded was marked by that co-ordinated opening of Thackeray's *Philip* with which the editor planned, according to the December 1860 'Roundabout Paper', to take his 'friend's place'[82] and to complete that volume.

If the other articles and their composition and register complemented the serial but are lost to the reader of the volume, there is a further strand to be explored in a 'bimodal' reading of the novel through the interaction of its illustrations with other illustrations across issues of the periodical. *Lovel the Widower* was illustrated each month by Thackeray and also included embedded figures and illustrated capitals such as the amusing black sheep for Chapter 4 (see Figure 5.1). It was not until the fourth instalment comprising Chapters 10 to 12 of *Framley Parsonage*, however, that Millais's first illustration for Trollope's serial appeared, prefacing the written text although the two characters illustrated will not meet for another nine periodical pages. The additional weight given to their meeting by the illustration with its proleptic message was further complicated by the fact that the meeting actually took place in a chapter entitled 'Griselda Grantly' which opened: 'It was nearly a month after this that Lucy was first introduced to Lord Lufton, and then it was brought about only by accident'.[83] In the illustration, Lord Lufton and Lucy Robarts appeared to be holding or at least shaking hands against a symbolic backdrop (see Figure 5.2). The figures were framed by a stone doorway with a

---

[77]   *CM* 2, 45; 54.

[78]   *CM* 2, 660.

[79]   This is discussed in Mary Hamer, *Writing by Numbers: Trollope's Serial Fiction* (Cambridge: Cambridge University Press, 1987), x; 67–8.

[80]   *CM* 3, 488.

[81]   *CM* 3, 62. The Grantlys, for instance, reappear in *The Small House at Allington* (serialized in the *Cornhill* 1862–64) and *The Last Chronicle of Barset* (published in parts 1866–67).

[82]   *CM* 2, 760.

[83]   *CM* 1, 457.

THE

CORNHILL MAGAZINE.

APRIL, 1860.

Lovel the Widower.

CHAPTER IV.

A BLACK SHEEP.

THE being for whom my friend Dick Bedford seemed to have a special contempt and aversion, was Mr. Bulkeley, the tall footman in attendance upon Lovel's dear mother-in-law. One of the causes of Bedford's wrath, the worthy fellow explained to me. In the servants' hall, Bulkeley was in the habit of speaking in disrespectful and satirical terms of his mistress, enlarging upon her many foibles, and describing her pecuniary difficulties to the many *habitués* of that second social circle at Shrublands. The hold which Mr. Bulkeley had over his lady lay in a long unsettled account of

Fig. 5.1   'A Black Sheep,' Illustration opening Chapter 4 of *Lovel the Widower*, *Cornhill Magazine* 1 (1860): 385.

LORD LUFTON AND LUCY ROBARTS.

Fig. 5.2   J.E. Millais, 'Lord Lufton and Lucy Robarts,' *CM* 1 (1860): facing
              page 449.

dovecote above Lucy's head. Lord Lufton's kill from his hunting trip was draped over his shoulder and hanging head first down his back. The other participants in the scene, Fanny Robarts and the lord's gamekeeper are notably absent from the illustration. For the serial reader, the threat of capture and confinement was already introduced through the placement of the illustration separated from the text. Despite the fact that this separation was for technical reasons of production and to provide better-quality paper, the original reader would have seen this illustration in its original place a whole chapter before their first encounter.

The illustration also followed on immediately from a poem called 'Strangers Yet' by R[ichard] Monckton Milnes in which it was suggested that there are divisions between spouses, old friends, parents and children which can be resolved only in heaven.[84] At the interface with the content of this poem, the meeting of the young people in the serial was threatened both by the poem's subject matter and by Lady Lufton's plans to unite her son with the aforementioned Griselda. In addition, another Millais illustration of two figures, mother and daughter, had already appeared two months before in February 1860 opposite and embedded in another Milnes poem entitled 'Unspoken Dialogue' (see Figure 5.3). The two women, like the prospective lovers, were holding hands as they passed each other on a significant physical and psychological threshold. There were birds flying free in the sky which acted as a backdrop to the scene as in the *Framley Parsonage* illustration. In the poem, the mother has renounced her claims to a man whom her daughter loved but the pose adopted by the two women was mirrored by that of Lucy and Lord Lufton two months later.

A third illustration of figures in this arrangement appeared in March 1861 showing the Robarts facing the crisis of the bailiffs in the penultimate instalment of the novel. This instalment opened by drawing attention to the actual experience of the reader, explaining how 'a month went by at Framley without any increase of comfort to our friends there'.[85]

The position of the illustration adjacent to this statement intensified the anticipation of a further reduction in comfort since Fanny Robarts's announcement of the arrival of the bailiffs ten pages later was used as the title: '"Mark," she said "The men are here"' (see Figure 5.4).[86] In this case, the forbidding doorway was replaced by the family fireplace, under threat as a result of Mark Robarts's financial and social naivety. This illustration was dramatic in its place but not, however, indicative of the final outcome since Lord Lufton would step in before the end of the instalment to satisfy Mark's creditors, so making the bailiff's visit a largely non-sensational event. The echo of the pose of Lucy and Lord Lufton reminded the reader, however, of the other long-running plot situation of their thwarted engagement which was also resolved in the same instalment. Barbara Schmidt suggests that within *Cornhill Magazine* 'the articles and poems interrogated the

---

84 *CM* 1, 448.
85 *CM* 3, 342.
86 *CM* 3, 352.

" Dear child! he comes.—Nay, blush not so
To have your secret known ; "

Fig. 5.3   J.E. Millais, Illustration for R. Monckton Milnes, 'Unspoken
               Dialogue,' *CM* 1 (1860): facing page 194.

" Mark," she said, "the men are here."

Fig. 5.4   J.E. Millais, "'Mark,' she said, 'the men are here,'" *CM* 3 (1861): facing page 342.

fiction',[87] and this concept should be extended also to the illustrations. The proleptic effect of the illustrations in the periodical added greater tension if not an ironic effect to the penultimate instalment as well as recapitulating the linked plotlines across the serial stretching over a year from April 1860 to March 1861. The echoes across the illustrations within the serial also encouraged the recognition of echoes from the accompanying poems.

A similar pattern was also apparent in the style of illustrations shared with a factual serial. This can be traced in the impact of Millais's June 1860 illustration which was the next to appear in *Framley Parsonage* after 'Lord Lufton and Lucy Robarts' of April. 'Was It Not a Lie' was the subject of a disagreement between Trollope and Millais who drew his cryptic title from the end of a chapter unpromisingly entitled 'Mrs Podgens' Baby'. The quoted line occurred some ten pages after the illustration which showed Lucy draped across her bed in despair, wearing a large crinoline (see Figure 5.5). The shape and opulence of Lucy's dress caused a heated exchange with Smith although Trollope was reconciled to the illustration later after seeing a dress with a similar pattern.[88] In context, 'Was It Not a Lie' made visual reference to the illustrations for the factual serial 'Studies in Animal Life' creating, in effect, a parallel study in human life. 'Studies in Animal Life' was densely illustrated for its first three instalments from January to March 1860 although there were no illustrations in April and May. The illustrations of the parasitic worm *cercaria* in January were fluent and detailed, like Lucy's dress, despite being labelled 'embryo' and 'excretory organ'.[89] One of the March illustrations depicted a male triton or water-newt which created a similar shape to that of the draped dress (see Figure 5.6). The single illustration for 'Studies in Animal Life' in June 1860 was of a *campanularia* polyp magnified to show its graceful, co-dependent parts (see Figure 5.7), and the elegant shape matched the designedly elegant figure of Lucy which was itself magnified to represent the serial instalment as a whole. The later 'Bird's Eye View of Society' carried on this theme of densely illustrated studies in human life, iterating these recurring patterns across the illustrations which were being developed and encouraged in the early volumes of the periodical.

In addition, there was another visual reference to Lucy's dress in a *Cornhill* illustration from May 1860, a month earlier. Emily Brontë's 'The Outcast Mother' had been followed in this number by an illustration for George Macdonald's *The Portent* which showed a fleeing woman who was effectively positioned to double as a character in both Brontë's poem and in this new serial. The illustration was by Frederick Sandys and used the same angle of dress across the page as Millais's in June (see Figure 5.8). The background to this illustration was not a cheval glass

[87] Barbara Q. Schmidt, 'The *Cornhill Magazine*: Celebrating Success,' *Victorian Periodicals Review* 32 (1999): 204.

[88] Anthony Trollope to George Smith, 27 May 1860, Trollope, *Letters*, vol. 1, 104; Anthony Trollope to George Smith, 21 July 1860, 111.

[89] *CM* 1, 71.

"WAS IT NOT A LIE?"

Fig. 5.5   J.E. Millais, 'Was it not a lie?' *CM* 1 (1860): facing page 691.

A glance at the contents of our glass vases will yield us samples of each of these five divisions of the animal kingdom. We begin with this Triton. It is a representative of the VERTEBRATE division, or sub-kingdom.

Fig. 17.

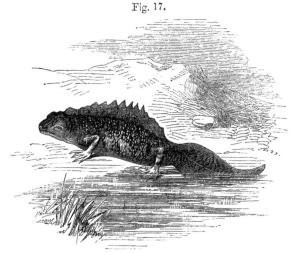

MALE TRITON, or WATER-NEWT.

You have merely to remember that it possesses a backbone and an internal skeleton, and you will at once recognize the cardinal character which makes this Triton range under the same general head as men, elephants, whales, birds, reptiles, or fishes. All these, in spite of their manifold differences, have this one character in common:—they are all backboned; they have all an internal skeleton; they are all formed according to one general type. In all vertebrate animals the skeleton is found to be identical in plan. Every bone in the body of a triton has its

Fig. 5.6   'Water-newt,' *Studies in Animal Life, CM* 1 (1860): 291.

as it was in Millais's but rather a violent scene of two brothers in the distance fighting over the woman in the foreground. Unlike the demure and contained Lucy, Sandys's woman reacted to the fight by reaching out dramatically from the page towards the reader and this reflected her tragic end, her neck broken when she was abducted by the dominant younger brother in the legend. The ghostly hoof-beats of the abductor's horse were the eponymous 'portent' of the story, and this visual cross reference is another echo of the plot of *Framley Parsonage* and perhaps of the silent screams of the novel's female characters.

If the reader of the *Cornhill* was encouraged to share in the register of the periodical from month to month, this reading of the illustrations seems to offer a similar system of knowing visual echoes and cross-referencing. It is clear that the deployment of the illustrations reinforced the seriality of the novel within the periodical, using the subject matter to visualize plotlines long under discussion

CAMPANULARIA (Magnified,
and Natural Size).

Fig. 5.7   '*Campanularia* polyp,' *Studies in Animal Life, CM* 1 (1860): 683.

such as the deferred engagement and averted bankruptcy discussed above. This also continued as a means of reinforcing the Barsetshire Chronicles as a series. The illustration of Lady Lufton and the Duke of Omnium in October 1860 prefigured by a few pages the meeting between the two characters which was much elaborated in the text.[90] It had been flagged up as an unlikely event since the first instalment of the serial when the reader was told that 'the great Whig autocrat' who featured in the earlier novels was regarded by Lady Lufton 'as the impersonation of Lucifer upon earth'.[91] Trollope drew Millais's attention to previous descriptions of his principals especially Miss Dunstable, and later proposed himself that the meeting of Lady Lufton and the Duke of Omnium should be the subject of the October 1860 illustration. The scene was itself illustrative of the whole instalment in which Miss Dunstable engineered a meeting between these two representatives of the

---

[90]   *CM* 2, opposite page 462; the meeting takes place on page 473. David Skilton discusses Millais's sources in 'The Centrality of Literary Illustration in Visual Culture: The Example of Millais and Trollope from 1860 to 1864,' *Journal of Illustration Studies* (2007), http://www.jois.cf.ac.uk/articles.php?article=30.

[91]   *CM* 1, 11.

LEGEND OF THE PORTENT.

Fig. 5.8   Frederick Sandys, 'Legend of the Portent,' *CM* 1 (1860): opposite page 617.

nobility and then recognised her weariness of society.[92] As with the echoes from the poetry illustrations, this illustration was also provided with a counterbalance in the introductory picture of 'The Crawley Family' of August 1860. Trollope announced 'it will be proper that the historian should drop a veil over their sufferings'[93] but the alternative lifestyle of the Crawleys helped to put Lucy's struggles into perspective pictorially as well as in the text despite the fact that magazine readers might prefer to be entertained by illustrations of higher society whatever the subject matter of the serial. In January 1861, the illustration for the serialized *Framley Parsonage* depicted Mrs Gresham and Miss Dunstable, recurring figures from Trollope's earlier un-illustrated fiction.[94] These appeared to readers as visual representations or recapitulations of existing characters, previously unrealised in illustrated form. The Crawleys were new characters who were immediately illustrated and would be carried forward into the Barsetshire series but, despite Trollope's advice to Millais to read *Dr Thorne* for a description,[95] Miss Dunstable was shown with her back to the reader who, like the artist, was also referred back to those 'county chronicles of Barsetshire'.

At one further level of meta-narrative, the texts of the serials also created a fluid pattern of cross-reference amounting to a dialogue. In the same number of the *Cornhill* as the illustration of Mrs Gresham and Miss Dunstable, the actions of recapitulation and of the intertwined serial and periodical re-crossed the factual boundary within the magazine. This demonstrates in microcosm how seeing the serial in context was a significant part of the reader's original experience of the novel. James Reddie's article 'Falling in Love' immediately preceded the twelfth instalment of *Framley Parsonage* beginning with Chapter 37. It is notable that Lucy Robarts and Lord Lufton did not feature in the instalment but they were kept in mind because Reddie used them as a 'true illustration'[96] and differentiated between their experiences of falling in love using very much the tone employed by Trollope's narrator. Reddie referred to their first meeting nine months before in serial time and to the 'lie' illustrated in June. These lovers could appear in the context of the serial while the fictional plot was recalling 'the early pages of this little narrative' and moving forward for Dr Thorne's proposal to Miss Dunstable, leading them all to become 'sighing lovers' in the final chapter three months later.[97] The later reader of the completed novel would not have such a reminder of the other plot strand to support the reading of these three chapters when they were reprinted in the volume edition.[98]

---

[92] In the text for October, she told Dr Thorne 'the game is not worth the candle' (*CM* 2, 482).

[93] *CM* 2, 144; the illustration was opposite page 129.

[94] CM 3, opposite page 48.

[95] Anthony Trollope to George Smith, 21 July 1860, Trollope, *Letters*, vol. 1, 111.

[96] *CM* 3, 43.

[97] *CM* 3, 52; 488.

[98] Chapters 37 to 39.

An unsigned notice in the *Westminster Review* called *Framley Parsonage* 'rather a series of anecdotes than a well-knit tale' and complained about the novel's 'great poverty of invention' with 'no evolution'. Against the grain of the serial – whose popularity was grudgingly acknowledged – the reviewer found only that 'the story progresses by constant aggregation of details'.[99] This aggregation using the intertwining of fact, poetry and illustrations with the serialized fiction was nonetheless the means by which the serial came to occupy a place in the lives of its readers. In his *Autobiography* Trollope described the novel as a 'hodge podge' and 'a morsel of the biography of an English clergyman'.[100] Many readers of the serial begged to differ and in particular because of the context of their reading experience over sixteen months. The *Saturday Review* described the novel as 'an inmate of the drawing room – it has travelled with us in the train … We feel as if we had met Lady Lufton at a country house.' The reviewer went on to complain, 'How is it possible, after so much friendly intercourse, to turn round upon the book and its leading characters, and to dissect and analyse them as a critic should?'[101] For such critics the seepage of the novel was a puzzling mark of its alternative value as reading in an open-ended context. Elizabeth Gaskell wrote to Frederic Chapman, 'How excellent & good & clever 'Framley Parsonage' is, – I never read anything in the way of fiction so true and deep!' She had already written to Smith about her wish that the serial should go on forever: 'every one I know is always dreading the last number'.[102]

Henry James regarded Trollope's methods as 'deliberately inartistic' and he complained after the novelist's death that Trollope 'took a suicidal satisfaction in reminding the reader that the story he was telling was only, after all, a make-believe'.[103] The reader of *Framley Parsonage* in *Cornhill Magazine* was encouraged to share in the verbal register of the periodical from month to month, and also to read the illustrations within a similar system of visual echoes and cross-referencing. This was a relationship forged through aggregation, recapitulation and familiarity where evolution and placement within the periodical affected the structure and interpretation of the novel. As *Framley Parsonage* concluded in April 1861, Richard Doyle requested in his 'Bird's Eye Views of Society' that 'my little fly-leaf may be preserved in the otherwise amber periodical in which it now appears'.[104] With a nod to the scientific articles in the periodical, he suggested both the fixed, decorative display which is the *Cornhill* and the means by which it was

---

[99] *Westminster Review* 76 (1861), 282–4; repr., *Trollope: The Critical Heritage*, ed. Donald Smalley (London: Routledge and Kegan Paul, 1969), 131; 134.

[100] Trollope, *Autobiography*, 142.

[101] *Saturday Review*, 4 May 1861: 451–2: repr., Smalley, ed., 121.

[102] Elizabeth Gaskell to Frederic Chapman, 22 August 1860, Gaskell, *Further Letters*, 214; Elizabeth Gaskell to George Smith, 1 March 1860, Gaskell, *Letters*, 602.

[103] Henry James, *Century Magazine* n.s. 4 (July 1883); repr., *The Barsetshire Novels*, ed. Tony Bareham (London: Macmillan, 1983), 65.

[104] *CM* 3, 497.

created, organically. Trollope, the evolving serial writer was at home in the context of a periodical which was constantly discussing its formation and patterns. The editorials and the other articles and serials reinforced the 'novel-spinning' pattern created by *Framley Parsonage*, and these complementary discourses contributed to the resonance of a novel which was both shaping and shaped by its magazine context.

Mistress and Maid in *Good Words*

Elizabeth Gaskell's reactions to *Framley Parsonage* demonstrate the influence of the serial amongst the reading public of the time. Dinah Craik's first serialized novel two years later was framed by the very different context of *Good Words* but shared some themes such as the observance of the Sabbath and the referencing of the South Seas. In February 1860, in the second instalment of *Framley Parsonage*, MP Harold Smith lectured the Barchester Mechanics' Institute on the subject of Borneo and the 'South Sea islands', and in *Mistress and Maid* Craik used references to such islands to develop the idea of missionary work at home. The maid Elizabeth was likened to 'a South Sea islander' and London servant-life was later described as 'a world essentially its own and a life of which the upper classes are as ignorant as they are of what goes on in Madagascar or Tahiti'.[105] In the October 1862 instalment, Elizabeth corrected her printer fiancé Tom about their place in the world 'with a strange gentleness, that no one could have believed would ever have come into the manner of South Sea Islanders'.[106] In *Framley Parsonage*, Mrs Proudie observed that 'these islanders can never prosper anything unless they keep the Sabbath holy'[107] and, in the second instalment of *Mistress and Maid* the novel, Elizabeth's education was improved on the Sabbath by her mistress Hilary who described these lessons as a 'Polynesian Academy'.[108] At the very least, the serials were referencing a subject of interest shared within periodicals of the early 1860s. Perhaps more significantly, *Mistress and Maid* also shared with *Framley Parsonage* the same illustrator in John Everett Millais.

The following section demonstrates how *Mistress and Maid* appeared as a serial embedded in the religious content of *Good Words*. The accompanying commentary for the serial was generated by religious, topical and educational articles together with Craik's own *A Woman's Thoughts About Women*. This section describes the use of complementary articles and then traces the impact of illustration on reading the novel. The tight control of subject matter within the bounds of Strahan's mission as a publisher was itself a type of serialization and

---

105 *GW* 3 (1862): 37; 615.

106 *GW* 3, 617.

107 *CM* 1, 174.

108 *GW* 3, 105.

the reading of complementary material offered up a pattern supplied by the named contributors writing within a defined space bounded by Macleod's editorship.

In 1862, it was Craik's authorship which provided a pattern to rival Macleod's as editor and the periodical framework proved mutually beneficial. *Good Words* flaunted its association with actual clerical figures rather than Trollope's fictional ones, not just Macleod himself but also Archbishop Whately, Andrew Kennedy Hutchison Boyd and William Fleming Stevenson. At the end of the first instalment of *Mistress and Maid*, the household read together from the New Testament to represent their affinity with readers of *Good Words*. This two-way influence was demonstrated by the Leaf family's reading their evening bible extract within the text followed in sequence by the suggested scripture reading promoted by *Good Words*. *Good Words* had been providing such structured reading for two years but at the same time the reading scenario was a device which positioned the family –'real ladies' as Elizabeth calls them – as readers of this type of periodical and therefore fit subjects for the unfolding serial.[109]

The religious discourse and register was prominent if not pre-eminent, and in 1862 every issue of *Good Words* concluded with 'At Home in the Scriptures', a series of family readings for the Sunday evenings of that year. Stevenson's 'On the Biography of Certain Hymns' also echoed the role of the periodical in the lives of its readers since, he explained, 'every true hymn … is writing its own life and yours as you sing it'.[110] Despite the developing pattern of educational pieces, when Macleod's article on the Netherlands was promoted to editorial it was immediately followed by the hymn 'How Wondrous are thy Works, O God!'[111] A Dissenting School was described as 'a link betwixt the angels in heaven and the souls of many little children on earth'[112] and in October the two-part 'Trial Sermon' began, concerning the temptations of plagiarism.

Against this and despite her reputation in the *Saturday Review*, Craik did set herself apart as an educator rather than a preacher, insisting for her servant audience 'I am not making Elizabeth a text for a sermon'[113] but there was nonetheless regular reference to prayers and to the will of God within the serial as well. When Hilary proposed teaching Elizabeth to write during two spare hours each Sunday, Craik scrupulously exonerated Macleod from the accusations of his Evangelical peers including Mrs Proudie. Craik insisted in a footnote to the text: 'The author of this tale wishes distinctly to state, that she alone must be held responsible for the opinions it expresses'. She also added, however, 'To any earnest, honest Christians who differ from her, she need only say, that to write otherwise than as one religiously and conscientiously believes, is simply impossible.'[114] Despite

---

[109] *GW* 3, 38.

[110] *GW* 3, 645.

[111] *GW* 3, 521–2.

[112] *GW* 3, 224.

[113] *GW* 3, 163.

[114] *GW* 3, 105.

thus setting itself apart, the serial was re-immersed in the background religious discourse the following month when the editor immediately opened the April issue by writing, in parallel with Craik's footnote, about Sundays. In his article, Macleod called for the expansion of the fixed idea of a Sunday which he believed should address the good of the whole man, his physical, social, intellectual and spiritual needs.[115] This was clearly part of the ongoing promotion of the content of *Good Words* itself and by association the serial too as 'Sunday reading for all the week'.

Mistress and Maid was set against a range of reading material designed not only to promote Macleod's principles of secular and Christian education but also to be topical and interactive. Other patterns arose, for example, from a colliery disaster, the American Civil War, the International Exhibition and child mortality. During a year of crisis in the American Civil War, MacLeod tackled 'A Year of the Slavery Question' and his October editorial was entitled 'War and its Gains'.[116] In March 1862, an article entitled 'Causes and Remedies of Colliery Calamities' was a response to the Hartley mine disaster of 16 January 1862 when 204 workers were entombed by an accident. In April 'Colliers in their Homes and at their Work' appeared as well as a poem called 'Pictures in the Fire' which described miners 'buried alive, fast bound/ In the cold arms of eternity'.[117] In August Macleod even experimented with the more knowing style of the *Cornhill* in his 'Rambling Notes on a Ramble to North Italy'. He announced on the penultimate page that 'The Editor commands the writer to stop' and then continued to mention anyway what might otherwise have been omitted though the 'paltry jealousy and tyranny of the Editor', that is himself.[118] This reflection on the structure of periodical writing appeared also in the serial that month when Craik eschewed sensation by hinting that Hilary would one day marry Robert Lyon and tell him 'the minute history of this painful day'.[119] Robert's return from India, still two months away in serial time, was in turn contextualized and anticipated by the article on Baird Smith in September[120] although Robert's Scottish connection was touched on lightly at a time when Strahan was endeavouring to move his business to London. 'AKHB', for instance, discussed Lands End in November: 'In Devonshire you have Scotch irregularity of outline in the landscape; but there is English luxuriance in the hedges'.[121] The impact of the serial within these variously complementary articles can be exemplified within that April number of *Good Words* between Macleod's

---

[115]   *GW* 3, 193–7.

[116]   J.M. Ludlow, 'A Year of the Slavery Question in the US (1859–60),' *GW* 3 (1862): 177–84; 'War and its Gains': 577–81.

[117]   J.R. Leifchild, 'Causes and Remedies of Colliery Calamities,' *GW* 3 (1862): 137–43; 'Colliers at their Homes and at their Work,' 213–20; Gerald Massey, 'Pictures in the Fire,' 199–200.

[118]   *GW* 3, 453; 454.

[119]   *GW* 3, 484.

[120]   'Colonel Richard Baird Smith CB,' *GW* 3 (1862): 559–63.

[121]   'At the Lands End,' *GW* 3 (1862): 693.

'Sundays' editorial and papers by Archbishop Whately at one end of the issue and the scripture readings at the other. The pages were becoming more varied with the poem and article about the colliery disaster accompanying the Dissenting School article. Following on from *Mistress and Maid* in this number there were articles on Jamaica and on time measurement and also the 'King Sigurd' poem. Queen Victoria's accession was named as being exactly 24 years before and the Leaf sisters' 'whirling through indefinite England in a way that compounded all their geography and topography'[122] enacted the article on 'time'. With the sisters themselves adjusting their boundaries by travelling to London, the number was simultaneously stretching and testing the boundaries of the religious periodical for 'all the week'.

The intertextual relationship between Craik's work and that of other women authors publishing in *Good Words* has been discussed in Chapter 2. Craik's *John Halifax, Gentleman* was invoked every week during the serialization because of her naming through prior authorship, and a range of intertextual associations with her earlier novel can also be traced in the periodical. The two-part eighteenth-century tale 'A Cast in the Waggon by the author of "Papers for Thoughtful Girls"' envisaged a John Halifax character, 'manly and serene in his failure'.[123] In *Mistress and Maid* in August, Ascott was described as a 'fatal sham' as head of the family but he told his 'half aunt, half sister' Hilary 'What a nice young man you would make', on the model of John Halifax.[124] It was as a result of the success of 'the Author of *John Halifax, Gentleman*' that Craik was also able to mobilize her celebrity to publish her particular views on women's rights and these were reflected from the pages of *Chamber's Edinburgh Journal* and *A Woman's Thoughts About Women* onto the pages of *Good Words*. In May, this was made explicit when she commented of her characters, 'In those days women's work and women's rights had not been discussed so freely as at present'.[125] Craik also used the serial to continue and expand her mission to champion the causes of single women. Miss Balquidder was described in June as one of the 'women going solitary down the hill of life', and in October, Elizabeth, observing Johanna, decided that 'it can't be such a dreadful thing to be an old maid after all'.[126] Craik's persona and its associated texts were thus highlighted across the periodical. In the same October issue, woman's mission as an old maid was discussed by 'the Author of *Memoirs of an Unknown Life*', and this was also the issue in which the Editor moved his 'Three Present-Day Tracts' to the inside pages leaving the Exhibition and Craik's authorship to take their topical lead for that month.

---

[122] *GW* 3, 231.
[123] *GW* 3, 212.
[124] *GW* 3, 485.
[125] *GW* 3, 292.
[126] *GW* 3, 358; 611.

In the serial, Craik explained that 'in most women–the heart is the key to the intellect'.[127] Her views were not, of course, revolutionary and they were largely based on making the best of an existing lot in life. She used dressmaking to illustrate the maxim that 'the whole of life [is] made up of infinitesimally small things' making up the mosaic which represents the full pattern of 'Eternal wisdom'.[128] As she did in her *Women's Thoughts* Craik brought herself into the novel as 'the author of this simple story' who was not herself below stairs and was writing about one domestic in that 'small but steadfast circle'.[129] In the second instalment where she referred to 'pre-Elizabethan days' before the arrival of the maid, Craik emphasized as in *Women's Thoughts* that it was a matter of kindness in Hilary to maintain the difference between herself and her servant.[130] In the third instalment of the serial Craik compared men with women in her *Women's Thoughts* voice, observing 'We can "stand alone" much better than they can' and enjoy more 'real self-sustaining independence than they'. She concluded, however, 'a woman is but a woman, be she maidservant or queen'.[131] What was most significant for the reader of the serial was the interaction of these views with the surrounding religious and educational material. Craik sought the corroboration of the Macleod/Strahan framework which would allow her ideas to percolate into the household of readers. The volume edition could not make use of this further context despite its attribution through prior authorship.

The material conditions of the original serial were influenced not only by the surrounding text but by the intertextual relationship amongst the illustrations within the issues of the periodical. The volume edition of 1863 was un-illustrated although the February 1862 *Good Words* illustration of Hilary and Elizabeth was reproduced as a frontispiece to the first volume of the novel. In *Good Words* each instalment of *Mistress and Maid* was stationed halfway through a number of the periodical, between the editorial at one end and the scripture commentary at the other. The second instalment in February was four pages earlier than halfway but the others all appeared 32 pages into the number. Nine of the instalments consisted of eight or nine pages covering two chapters with April comprising three chapters but at the usual length overall. The remaining instalments for August, October and December comprised three chapters and were about half as long again, and there were occasional discrepancies in chapter division during these three months probably caused by additional material. Each instalment apart from the last was illustrated, with the illustration being positioned in the middle of the first page of text irrespective of the relationship between text and illustration.[132]

The periodical contained roughly five illustrations per number in addition to the illustrations for the serial, about 80 altogether in 1862. In addition to Millais

---

[127] *GW* 3, 104.

[128] *GW* 3, 100.

[129] *GW* 3, 615; 161.

[130] *GW* 3, 102; 106.

[131] *GW* 3, 162; 166.

[132] The illustrations all appear in *DMVI* albeit divorced from the text of *Good Words*. The page layout is shown at Figure 5.9.

and the named artists on the title page of the volume of *Good Words* for 1862, illustrations were supplied by J.D. (John Dawson) Watson, W.P. (William Paton) Burton, Samuel Solomon, John Whistler and A.B. (Arthur Boyd) Houghton. The profusion of illustration was more in the style of the penny journal but, of course, Strahan was intent on using the periodical as an educational tool and so provided pictures also for the scientific pieces such as 'Above the Clouds' in January, 'The Eye' in March and 'Glaciers' in June and July.[133] Twenty two of the twenty seven poems were also illustrated in 1862 and the style complemented that of the illustrations for the serial which were predominantly of the women in the novel with the notable exceptions of Robert Lyon (with Hilary) in March and Ascott's arrest in July. Simon Cooke suggests that the illustrations in *Good Words* provided 'visual reinforcement of the readers' unquestioning faith'[134] but it is rather the articles which performed this function since, like many of the poems, they tended to revert to the question of heavenly reward whatever their initial subject matter. The use of illustrations indicated that the serial was valued alongside the poetry with its advice on the conduct of life and its messages from scripture.

If the illustrations for the serial helped to integrate *Mistress and Maid* into the periodical, however, they had a more uneasy relationship with their own text since they frequently anticipated the plot and revealed prematurely the outcome of Craik's rhetorical discussions. The illustration for the first instalment plainly presented the mistresses meeting the maid; the 'rather tall, awkward, and strongly-built girl of fifteen' was the subject of the first line of the novel itself[135] and the illustration thus prefaced rather than anticipated the content of the serial. For the second instalment, Hilary was depicted teaching Elizabeth to read and write, and although this anticipated the action of the second chapter of that month's material, the scene was neutral in the context of the periodical as a whole, apart, that is, from its secondary role in illustrating Craik's overt challenge to the observance of Sunday. The third instalment, however, opened 'A household exclusively composed of women has its advantages and disadvantages'[136] but pictured Hilary and Robert on a dark street with their hands clasped. This was in contrast with the '*Woman's Thoughts*' discussion of the safe, female-populated fireside which was presented in the text immediately below the illustration on the page. This illustration was of the couple's later walk in the lamplight, a scene taking place again towards the end of the second chapter for that month and with its significant statement: 'Then they loosed arms, and Hilary knew that they should never walk together again till – when and how?'[137] (see Figure 5.9). The reader of the serial

---

[133] 'Above the Clouds,' *GW* 3 (1862): 48–54; 'The Eye,' 170–76 and 'Glaciers,' 342–9; 404–10.

[134] Simon Cooke, *Illustrated Periodicals of the 1860s: Contexts and Collaborations* (London: British Library, 2010), 67.

[135] *GW* 3, 33.

[136] *GW* 3, 161.

[137] *GW* 3, 168.

MISTRESS AND MAID.

A HOUSEHOLD STORY.

BY THE AUTHOR OF "JOHN HALIFAX, GENTLEMAN."

CHAPTER V.

A HOUSEHOLD exclusively composed of women has its advantages and its disadvantages. It is apt to become somewhat narrow in judgment, morbid in feeling, absorbed in petty interests, and bounding its vision of outside things to the small horizon which it sees from its own fireside. But, on the other hand, by this fireside often abides a settled peace and purity, a long-suffering, generous forbearance, and an enduring affectionateness, which the other sex can hardly comprehend or credit. Men will not believe what is nevertheless the truth, that we

III—11

Fig. 5.9   J.E. Millais, Illustration accompanying Chapters 5–6 of *Mistress and Maid*, *GW* 3 (1862): 161.

saw the couple frozen in this attitude, their arms linked despite their being parted in the novel for many years. In the manner of the illustrated poems seeking the goal of heaven, the instalment ended: 'He alone can know, who … is educating us into the infinite goodness of His and our immortality'.[138]

In April, the picture of the Leaf sisters on a station platform pre-empted the events of the instalment since the first of the instalment's three chapters concerned the intervening three years which have passed since Robert Lyon's departure. By contrast with this temporal shift, the day when the sisters decided to leave was dated exactly as that day of Queen Victoria's coronation on 28 June 1838. This illustration therefore anticipated their decision. In May the illustration adopted the more general character of showing the women in their London lodgings although it specifically represented Elizabeth reading about servanthood from the Bible whilst the lodging-house's dirty servant presented Peter Ascott's card to her employers, with Hilary offstage and Miss Leaf making the best of their dreary home. This was less proleptic as an illustration than its predecessors. In June the instalment began 'Months slipped by' and the illustration, showing the first meeting of Hilary with Miss Balquidder at a shoe-fitting, supplemented the discussion of shaping Providence two pages further on.[139] The illustration was also more representative of the events of the instalment although the plump little woman depicted was at odds with Craik's description of the 'hard-featured' Miss Balquidder.[140] In July the introductory illustration showed Ascott already writing his address for delivery to Hilary, the sheriff's officer having tricked Elizabeth into opening the door. Despite the twin encouragement of Peter Ascott's offer of marriage and Miss Balquidder's of employment which will occur on the same day within this instalment, the reader would have already known that the bubble of debt was about to burst as symbolized in the instalment by Ascott's poking the fire and leaving no coal for the evening.[141] The plot described his acts and ruses as a 'deliberate debtor'[142] but the opening page had already betrayed that he will be caught, and the illustration was especially darkened by the long black coats of the bearded arresting officers lit from behind by Elizabeth's despairing candle.

In August, the thematic watching of the two younger women closed the episode in which they have found out that Ascott has also forged a cheque. They have already been illustrated 13 pages earlier sitting up 'till candles burnt up, and shutters were opened, and upon their great calamity stared the broad unwelcome day'.[143] In September the illustration once more showed the three sisters, this time stitching Selina's wedding dress 'sitting silently in the midst of white finery, but

---

[138] *GW* 3, 169.

[139] *GW* 3, 354.

[140] *GW* 3, 554.

[141] *GW* 3, 419.

[142] *GW* 3, 422.

[143] *GW* 3, 494.

as sadly as if it were a funeral'.[144] The opening disquisition '"Missing" – "Lost"' again competed with the pictured activity where Hilary was shown gazing off to the right, forward into the serial and towards the opening of the next chapter which began 'ASCOTT LEAF never came home'.[145] The scene represented Hilary searching for a solution to the payment of Ascott's debts while the other two Leaf sisters remained out of focus amongst the 'finery' described. It was she who was pictured as 'lost' so that the opening of the instalment supplied an absent title for the illustration. This was not an unfamiliar topic for Craik's readers and an illustration entitled 'Lost' by Holman Hunt had acted as the frontispiece to Craik's *Studies from Life* published in 1861.

The last two illustrations which appeared in the original text of the serialized novel particularly demonstrate how the serial became enmeshed in and contextualized by the subject matter of the periodical. The sisters were regrouped for the October instalment which stated immediately and starkly as a commentary on the illustrated scene, 'It was not a cheerful morning on which to be married' with fog outside and the Leafs 'breakfasting drearily by candlelight, all in their wedding attire' (see Figure 5.10). This number of *Good Words* heaped up intertextual references to the serial. The illustrated poem 'The Veiled Bride' mirrored the illustration of the wedding morning breakfast. It concerned the arrival of Rebecca as a replacement for Leah in the bible story with a transferred echo to the serial: 'Veil'd the future comes' (see Figure 5.11). This instalment of *Mistress and Maid* closed with the birth of Selina's son and was then followed immediately by a one-page article called 'A Social Riddle' which reflected on class structure through a child's question. This article was ostensibly accompanied by an unrelated half-page illustration by Arthur Boyd Houghton in which a mother on a cliff top, having contemplated suicide, appeared to have drawn back from the edge to return to her baby. Paul Hogarth suggests that illustrations by Houghton were commissioned for Strahan by his engravers the Dalziel Brothers[146] with poems then being written to fit. It would appear, therefore, that no poem was written to accompany 'On the Cliffs' which nonetheless appeared in proximity to the birth of Selina's son. By this time, the fate and mortality of young children had emerged as a theme of the illustrations for which poems came to be written for *Good Words* including 'Rung into Heaven' which concerned a child accidentally killed by bells and 'Love in Death' where a child survived a snowstorm in Vermont'.[147] Houghton was a named contributor to the magazine whose work was accompanied in August 1862 by the poem 'My Treasure' by 'R.M.'. The sitter for this illustration in the Pre-Raphaelite style has been identified as Houghton's wife playing with two children including 'a little babe upon my knees/ To toss and pull my brown, brown hair'.[148] The

[144] *GW* 3, 550.

[145] *GW* 3, 549.

[146] Paul Hogarth, *Arthur Boyd Houghton* (London: V&A, 1975), 10.

[147] 'Rung into Heaven,' *GW* 3 (1862): 153–4; 'Love in Death,' *GW* 3 (1862): 184–5.

[148] *GW* 3, 504.

MISTRESS AND MAID.

A HOUSEHOLD STORY.

BY THE AUTHOR OF "JOHN HALIFAX, GENTLEMAN."

CHAPTER XXI.

It was not a cheerful morning on which to be married. A dense, yellow, London fog, the like of which the Misses Leaf had never yet seen, penetrated into every corner of the parlour at No. 15, where they were breakfasting drearily by candle-light, all in their wedding attire. They had been up since six in the morning, and Elizabeth had dressed her three mistresses one after the other, taking exceeding pleasure in the performance. For she was still little more than a girl, to whom a

Fig. 5.10   J.E. Millais, Illustration accompanying Chapters 21–23 of *Mistress and Maid*, *GW* 3 (1862): 609.

Fig. 5.11   Simeon Solomon, Illustration for William Robertson, 'The Veiled Bride,' *GW* 3 (1862): 592.

original print of the illustration is in Tate Britain and, by contrast with the poem, all three subjects are portrayed as miserable. Houghton's 'On the Cliffs' in October echoed some of the pose of this August offering but was neither an illustration for the 'riddle' article nor for the ensuing poem, 'Garibaldi' by Gerald Massey.[149] In the October issue of *Good Words*, serial readers accustomed to these unplanned juxtapositions were thus given a situational portent of Selina's future and a context in which to put both her newborn son and the spoilt and absent Ascott.

The deathbed scene between Elizabeth and Selina opened the penultimate November instalment and offered a number of intertextual enhancements to Craik's text (see Figure 5.12). Millais had used a similar deathbed illustration for 'Last Words' in the *Cornhill* in November 1860.[150] The illustration of Elizabeth and Selina had also been anticipated by that of Matthew Lawless in *Good Words* for October of a similar scene accompanying 'The Bands of Love' (see Figure 5.13). This was a poem recounting the Lancashire superstition that a person cannot die in the arms of someone who resists their death and the deathbed scene in the serial was thus foreshadowed by both the parallel scene of the poem and by the proleptic opening illustration in November. In discussing the shared pictorial iconography of death, Julia Thomas points out that the illustration for 'Bands of Love' is deceptive in itself since the apparent display of maternal affection is subverted by the subject matter of the poem in which the daughter actually wants to die.[151] In addition, on the page opposite Selina's deathbed scene in *Good Words* and immediately preceding the instalment of the serial was concluded a selection of reflections 'from a Roman Catholic Pulpit' in which one paragraph appeared to be very deliberately spaced to support the account of Selina's baby, reading: 'The child in thy house is the saint image, which God has placed there for thy contemplation and imitation; a living sermon telling you what you are to be and do'.[152] In the serial, the baby was then designated 'the good angel of the household ... trusting that the ghastly skeleton therein might in time crumble away into harmless dust',[153] a reference which recapitulated the skeleton illustration for Craik's 'Until Her Death' back in May. Selina's tender thoughts as a mother were allowed to undermine the suspense of the serial – 'How far they might have influenced her life to come, none knew, and none ever did know' – but, in fact, the illustration and its other portents have already suggested that she will die. The baby must be 'baptized in a great hurry' owing to 'apprehensions of it dying' mentioned immediately under the illustration but the overall suggestion from Craik's text in the magazine and the contextual material is that these apprehensions should rather be transferred to his pictured

[149] *GW* 3, 623–4; 624.

[150] *CM* 2, opposite page 513.

[151] Julia Thomas, 'Happy Endings: Death and Domesticity in Victorian Illustration,' in *Reading Victorian Illustration, 1855–1875: Spoils of the Lumber Room*, ed. Paul Goldman and Simon Cooke (Farnham: Ashgate, 2012), 95.

[152] *GW* 3, 672.

[153] *GW* 3, 674.

MISTRESS AND MAID.

A HOUSEHOLD STORY.

BY THE AUTHOR OF "JOHN HALIFAX, GENTLEMAN."

CHAPTER XXIV.

A FORTNIGHT'S time rather increased than diminished the excitement incident on the event at Russell Square.

Never was there such a wonderful baby, and never was there such a fuss made over it. Unprejudiced persons might have called it an ugly weakly little thing; indeed, at first there were such apprehensions of its dying, that it had been baptized in a great hurry, "Henry Leaf Ascott," according to the mother's desire, which in her critical posi-

Fig. 5.12   J.E. Millais, Illustration accompanying Chapters 24–25 of *Mistress and Maid*, *GW* 3 (1862): 673.

632   GOOD WORDS.   [Edited by

And the last of all wert thou, mother !
  That I had told of my woe ;
And I had not told it now, even now,
  But to make you let me go.

Oh ! let my soul go free, mother !
  I will come with the birds again ;
I will wake you at morn from the old plane-tree
  With a song that knows not pain.

When you think what you cannot speak,
  At evening, a kiss will steal,—
A kiss to dry the tears on your cheek,
  A kiss that you will not feel.

And I know I can scarce be dearer
  To your heart than I have been ;
Yet, perhaps, I may then be nearer
  With nought to come between ;

With no shadow from the grieving
  That walks on earth with love ;
Its footsteps never leaving,
  For it knows they must part above.

Oh ! let my soul go sleep, mother ;
  Why, why should love's excess
Still strive within its hold to keep
  What it can no longer bless ?

It is but the vain, vain yearning
  Of an eye that follows still ,
On a step no more returning,
  That it cannot shield from ill.

And such hath been thy love, mother,
  Thy mother-love ; but *there*,
In my Father's house above—above,
  There is bread enough and to spare.

We part from one another
  In grief, but we meet in bliss ;
We part with the kiss and the tear, mother !
  We meet with the smile and the kiss.

And the dark will grow to light,
  But the light will not pass away.
We part, we part in the mirk midnight,
  But we shall meet i' the day.   .   .

There is a sore strife for my breath,
  But on it rest begins ;
Oh, love is strong— is strong as death,
  But it is not *now* it wins !

And thine, and thine is my love, mother !
  But I should not pray *to thee ;*
I would speak with One above, mother !
  Oh, let my soul go free !

                          D. G.

Fig. 5.13   Matthew Lawless, Illustration for [Dora Greenwell], 'The Bands of Love,' *GW* 3 (1862): 632.

mother, who will die at the end of the first of the two chapters of this instalment and be commemorated at the beginning of the second.[154]

A picture of Hilary at Selina's large marble monument in Stowbury six months later in fictional time was used to illustrate the 1862 volume edition of *Good Words* although this scene had no place in the serial itself. Paul Goldman describes the illustration as being of Elizabeth at Tom's grave, but the seated female figure closely resembles Hilary and the monument is far too grand to be that of an impoverished printer.[155] The final December instalment of *Mistress and Maid* had no illustration, but the reader's conditioned expectations might be satisfied by the surrounding material, reading across the complementary subjects as in the previous month. Thus Adelaide Proctor's poem 'True or False' was accompanied by another Houghton illustration of a child and its parents, identified by Hogarth as Houghton himself, together with his wife and son Arthur.[156] Once again poem and subject matter were at odds but the figures could be viewed as substitutes for Elizabeth and her master Peter Ascott. Similarly Houghton's illustration for J. Hamilton Fyfe's 'About Toys' immediately following the instalment of *Mistress and Maid* showed children playing and was written by 'an old bachelor – quite a hopeless, hardened case of that social disorder', who might also have been Peter, softened by the immediately preceding events of the serial.[157] The illustration is very similar to those produced by Houghton for *Home Thoughts and Home Scenes*, a Dalziel Brothers gift book of 1865 to which Craik contributed three poems.

Cooke describes these illustrations as 'framed by a set of circumstances'[158] but they clearly functioned also to affect the reading of the serial and the periodical. They offered the shared and distinctive themes of *Good Words* at the same time as anticipating the events of the novel in ways which both rationalized sensation and supported the periodical's religious mission. Robert Lyon's return was made deliberately low-key but the frozen illustration of him from March could then return to life when, as Craik observed, 'Nobody screamed, nobody fainted. People seldom do that in real life'.[159] In a parallel with the fate of the serial itself being read below stairs, Elizabeth identified where her former fiancé Tom was living through charitable magazines sent downstairs as firelighters. Through her, the events of the novel were reviewed and, despite the setting in the completed past, the maid was highlighted at its ending as 'still living' among the readers of *Good Words*.[160] Overall, the framing of the text was significant for the novel serialized

---

[154] *GW* 3, 675; 673.

[155] Paul Goldman, *Beyond Decoration: The Illustration of John Everett Millais* (London: British Library, 2005), 239. The use of this illustration as the frontispiece to *Good Words for 1862* is discussed in Chapter 6.

[156] *GW* 3, 721; Paul Hogarth, *Arthur Boyd Houghton* (London: Gordon Fraser, 1981), 25.

[157] *GW* 3, 753; 752.

[158] Cooke, *Illustrated Periodicals of the 1860s*, 163.

[159] GW 3, 682.

[160] GW 3, 751.

in a periodical. On the opening pages of the first eleven instalments of *Mistress and Maid* the serial, the public images of Craik and her collaborators were held in a synchronous tension – the periodical dispensing good words, the editor with his DD, the novelist trading on her success to reach a designated audience and the artist signing the illustrations which allude to the subject matter of serials across periodical reading. The serial was itself at home among the complementary educational and religious articles which would continue to appear in the next annual progression of the periodical. In 1862, it was a self-reflexive act for the women in the serial to read from the scriptures and for the readers of the periodical to read the women in the context of Craik's lay preaching as a woman with a respectable and respected public face.

The Moonstone in *All the Year Round*

There is a sense in which *Mistress and Maid* thus had multiple narrators in its serial context, not just Craik herself but her designated authorial personae and the complementary contributors deployed by Strahan and Macleod. The successive narrators of *The Moonstone* reproduced the multiple authorship of the periodical itself but the serial in context reveals a competitive as well as a complementary discourse during the serialization in *All the Year Round*. Dickens wrote of *The Woman in White* in January 1860, 'it grips the difficulties of the weekly portion and throws them in a masterly style',[161] and he held Collins up as a model of the serial author. Collins refined his craft under Dickens's editorship and later Smith's at the *Cornhill* and in many ways *The Moonstone* eight years later was the apotheosis of the novel designed for serialization within the periodical; it reflected the tone and structure of the periodical context whilst using segmentation to hold the readers' attention between instalments. This section explores the novel presented in *All the Year Round* by considering the expectation created by advertising prior to the serialization, and then discussing a range of intertextual features created by both fictional and factual material. This leads into examples of the 'weekly portion' and its interaction with the narrative techniques used by the intradiegetic contributors to the novel. Finally, the section demonstrates how Dickens's endorsement of Collins turned the complementary serial narrative into competitive editing.

By 1868, Wilkie Collins's long association with periodical publishing had made him adept in the organization of texts by multiple authors. The group authorship of *The Moonstone* has been discussed in Chapter 2. The multiple narrators of the novel mirrored the pattern of the periodical with its multiple authors smoothed into their weekly whole and his deployment of this technique reflected Collins's confidence in his medium. The new serial was trailed in *All the Year Round* from 5 October 1867, three months before the commencement of the serialization, and

---

[161] Charles Dickens to Wilkie Collins, 7 January 1860, Dickens, *Letters*, vol. 9, 195. See also J. Don Vann, 'Dickens, Charles Lever and Mrs Gaskell,' *Victorian Periodicals Review* 22 (1989): 64–71.

this reflects Dickens's reciprocal confidence in Collins. The advertisement offered the possibility of a relationship stretching out across the turn of the year since it also included notice of the preceding serial by Percy Fitzgerald:

> In No. 443, for October the 19th, will be commenced a NEW SERIAL STORY by the Author of "BELLA DONNA," "NEVER FORGOTTEN," &c., entitled THE DEAR GIRL.
>
> To be continued from Week to Week until completed in Four Months.
>
> A NEW SERIAL STORY, BY WILKIE COLLINS, Will also soon appear in these pages.[162]

On 23 November, the commencement date of 4 January 1868 was finally announced and the title '*The Moonstone*' on 30 November.[163] These inducements were intertwined with advertising for the double Christmas number for 1867 'Written entirely BY CHARLES DICKENS AND WILKIE COLLINS' and named 'No Thoroughfare' on 23 November.[164] The serials and other material to be marketed were woven together to spark interest and desirability, and at this stage both Dickens and Collins appeared to be benefiting from the association. The reader of *All the Year Round* would be reading the beginning of *The Moonstone* with the anticipation created by this long-running marketing effort as well as with the knowledge that the new serial had the endorsement of Dickens himself.

Mabel's Progress 'a novel by the Author of "Aunt Margaret's Trouble"' had been in lead station since 6 April 1867 but the last three of its 31 instalments were moved to make way for Fitzgerald's *The Dear Girl* in the manner of other about-to-be-completed serials. The author was Frances Eleanor Trollope, sister of Ellen Ternan and wife of Thomas Adolphus Trollope. *The Dear Girl* took over as lead serial on the advertised date of 19 October, and after 11 instalments Fitzgerald's novel in turn made way for *The Moonstone* on 4 January 1868, taking up the final station from that date in preparation for its anticipated conclusion which took place on 8 February. *The Moonstone* remained in first station throughout its serialization and was not accompanied by any other substantial piece of fiction during the remainder of the period of its appearance in *All the Year Round*, and the dependability of its position allowed some manipulation of recurring fictional material written by Dickens himself. In January and February 1868, there was a complicated series of advertisements for two short serials by Dickens: 'Holiday Romance' and 'George Silverman's Explanation' in 'monthly portions'. The latter comprised nine chapters although the first two were only halting paragraphs and the

162   *AYR*, 5 October 1867, 360.
163   *AYR*, 23 November 1867, 528; 30 November 1867, 552.
164   *AYR*, 23 November 1867, 528.

story actually appeared in alternate numbers of *All the Year Round* in February.[165] The monthly treatment of 'Holiday Romance' in the first four months of 1868[166] was rather a ponderous process for such a slight piece although the discussion below demonstrates how the use of narrators in these shorter serials interacted with the longer. What seems apparent, however, is that the consistent and fixed appearance of *The Moonstone* was designed to support this more fragmentary process and re-patterning in the rest of the periodical.

There were other accompanying pieces which complemented and competed with the novel both as fiction and fact, in subject matter and in narrative style. References to India and references back across numbers of the periodical were particular features. The first two instalments of *The Moonstone* appeared in the same number of *All the Year Round* as the two final chapters of 'Sir John's Troubles'. This was a story set against the backdrop of India and its impact on returning servants of the empire but in wholly domestic contrast with the dramatic siege and theft of the Moonstone. Clearly the treatment of empire was a significant topic which both novel and periodical could cross-reference, although Hyungji Park argues that Dickens's periodicals were overall comparatively silent about India.[167] The article 'My First Tiger' which immediately preceded the first instalment of 'George Silverman's Explanation' provided a link too: 'In London we are always running a race against time and losing it. Not so in India'.[168] In the serial that week, Mr Murthwaite has explained about the caste system and the loss of the Moonstone's sacred identity if it were cut up. He has reinforced the domestic and the dramatic through a direct reference to the subject of the hunting article: '[t]hose men will wait their opportunity with the patience of cats, and will use it with the ferocity of tigers'.[169]

The referencing of back numbers which was a feature of periodical discourse and its proponents was also employed by the narrators of *The Moonstone*. On 18 January, when the advertisement for 'Holiday Romance' appeared, the narrator Betteredge observed that 'we only believe in a romance when we see it in a newspaper'.[170] In the same number accompanying Chapters 6 and 7 of the serial, there was an article entitled 'Another Species of Official Midge' which itself referred back to 'Midges in Office' on 'page 31 of the present volume' of *All*

---

[165] *AYR*, 1 February 1868, 180. 'George Silverman's Explanation,' *AYR*, 1, 15 and 29 February; also in *Atlantic Monthly*, January–March 1868.

[166] 'Holiday Romance,' *AYR*, 25 January, 8 February, 14 March and 4 April; also in *An Illustrated Magazine for Boys and Girls*, January–May 1868.

[167] Hyungji Park, '"The Story of Our Lives": *The Moonstone* and the Indian Mutiny in *All the Year Round*,' in *Negotiating India in the Nineteenth-Century Media*, ed. David Finkelstein and Douglas M. Peers (Basingstoke: Macmillan, 2000), 84–109.

[168] *AYR*, 1 February 1868, 177.

[169] *AYR*, 1 February 1868, 172.

[170] *AYR*, 18 January 1868, 122.

the Year Round and to *Household Words* of fifteen years before.[171] There was an explanatory footnote on page 135 'of the volume' referring back to three articles in *Household Words* of 1854. These were two separate linked pieces (one a 'Chip') from 7 and 28 January by 'Roving Englishman' Grenville Murray and a third on 8 July 1854 also by Murray which had originally followed on from the fifteenth instalment of *Hard Times*.[172] Collins was used to playing his part in this complex system from the earliest days of his contributions to Dickens's periodicals. In fact, on 27 June 1868 when Franklin Blake announced 'We are already in the month of June' for the 26th instalment of the serial,[173] the article 'Crédit Mobilier in Discredit' referred back to *Household Words* for 3 January 1857 where Edmund Saul Dixon's 'Crédit Mobilier' had appeared immediately before the first instalment of Collins's first serialized novel, *The Dead* Secret.[174] The intertextual manipulation continued into Collins's last ever instalment in *All the Year Round*. In the number containing the penultimate instalment of *The Moonstone* on 1 August there were three backward references, two in 'The Coming Eclipse' referring to the transit of Venus and one declaring that 'no beaver story surpasses one which appeared in this journal, Number 278, August 20, 1864.'[175] Collins's narrator Sergeant Cuff then employed the same technique in the final instalment the following week for the Sixth Narrative of the Second Period of *The Moonstone*, when he referred back to Betteredge's earlier narrative in the First Period.[176]

The most significant intertextual flashback, however, referred to an incident much closer to home than Venus or even India. On 14 March, the eleventh instalment of *The Moonstone* was succeeded by an article entitled 'Some Very Light Literature' which discussed *La Belle Assemblée* of 1809. The writer pointed out 'how queerly some of the facts and opinions contained in such works show when looked at with the knowledge of subsequent events present in our mind'.[177] He mentioned some *post hoc* references to Walter Scott, to the qualities of iron and to the fire-proofing of theatres. In the serial, the incidents of the laundry list and missing nightgown have already taken place but the trail of the theft of the Moonstone was further sidetracked for the serial reader by an apparently random

---

[171] 'Another Species of Official Midge' (*AYR*, 18 January 1868, 132–5) referring to 'Midges in Office' (*AYR*, 21 December 1867, 31–4) which was actually 14 years before.

[172] 'On Her Majesty's Secret Service,' *HW*, 7 January, 433–7; 'Chip: Her Majesty's Service Again,' *HW*, 28 January 1854, 523–4; 'Her Majesty's Consular Service,' *HW*, 8 July 1854, 482–7.

[173] *AYR*, 27 June 1868, 50.

[174] 'Crédit Mobilier in Discredit,' *AYR*, 27 June 1868, 57–60; 'Crédit Mobilier,' *HW*, 3 January 1857, 8–12. *The Dead Secret* followed on pages 12–18.

[175] 'The Coming Eclipse,' *AYR*, 1 August 1868, 185; 186; the references were to 'A Long Look-Out,' *AYR*, 1 February 1868, 174–7 and 'Photological Facts,' *AYR* ,11 and 25 March 1865, 149–53; 208–12; 'Beavers,' *AYR*, 1 August 1868, 177.

[176] *AYR*, 8 August 1868, 197.

[177] 'Some Very Light Literature,' *AYR*, 14 March 1868, 319.

reference to Collins's source story for these incidents, the Road Murder of 1860. In December 1860 James F. Stephen's article in *Cornhill Magazine* on 'The Criminal Law and the Detection of Crime' referred to the media attention attracted by the murder at Road.[178] Some elements of Collins's plot of 1868 such as Blake's actions on leaving the house after the theft of the Moonstone reflected the possibility discussed in the media at the time that Samuel Kent was guilty of the murder of his son. In the same number of that periodical as the twelfth instalment of *Framley Parsonage*, Stephen called for a 'more efficient mode of detecting' but also raised concerns about 'the pressure of temporary excitement' and the 'moral and dramatic interest' in the reporting of the crime.[179] In 1868 when *The Moonstone* was being serialized, the Road case had been more recently in the public eye since Samuel's daughter Constance Kent had been tried and found guilty in 1865 after confessing to the murder of her half brother Saville.

During the serialization of *The Moonstone*, the writer of an article on 'Light Literature' was completely diverted from the discussion of the 'elegant and feeble work' of *La Belle Assemblée* to announce:

> It was but the other day, after an interview with Constance Kent at the Penitentiary, Milbank – where I found her engaged in the harmless occupation of ironing linen –that, on referring back to a number of the Annual Register for the year in which the Road murder was committed, I found it stated as an instance of what absurd theories people will sometimes put forward, that certain persons had even gone so far as to suggest that the murdered child had been the victim of Miss Constance Kent, a daughter of the house![180]

The article writer added darkly: 'Knowing what we do now, this paragraph reads oddly enough.' Readers of the serial were here reminded of the original context for the clues being unearthed in the novel. Like Samuel Kent, Blake has left the scene in search of police assistance. A missing nightgown believed to be blood-stained was a key feature of the original reporting of the murder in 1860. During the serialization of *The Moonstone*, the description of Kent in the periodical followed on from Rachel Verinder's suspicious behaviour in the novel and it also prefigured Blake's discovery of his own nightgown at the Shivering Sands. This latter occurrence would conclude a later instalment on 30 May with dramatic capitalization, that 'on the unanswerable evidence of the paint-stain, I had discovered Myself the Thief'.[181] In the serial as in the Road Murder, the past has had to be revised in the present. If the novel reader continued to read this number of *All the Year Round*, there was, of course, no need for any annotation

---

[178] [James F. Stephen], 'The Criminal Law and the Detection of Crime,' *CM* 2, 697–708.

[179] *CM* 2, 697.

[180] 'Some Very Light Literature,' 319.

[181] *AYR*, 30 May 1868, 583.

of Collins's source for the serial, an annotation which needs to be supplied for a modern edition of the novel.

It may perhaps be deduced that the presence of the serial in the periodical had given the writer of the article his idea. Since, as discussed below, Collins was acting as visiting editor for *All the Year Round*, the inclusion of this paragraph or use of the historical document might be attributable to him. The original serial reader who picked up associations from the factual article would have been even more baffled and thrilled by the chain of events which were being simultaneously reread in the magazine context of those much-publicized incidents at Road.

A historical document such as *La Belle Assemblée* of 1809 might thus be called into use for quiet weeks in a weekly periodical, although clearly this was a heavily weighted piece in terms of the ongoing serialization. This approach also, however, reflected the use made of dating and documents already called into service to open the serial five months earlier. The Prologue to *The Moonstone* on the Storming of Seringapatam was dated 1799 and was described as '(*Extracted from a Family Paper*)'[182] in the manner of other instances of factual fiction in the periodical. In the serial, contemporary and fictional dating continued to be manipulated as they had been in *The Woman in White*. The unidentified editor of the family papers announced the title of the 'First Period' three pages into the instalment dating 'The Loss of the Diamond' to 1848, and this first period was then narrated by Gabriel Betteredge for 23 chapters or a further 12 instalments which appeared between 4 January and 28 March 1868 in real time. Betteredge firstly indicated that he was writing his account after 21 May 1850 in fictional time but struggled to control his narrative. Retaining the textual reinforcement of documentary evidence used by the editors of both the magazine and the serial, he then offered to tell the story 'day by day' dating from 24 May 1848 with the aid of his daughter Penelope's diary.[183]

The steward or guardian Gabriel Betteredge was a type of the fictional narrator of fact common in periodical discourse. On 4 January 1868 he demonstrated the self-conscious reflexivity of the fictionalized journalists in *Household Words* such as the 'Scotchman' or 'Roving Englishman' by wondering 'whether the gentlemen who make a business and a living out of writing books ever find their own selves getting in the way of their subjects, like me?'[184] There was also copious intertextual reference in his narrative to *Robinson Crusoe* which became an advice manual and almanac combined.[185] Betteredge thus had a range of precedents as a narrator in a periodical which would be familiar to contemporary readers but which are lost to the later reader of the volume edition. After his hesitant start in the periodical, the steward demonstrated that he was fully aware of the job of organizing his

---

[182] *AYR*, 4 January 1868, 73. Seringapatam was cross-referenced on 11 July in an article on 'Animal Intelligence' (115).

[183] *AYR*, 4 January 1868, 75; 78.

[184] *AYR*, 4 January 1868, 77.

[185] See also Katie Lanning, 'Tessellating Texts: Reading *The Moonstone* in *All the Year Round*,' *Victorian Periodicals Review* 45 (2012): 1–22.

material 'in its proper place'.[186] By Chapter 8 he was able to fix certain dates and to summarize events before suspending time to cover the birthday dinner and its immediate aftermath so that Chapters 9, 10 and 11 spanned four instalments, a pattern of suspense lost in the volume edition. Chapter 9 was the second half of the instalment on 25 January and Chapter 10 comprised the whole of the 1 February instalment which closed: 'The next thing to tell is the story of the night'. Chapter 11 began on 8 February and was concluded a short way into the next instalment on 15 February: 'so much for the day that followed the birthday'.[187] The effect is both self-referential and knowing in the periodical context. At the end of the first instalment and of Chapter 3, 'later on that same day' became the following week of the serial and when the second instalment opened (on the same page in the volume edition of the novel) Betteredge was still in his chair protesting that 'things must be put down in their places, as things actually happened'.[188] The suggestion might be that for many periodical writers their lives and experiences were their own subjects and that Betteredge himself was in his 'proper place' within the periodical. This was reinforced when he also demonstrated his grip of 'the weekly portion' not visible to the reader of the volume. He referred to the jewel as 'the Diamond' throughout the first instalment and only named it in his dramatic final sentence: '"It" meant the Moonstone'.[189]

The other narrators are urged by their editor Blake to retain the proper place for their narratives. Lewis Roberts has observed that 'the narrators are both part of the narrative action and observers of the narrative structure'[190] and this mirrored periodical production with some of the self-consciousness demonstrated by the *Cornhill* contributors discussed above. The place of the narrators of the serial was also both compromised and complemented by other elements of the periodical in which the instalments were embedded. Betteredge has been discussed above. On 4 April his successor, Miss Clack, described herself as 'condemned to narrate'[191] but, as a parody of the reader of *Good Words*, she nevertheless managed to embroider her account with the improving religious advice she has tried unsuccessfully to foist on her aunt, Lady Verinder. As the Clack narrative began in *All the Year Round*, the overall control of the text was highlighted by a footnote precisely fitting the page of the periodical and authored by Franklin Blake. There was the barely detectable hint that Blake was now married to Rachel in 1850. He and the unidentified object of Miss Clack's pen regard that pen as having 'unquestionable value as an instrument for the exhibition of Miss Clack's character'.[192] The

[186] *AYR*, 4 January 1868, 80.

[187] *AYR*, 1 February 1868, 174; 15 February 1868, 219.

[188] *AYR*, 10 January 1868, 97.

[189] *AYR*, 4 January 1868, 80.

[190] Lewis Roberts, 'The "Shivering Sands" of Reality: Narration and Knowledge in Wilkie Collins's *The Moonstone*,' *Victorian Review* 23 (1997): 169.

[191] *AYR*, 4 April 1868, 388.

[192] *AYR*, 4 April 1868, 388.

appearance of the text so neatly fitting the page counterpointed Clack's apparently disorganised waffle and demonstrated that this placement was significant as part of the control over the novel in serial. Not only was her fictional editor allowing her to condemn herself out of her own mouth, but Miss Clack's account of 'the unrelenting pecuniary pressure of Mr Blake's cheque' was also followed in *All the Year Round* by an account of the uses to which 'Margins' (or disposable income) might be put.[193]

At the horizontal level of periodical discourse, the narrative of Miss Clack also appeared in conjunction with three other stories apparently about single women in *All the Year Round* in 1868. The five-part 'The Late Miss Hollingford' narrated by the unmarried Margery Dacre was much in the style of a Gaskell story with a plot which included three sisters running a school, an account of the trials of poverty and the results of a failed bank. Hollingford was the Cranfordian town in *Wives and Daughters* which, like 'The Late Miss Hollingford', also concerns a family called Gibson. The missing Miss Hollingford called herself Rachel Leonard at the same period as Rachel Verinder was appearing in Miss Clack's narrative.[194] The three-part 'Sister Anne' by Julia Kavanagh which began in the week of the last Miss Clack instalment was apparently narrated in retrospect by 'a lonely old maid'[195] but like 'Miss Hollingford' this was a type of disguise since the narrative closed three weeks later with Anne a happily married woman as she would have been when the story began. These two short stories between them occupied the final station of *All the Year Round* for seven weeks, to be followed by Harriet Parr's 'Polly's One Offer' whose title was also a deception since the eponymous Polly received and accepted a second offer of marriage in the third and final instalment of the story on 27 June. The apparent singleness of these women who were actually married all along was a studied alternative to and context for the spinster Clack within the magazine.

Following on from Miss Clack, Mr Bruff took a lawyerly stance to justify his 'claims to fill [his] position ... in these pages'.[196] As a more traditional type of periodical contributor, he was both more scrupulous and briefer in presenting the information peculiar to him. He handed over in mid-instalment to Franklin Blake who has returned to England in the fictional spring of 1849. Having been a character, critic and editor behind the scenes, Blake now migrated into the role of contributor and this complicated his role within the serial, particularly as editor. He had barely begun his narrative before the instalment concluded with his tears on meeting Betteredge such that he 'was obliged to wait for a moment', which became a week for his readers in *All the Year Round*.[197] Blake was now controlling the structure of the narrative within the framework of his edited but ostensibly

---

[193] *AYR*, 11 April 1868, 413; 'Margins,' *AYR*, 11 April 1868, 413–7.

[194] *AYR*, 11 April 1868, 431.

[195] *AYR*, 9 May 1868, 524.

[196] *AYR*, 16 May 1868, 529.

[197] *AYR*, 23 May 1868, 559.

evidence-driven narrative. Through a tortuous manipulation of her testimony and the assumption of editorial control, he allowed Rosanna's letter to narrate within his own and then admitted Jennings's journal directly into his miscellany in order to corroborate his own innocence.

The final instalment of *The Moonstone* showed the most varied approach to serial content in the scope of its narratives ranging back over previous numbers. In *All the Year Round* dated 8 August 1868, Cuff dated his report 30 July 1849. He wrote in a linear manner to fill in the gaps of the other narratives at the same time as endorsing the previous narrative of Betteredge in a concluding footnote: 'Wherever the Report touches on the events of the birthday, or of the three days that followed it, compare with Betteredge's Narrative – Chapters VIII to XIII.'[198] Mr Candy supplied the 'Seventh Narrative' dated 26 September 1849 which explained how the dying Jennings tore the relevant pages out of his Journal so that they could be included in the serial. Betteredge then returned as steward 'left behind to close the story up' to supply the date of Rachel's marriage on 9 October 1849 concluding, 'I make my bow, and shut up my story'.[199] This made way for the three-part Epilogue which explained in three separate voices the return of the Indians all laid out in the form of articles within a number of the periodical, a layout lost in the volume editions whose text does not migrate back into the periodical series. This final instalment acted to disintegrate the form of the novel whilst reintegrating the future content of the periodical which would carry on though the serial was concluded.

After only four instalments of *The Moonstone*, the critic Geraldine Jewsbury complained in the *Athenaeum* of these 'tantalising portions'.[200] More recently, David Blair has seen the puzzle of *The Moonstone* as a 'closed system'[201] but its original readers would have looked forward to the solution at the same time as being given the space by their reading practice to read laterally within the numbers of *All the Year Round*. Jenny Bourne Taylor sees the narratives of *The Moonstone* as 'marginal and half-hidden texts'[202] but in addition the forms of storytelling chosen by Collins reflect the stylistic choices of periodical writers which were understood and recognised by periodical readers. During the serialization, these articles were in plain sight and it is thus the periodical matter which is made 'marginal' when the volume edition becomes the definitive text. Sue Lonoff believes that the narrative is limited by the narrators' perceptions and that 'the characters ... also

---

[198] *AYR*, 8 August 1868, 197.

[199] *AYR*, 8 August 1868, 198; 199.

[200] *The Athenaeum*, 25 January 1868, 106; repr., *Wilkie Collins: The Critical Heritage*, ed. Norman Page (London: Routledge and Kegan Paul, 1974), 170.

[201] David Blair, 'Wilkie Collins and the Crisis of Suspense,' in *Reading the Victorian Novel: Detail into Form*, ed. Ian Gregor (London: Vision Press, 1980), 44.

[202] Jenny Bourne Taylor, *In the Secret Theatre of Home: Wilkie Collins, Sensation Narrative and Nineteenth Century Psychology* (London: Routledge, 1988), 179.

colour and distend their narratives by the force of their personalities'.[203] In fact, the 'coloration' from the context and intertextual relationships within the weekly numbers redefined these limits and extended both the system of the puzzle and the narrative growth of the story into the whole issue of the periodical.

This open system comprised also the interaction of the narrators across *All the Year Round* in early 1868 including George Silverman, Margery Dacre and Sister Anne, and the techniques of Collins's narrators were significantly shared and imitated. Gabriel Betteredge expressed concern about his commencement in the first instalment of *The Moonstone*, and Dickens also used this conceit of the tentative narrator in 'George Silverman's Explanation' which appeared during the second month of the serialization of Collins's novel. The allusions were not always supportive, however. 'Holiday Romance', Dickens's other short serial from the early part of 1868, was narrated successively by little Alice Rainbird aged seven, 'Lieutenant-Colonel' Robin Redforth aged nine and Nettie 'Aged half-past six'.[204] In addition to these infant replicas of Clack, Betteredge and Bruff, their editor William Tinkling, aged eight seemed to mock the arrangement of Collins's serial insisting, 'This beginning part is not made out of anybody's head you know. It's real.'[205] Later on in 1868, a further competing pattern emerged from Dickens's reassertion of his editorship on his return from America.

Dickens sailed for America in November 1867 leaving Collins as visiting editor on *All the Year Round* with strict instructions which, according to Lillian Nayder, limited his ability to shape the journal.[206] As we have seen, Dickens's own short serials were promoted in the periodical and, of course, his conductorship was still advertised on every page. Collins wrote to his mother on 26 November 1867: 'I am finishing the 3rd act of the play [No Thoroughfare]–conducting All the Year Round–and correcting The Moonstone for its first appearance in London and New York–all together. My very minutes are counted.'[207] The control exerted over the serial's context can be illustrated not only by the miniature narrators of 'Holiday Romance' but through the horizontal pattern created in the periodical around Ezra Jennings's journal. On 15 February 1868, there had been a review in *All the Year Round* of 'English Royal Authors', including Queen Victoria whose 'Highland Journal' was described as the 'reflected light from the sunshine which fills the heart of the writer'.[208] Jennings's brief journal, suggesting a life of great suffering, was in stark contrast when it appeared on 18 and 25 July. After Dickens's return, however, the anonymous and rather scurrilous diary of a Scottish naval surgeon

---

[203] Sue Lonoff, *Wilkie Collins and His Victorian Readers: A Study in the Rhetoric of Authorship* (New York: AMS Press, 1982), 74; 201–2.

[204] *AYR*, 8 February 1868, 204; 14 March 1868, 324; 4 April 1868, 396.

[205] *AYR*, 25 January 1868, 156.

[206] Lillian Nayder, *Unequal Partners: Charles Dickens, Wilkie Collins and Victorian Authorship* (Ithaca: Cornell University Press, 2002), 161.

[207] Wilkie Collins to Harriet Collins, Collins, *The Public Face*, vol. 2, 92

[208] 'English Royal Authors,' *AYR*, 15 February 1868, 240.

was presented as another fragmentary testament on 26 September. The collator of this alternative medical practitioner's diary indicated that: 'The notes or additional memoranda to each name of interest, are added within brackets to preserve the context of the little narrative'.[209] In the 25 July instalment of the earlier serial, Jennings has laid down his pen on two occasions and each time five asterisks indicated a gap in the timing of his narrative. The editing of the Scottish surgeon's diary two months later reflected and mocked that of the narrative in *The Moonstone* down to the asterisks which closed the incomplete text.[210] In addition, the use of layout to accommodate the pattern of the periodical and to re-exert control was also deployed at the boundaries of the serial instalment containing the journal of Collins's doctor's assistant. Thus on the last page of Jennings's narrative, a veil was drawn over Blake's reunion with Rachel, but Jennings's last words in the periodical were made to flow into the text of the next article:

> God be praised for his mercy! I have seen a little sunshine – I have had a happy time.
>
> LEAVES FROM THE MAHOGANY TREE. A CUP OF TEA.
>
> A CUP of tea! Blessings on the words, for they convey a sense of English home comfort.[211]

This demonstrates how the serial was elided into the number of the periodical which could then carry on from week to week. At the level of contributor Jennings was no longer the narrator and three weeks later *The Moonstone* was no longer the serial but 'Leaves from the Mahogany Tree' continued until the end of the volume of *All the Year Round* to its 21st instalment on 28 November.[212] Dickens, of course, also continued as Conductor.

The editor had returned from America in May 1868. On 6 June 1868, the first advertisement for his Farewell Series of Readings appeared in *All the Year Round* as well as a new pattern emerging of backward references to his earlier novels. The Farewell Readings continued to be advertised each week until the end of the serialization of *The Moonstone*, and articles were interwoven with references, as discussed above, to previous issues of Dickens's periodicals as well as other allusions to his novels. On 4 July, an article on the poor rate was entitled 'Saint Bumble' after the beadle in *Oliver Twist* and another – 'Growth of a London Myth' – described Bleeding Heart Yard, the setting for parts of *Little Dorrit*.[213] In an article the following week entitled 'Queer Street' which immediately followed the

---

[209] 'An Anonymous Diary,' *AYR*, 26 September 1868, 381.

[210] *AYR*, 25 July 1868, 145.

[211] *AYR*, 25 July 1868, 153.

[212] The first in the series appeared on 30 April. There was no 'Leaf' on 26 June, 1 August, 8 August, 3 October or 30 October.

[213] *AYR*, 4 July 1868, 83–4; 88–93.

28th instalment of *The Moonstone*, Fagin and the Artful Dodger were referenced at a time when Dickens was beginning his preparations for the *Sikes and Nancy* element of his reading tour.[214] Most noticeable, however, was the 'Debt of Honour' article which reprinted Dickens's conciliatory speech given on 18 April at a dinner in New York. In it, Dickens announced his intention to add this statement to any future reprints of *Martin Chuzzlewit* originally published in 1844, and the printed version in the periodical was entitled 'Postscript' to indicate the position of this statement within another printed book. It was also to appear in reprints of *American Notes*, originally published in 1842. In the speech Dickens had endeavoured to repair some of the damage done by his treatment of America in *Martin Chuzzlewit* which was originally serialized in monthly parts from January 1843 to July 1844 and which contained anti-American satire in response to his treatment at the hands of the American press after his first tour there in 1842.[215]

Although the presentation of Dickens's speech was to be 'done in the plainest and simplest manner possible',[216] the Postscript of 1868 was manipulated within the number of *All the Year Round* in a way which undermined the progress of the serial. The Postscript sat not at the end of the issue as was usual for editorial corrections and as its title implied, but exactly in the middle of the number which also carried an advertisement for his reading tour at the end. The concluding announcement of the tour reinforced both the sense of competition with the ongoing serial and the control to be exerted by Dickens over the content and context of the periodical:

> MESSRS. CHAPPELL AND Co. beg to announce that, knowing it to be the determination of MR. DICKENS finally to retire from Public Reading soon after his return from America, they (as having been honoured with his confidence on previous occasions) made proposals to him while he was still in the United States achieving his recent brilliant successes there, for a final FAREWELL SERIES OF READINGS in this country.[217]

The impact of the two announcements was in stark contrast to the beginning of the serialization of *The Moonstone* where the collaborative announcement of 'No Thoroughfare' had allied the two authors and projected their joint authorship which was now shown to be interrupted. In the 6 June number containing the Postscript, the serial had reached its 23rd instalment where the documentary narrative was additionally complicated by having Blake recount Betteredge's reading of the letter left for him by Rosanna Spearman. In the serial that week, Blake has asked Betteredge to tell him any important facts out loud but has in fact copied and printed 'the continuation of the letter from the original' which he admits to having in his 'own possession'.[218] The rhythm of the narrative was

214   *AYR*, 11 July 1868, 103–4; see Slater, *Charles Dickens*, 589–90.

215   See Slater, *Charles Dickens*, 215.

216   'Postscript,' *AYR*, 6 June 1868, 610.

217   *AYR*, 6 June 1868, 620.

218   *AYR*, 6 June 1868, 604.

then once again interrupted by the arrival of Ezra Jennings 'the man with the piebald hair'[219] whose name closed the instalment and whose text will also be hijacked for Blake's own purposes. These narrative interruptions and corrections were heightened in the periodical context of 6 June by the postscript and the linked advertisement. Blake announced at the beginning of the instalment: 'The picture which I am now presenting of myself will, I suspect, be thought a very strange one',[220] and the instalment both reflected and rebelled against the construction of the periodical number which surrounded it. Blake, like Dickens, was asserting himself as the controller of his text with Jennings, like Collins, relegated to the role of a fictional curiosity.

The Moonstone within *All the Year Round* imitated a periodical edited by Dickens with all the boundaries and thresholds orientated towards control but where no control was finally possible. Dickens was himself impatient with the serial despite its success. He complained to Wills of the novel's 'obstinate conceit' and Lillian Nayder has seen Dickens's subsequent novel *The Mystery of Edwin Drood* as a response to the criticism of empire in *The Moonstone*.[221] Catherine Peters suggests that Dickens was also uncomfortable about Collins's private life and exasperated with his son-in-law, Wilkie's brother Charles Collins.[222] Dickens seems to have recognized that his methods were effectively being satirized and moved to reassert editorial control. Lewis Roberts has observed that in *The Moonstone* 'the narrators both disclose their knowledge of what happened, and suppress their understandings of the importance of that knowledge'.[223] In fact, like staff writers under the control of their editor, they have been required to conform to a pattern which has allowed the story to unfold as a mystery, but yet a mystery in which it was finally the editor, Blake 'whodunnit'. Betteredge has urged Blake on 6 June to use Rosanna's nightgown as a witness and to '[l]et her speak for herself', her story has been 'told quite often enough in the newspapers'.[224] The boundaries of this periodical discourse extend outwards from the serial in the magazine to integrate not just the story of a fallen woman but the story of Constance Kent and the story of Dickens in America.

Poor Miss Finch in Cassell's Magazine

The article on *La Belle Assemblée* in *All the Year Round* might have been describing Cassell's *Illustrated Family Paper*:

---

[219] *AYR*, 6 June 1868, 606.

[220] *AYR*, 6 June 1868, 601.

[221] Charles Dickens to W.H. Wills, 26 July 1868, Dickens, *Letters*, vol. 12, 159; Nayder, 163–97.

[222] Catherine Peters, *The King of Inventors: A Life of Wilkie Collins* (London: Minerva Press, 1991), 311.

[223] Roberts, 170.

[224] *AYR*, 6 June 1868, 602.

> Its contents consist of long extracts from books of tales, of letters from fancifully named correspondents, of occasional theatrical criticisms, of biographical sketches, and of selections from the works of the British poets ... with occasionally some original verses, by unknown hands, and of inscrutable badness. Lastly, there is ... an elaborate article on ladies' costumes, which, with two coloured illustrations, is appended to each monthly number.[225]

By January 1870, the editor of the *Paper*'s successor *Cassell's Magazine* could boldly quote complaints from similar critics that 'the poems are trash; ... the pictures ... badly drawn, worse cut, and worst of all printed',[226] safe in the knowledge that the very same issue also contained the ninth instalment of Wilkie Collins's latest serialized novel. Cassell, Petter and Galpin redefined the fictional content of the *Paper* in *Cassell's Magazine* under its existing umbrella of lower middle-class respectability, and *Man and Wife*, Collins's first novel after *The Moonstone*, increased the audience of the *Magazine* to 70,000. Nevertheless, the original format and editorship of the *Paper* cast a long shadow over its future incarnation as *Cassell's Magazine*. Collins's subsequent serial *Poor Miss Finch* was described in the *Athenaeum* as 'a sensation novel for Sunday reading', and in his review, the critic D.E. Williams also claimed on behalf of the literary establishment that Collins had been tamed by Cassell's 'sanctifying influence'.[227] The following section examines the sources of this tension in the novel's original magazine context, drawing particular attention to the intertextual relationship with other material before reading the serial against the established reputation of *Cassell's Magazine*. The novel is found to be competing with the discourse of the periodical but at the same time there are clear indications that other magazine content was also being redefined by the proximity of the serial. The following discussion contextualizes the treatment of blindness in the novel and periodical by examining the poetry and illustrations which accompanied the serial. Reference is also made to the pattern previously established by *Man and Wife*. Over 26 weeks, the instalments of *Poor Miss Finch* occupied various stations. Where Miss Finch herself relies on others to do her reading of print for her, the sighted reader of her story had opportunities to contextualize the events of the novel through the poems, articles and illustrations in which it was embedded. When the cure of Lucilla's blindness was attempted in the serial, the women of the published poems – illustrated by a female artist – looked directly out from the cover of the magazine issues and their gaze acted as a further counterpoint to the events within the novel.

 Cassell's Illustrated Family Paper was aimed at the working- and lower middle-class reader but the *Magazine* was seeking a more upwardly mobile audience, especially in its choice of new fiction writers. The *Magazine* ostensibly maintained audience interest in domestic subjects and appeared to reinforce the

---

[225] 'Some Very Light Literature,' 319.

[226] 'On Reading Magazines,' *CassM*, 15 January 1870, 140. See the discussion in Chapter 3.

[227] *The Athenaeum*, 17 February 1872; repr., Page, ed., 191.

joint respectability of reader and periodical at a time when that family audience was growing. Four years into this project, the first four chapters of *Poor Miss Finch* occupied the first station on 2 September 1871. Collins was named as the author of the serial and the text of the first instalment offered a 'twilight view of the man', still unnamed, who might prove to be the new Franklin Blake or Walter Hartright. Significantly the appearance of Oscar Dubourg was revealed at once to the reader of the periodical because an illustration anticipating the meeting between this mysterious young man and Lucilla Finch (together with her companion Madame Pratolungo) appeared in the upper portion of the first page of the first instalment. It was, of course, Lucilla herself who had a 'twilight view' because of her blindness. Picking up the situation of the blind heroine, the magazine issue closed with a poem ominously entitled 'Darkness' by 'W.A.S.' where 'Empty and blind the landscape lies/ In darkness' hold'.[228]

Other blind women in the literature of the time included Margaret Legh in Gaskell's *Mary Barton* (1848) who asserts herself through her singing ability. More characteristic of the type was Bertha Plummer in *The Cricket on the Hearth* (1845) who initially lives in a world of her father's creation and loves the miserly Tackleton. Dickens lists unflinchingly the deceptions practised on her, the things '[t]he Blind Girl never knew' about her life. Dickens also provided a sentimental account of the blind deaf mute woman Laura Bridgman in his *American Notes* of 1842; she was an object of curiosity, made safe by living in an institution.[229] The independence of Margaret Legh may indeed have been a challenge to these representations in the later 1840s. Dinah Craik, however, erred on the side of sentiment in her account of Mrs Rothesay, Olive's blind mother in the novel *Olive* (1850) and in 1856, the year of Millais's painting of 'The Blind Girl', Craik expanded her portrayal of blindness in her landmark novel *John Halifax, Gentleman*. The doomed character of Muriel Halifax is a saintly child blind from birth who dies on her eleventh birthday. Wilkie Collins's first serialized novel *The Dead Secret* which appeared in *Household Words* in 1857 also concerned a blind character. In the novel, Leonard Frankland repeatedly asks his wife to 'lend' him the eyes he needs to conduct his life. His wife Rosamond, whose identity is at the heart of the plot, is freed from some of the constraints of Victorian womanhood by her acts of writing, describing and guiding on his behalf. This is significant for the representation of Lucilla who is shown using her blindness as a gift which gives her liberty. In Chapter 11 of *Poor Miss Finch* Madame Pratolungo observes that 'blindness is never bashful, for the one simple reason that blindness cannot see. The most modest girl in existence is bolder with her lover in the dark than in the light'.[230]

---

[228] W.A.S., 'Darkness,' *CassM*, 2 September 1871, 16.

[229] Charles Dickens, *American Notes*, ed. Patricia Ingham (2000; repr., London: Penguin, 2004), 40–50 (Volume 1, Chapter 3).

[230] *CassM*, 23 September 1871, 58.

A poem which preceded the fourth instalment of *Poor Miss Finch* in *Cassell's Magazine* firmly asserted the typical attitude towards blind women purveyed by Dickens and Craik. In 'The Blind Sleeper', some scented roses are placed for a sleeping woman whose 'heart is weary of the dark.' The poem's narrator continued: 'She dreams perchance of sight;/ Shall we wake her to life's night?/ No let her be.' There is a sense of control over the blind person, of condescension and knowing, and of a belief that it is only in the alternative world of dreams that '[s]he feels no more the cross she bears'.[231] Samuel Gladden points out that Madame Pratolungo and Nugent Dubourg also regard blindness as a type of death with its accompanying fear and anxiety but that for Lucilla it actually brings knowledge and empowerment.[232] Her blindness releases her from constraints and she relies on her other senses to decode the world and her relationships, including those with young men.[233] The twins Oscar and Nugent in *Poor Miss Finch* are initially indistinguishable from one another and Lucilla is able to assert some power over her domestic circle by recognizing Oscar as her fiancé by touch. She is disadvantaged over the world when she regains her sight. It is then that she mistakes the duplicitous Nugent for Oscar who has a visibly blue face as a consequence of his epilepsy medication. Sight does not in this case serve Lucilla well and these distinctions were made more pronounced by the illustrations for the serial and the filler poems which surrounded it.

In the fifth chapter of *Poor Miss Finch* in *Cassell's Magazine*, Lucilla was illustrated demonstrating her ability to touch and to describe her world in a way which anticipates twentieth-century accounts of the developed senses of the blind (see Figure 5.14). The phenomenon is used by H.G. Wells in his short story 'The Country of the Blind' (1904) where it is sight which becomes the disability. The illustration portrayed Lucilla's own sight as being veiled while she was reading an object with her fingers, but the instalment of the novel was prefaced for the serial reader by another poem with its accompanying illustration entitled 'Found – A Veil'. In it, H.G.B. Hunt, who will later become the long-term editor of *Cassell's Family Magazine*, speculated on the 'untold tale' which 'Might cling unseen in the folds of a veil' found soiled, torn and dusty in a busy city street (see Figure 5.15). The poem bemoaned the fashion for veils which cover women's eyes, '[t] o hide such light from the eyes of man!'[234] The illustration depicted a coy and demure young lady from the earlier lines of Hunt's 'ditty' where he described 'a jealous glimpse/ Of lips that laughed of a very pureness'. Ultimately, however, the poem's meaning was twisted. It concluded that the veil had been lost by a fallen woman on her 'hurried march through the ways of men' and that this scrap of material ultimately offered 'A watery glimpse of worldly glory;/ … The dreary end of a dreary story.'[235] The illustration and the poem's subject matter were thus at

---

[231] W. Sawyer, 'The Blind Sleeper,' *CassM*, 16 September 1871, 56.

[232] Samuel Lyndon Gladden, 'Spectacular Deception: Closets, Secrets and Identity in Wilkie Collins's *Poor Miss Finch*,' *Victorian Literature and Culture* 33 (2005): 471.

[233] See Catherine Peters, 'Introduction' to *Poor Miss Finch* (Oxford, 2000), xi–xii.

[234] H.G.B. Hunt, 'Found – A Veil,' *CassM*, 9 September 1871, 17.

[235] Hunt, 18.

"HER CLEVER FINGERS WERE PASSING OVER IT RAPIDLY."

Fig. 5.14   Edward Hughes, 'Her clever fingers were passing over it rapidly,'
            Chapter 5, *Poor Miss Finch*, *CassM*, 9 September 1871, 25.

odds with one another, the illustrated woman acting as textual cover for the darker
subject matter of the poem. The poem also seemed to signal that losing her veil
and seeing clearly would make Lucilla a fallen woman too although it has already
become clear that her blindness gives her freedom. The illustrations for the serial
were in effect operating like the illustration for the poem since the text of the novel
also contradicted the picture of the demure heroine.

   This juxtaposition and the attempted reassertion of sanctification can be traced
in 'Chapter the Eleventh' which appeared as the fourth instalment of the serialized
novel on 23 September 1871. The instalment entitled 'Blind Love' followed
on immediately from 'The Blind Sleeper' and was especially arranged so that
its closing lines also closed the issue of the magazine. During the instalment,
Lucilla's half sister the three-year old Jicks has returned from a walk with blood
on her white dress and Madame Pratolungo's last words of the instalment were:
'Yes! – traced on the back of the child's frock, with a finger dipped in blood –
"HELP".'[236] This pronouncement had, however, been prefigured if not diluted by
the Hughes illustration on the first page of the serial instalment (see Figure 5.16).

---

[236] *CassM*, 23 September 1871, 64.

FOUND—A VEIL.

"PERCHANCE IT GAVE BUT A JEALOUS GLIMPSE."

SAUNTERING idly down a street,
   The busiest street in the busy city,
   I found—by the dust of a thousand feet,
      Soiled and torn—the theme o' this ditty:
Wondering much what untold tale
Might cling unseen in the folds of a veil.

Fancy was busy, and covered o'er,
   Unveiling again, a host of faces—
Blonde, brunette, and a myriad more
   Than tongue can tell for their unnamed graces :
A pity it was, when the mode began,
To hide such light from the eyes of man !

Fig. 5.15   Mary Ellen Edwards, 'Perchance it gave but a jealous glimpse,' illustration for H.G.B. Hunt, 'Found – AVeil,' *CassM*, 9 September 1871, 17.

POOR MISS FINCH.

A Domestic Story.

BY WILKIE COLLINS.

CHAPTER THE ELEVENTH.

BLIND LOVE.

LUCILLA was at the piano when I entered the sitting-room.

"I wanted you of all things," she said. "I have sent all over the house in search of you. Where have you been?"

"What are you going to do?" I asked.

"I want my hat and my stick," she answered.

"You are going out?"

"Yes."

"Where?"

"Can you ask the question? To Browndown, of course!"

"TRACED WITH A FINGER DIPPED IN BLOOD."

I told her.

She sprang to her feet with a cry of delight.

"You have persuaded him to trust you—you have discovered everything. You only said 'I have been at Browndown'—and I heard it in your voice. Out with it! out with it!"

She never moved—she seemed hardly to breathe —while I was telling her all that had passed at the interview between Oscar and me. As soon as I had done, she started in a violent hurry—flushed and eager—and made straight for her bedroom door.

I begged her to wait a moment, and hear a word or two that I had to say. It is, I suppose, almost needless to add that my object in speaking to her was to protest against the glaring impropriety of her paying a second visit, in one day, to a man who was a stranger to her. I declared, in the plainest terms, that such a proceeding would be sufficient, in the estimation of any civilised community, to put her reputation in peril. The result of my interference was curious and interesting in the extreme. It showed me that the virtue called

Fig. 5.16   Edward Hughes, 'Traced with a finger dipped in blood,' Chapter 11, *Poor Miss Finch, CassM*, 23 September 1871, 57.

In effect, Madame Pratolungo and Mrs Finch have already proleptically made their discovery of this message written on Jicks with the accompanying paraphrase which forms the title of the illustration "Traced with a finger dipped in blood".[237] The reference to blood was essential to create the required impact within a black-and-white illustration and there was little evidence that a finger had traced it other than in the explanation which was not supplied until the following week. In context, however, and despite the horror of the bloodstained child emphasised in word, this act of textual positioning was in fact designed both to defuse sensation and to distract the reader from Lucilla's forward and independent behaviour in wanting to visit Oscar at his house during this same instalment.

Such an approach by Cassell's can also be identified in the distraction techniques surrounding a miscarriage in *Man and Wife* serialized two years before, where another illustration competed with the written text. The governess Anne Silvester's pregnancy was portrayed and rewritten through the actions of both the illustrator William Small and the unsympathetic landlady of the Sheep's Head Hotel, Mrs Karnegie. In Collins's text Anne's miscarriage was daringly presented although still necessarily veiled. The dramatic illustration 'Done' depicted her faint which concluded the 13th instalment on 12 February 1870 and in the following week in the 22nd chapter of *Man and Wife*, Anne was reported to be 'in delicate health'. [238] On visiting a lawyer in Glasgow under an assumed name in episode 18 four weeks later she was 'seized with giddiness, and with some sudden pang of pain'.[239] In the next chapter on the same page of the magazine her landlady found her trying to write a letter 'her handkerchief twisted between her set teeth, and her tortured face terrible to look at'. The landlady later reported "'A child born dead"' and the blotted fragments of the letter were read by two witnesses.[240] The illustration for this episode was prioritized – as was 'Done' – on the front page of the magazine issue six pages before the incident, using the landlady's earlier words as a strapline: 'I say you are a married woman' which became as usual a secondary title for the instalment,[241] and appeared on the surface to reinforce a respectable married status.

Critics might read here a conflict between the illustrator and the novelist as well as a technical effect arising because of some delay in commissioning the illustration, situations which are documented in the careers of most serial novelists. William Small's collaboration with Collins has prompted some commentary from art historians about 'unpleasant' themes, and Forrest Reid observes of the *Man and Wife* illustrations in his seminal account of the period, 'No doubt they admirably fulfil their purpose as an echo of the text'. [242] The illustrations actually offered a

---

237   *CassM*, 23 September 1871, 57.

238   *CassM*, 12 February 1870, 193; 19 February 1870, 213.

239   *CassM*, 19 March 1870, 278.

240   *CassM*, 19 March 1870, 279.

241   *CassM*, 19 March 1870, 273.

242   Forrest Reid, *Illustrators of the Eighteen Sixties* (1928; repr., New York: Dover, 1975), 218.

superficial interpretation which competed with the final conclusions within the written text since Anne was not 'a married woman'. At the same time there were other items for the reader of the magazine which had already been presented in an intertextual relationship to this episode. The back page of the issue containing episode eight, ten weeks earlier had been occupied by an illustration and poem about a mother nursing at the fireside, 'All in White' by the enigmatic 'H'. At this point, Anne was still expecting the father of her child, Geoffrey Delamyn, to marry her, but the otherwise sentimental poem predicted death for mother and baby: 'They shall troop and sing with angels,/ All in white, all in white'.[243] In the instalment immediately preceding the miscarriage, a full-page poem and illustration was entitled 'The Broken Vow' in which a spurned woman was horribly disfigured when she saved her nephew, a 'baby-angel,' from death in a fire.[244] Later, when, for complicated legal and proper reasons, Anne did become Geoffrey's wife, this was picked up again in the poem 'Spinning' by Julia Goddard: 'She spins and dreams o'er the broken thread/ A dream of a broken vow'.[245]

It is partly because this was a family magazine that the intertextual commentary was so unrelenting. On 26 February, when Anne took flight to avoid Geoffrey's plot to marry her to another man, a filler poem defined the 'Model Husband' with a levity which was a gruesome juxtaposition with the situation in the novel.[246] On 7 May Edward Capern acclaimed 'Wedded Love' at the juncture when Geoffrey's wealthy alternative fiancée headed for the Lundie family's Scottish house, although this was tempered by the ensuing prose reflection 'In the Twilight', where 'the true heart and the ruined life are alike beyond your reach now'.[247] Similarly in Chapter 11 of *Poor Miss Finch* read in serial, the whole instalment competed with the representations of the veiled woman, the blind sleeper and an ongoing three-part serial entitled 'The Best Wife in the World' in which Amy Maitland collapsed dramatically in her quest to protect her husband's family honour and would be ill for three months to recover from it. This latter was an anonymous long short story serialized alongside the third, fourth and fifth instalments of *Poor Miss Finch* and given first station with dramatic illustrations for its first and third instalments.[248] The intervening un-illustrated instalment was displaced by another poem by 'H.' illustrated in imitation of an Old Master by Edward Hughes, ongoing illustrator of *Poor Miss Finch*. Amy must engage in some unwomanly detection in this instalment and so the story was masked for the reader by the poem which concluded, by way of introduction to the middle two chapters of 'The Best Wife', with an alternative 'song of love to a womanly Wife'.[249]

---

[243] *CassM*, 8 January 1870, 128.

[244] *CassM*, 12 March 1870, 272.

[245] *CassM*, 4 June 1870, 456.

[246] *CassM*, 26 February 1870, 240.

[247] *CassM*, 7 May 1870, 392.

[248] *CassM*, 16 September 1871, 33; 30 September 1871, 64.

[249] *CassM*, 23 September 1871, 50.

If the poems early on in the serial reinforced stereotypical compassion and resignation for a blind woman, the illustrations for the poems presented in the periodical during Lucilla's attempted cure and period of sight offered a different counterpoint. The illustrator of the poems was the popular female artist Mary Ellen Edwards who signed herself 'MEE'. Edwards worked for many of the periodicals of the day and continued to do so for some thirty years through two marriages although she is firmly termed a 'secondary illustrator' by art historian Simon Houfe, who adds that 'her drawings of domestic life never advanced beyond the competent and pretty.'[250] Forrest Reid describes her work as repetitive and monotonous, 'always precisely the same pretty maiden' although, by contrast, Barbara Onslow commends 'the versatility of her appeal'.[251] This was not the first time that Collins's text and Edwards's illustrations had appeared together. Edwards supplied 32 illustrations for *The Claverings* in *Cornhill Magazine*, and for five months between February and June 1866 Collins's much vilified novel *Armadale* appeared in tandem with Trollope's novel as the *Cornhill*'s second serial. In *Cassell's Magazine*, Edwards's women and their relationship with the poems acted as a foil to Edward Hughes's illustrations for *Poor Miss Finch* at the same time as adding materially to the contradiction of the blind woman's experiences.

A characteristically bold Edwards young lady 'Stood at Gaze' (see Figure 5.17) to adorn the opening page of the magazine on 2 December 1871. This effectively acted as a cover for the instalment of *Poor Miss Finch* in which Lucilla familiarly fingered the oculist Herr Grosse's sharp instruments. In the number where Lucilla mistook Nugent for Oscar through the collaboration of the sighted characters, Edwards illustrated the poem 'Led Captive' in which a bachelor was undone by the flowerily named Lily with her '[e]yes whose brightness could calm me or kill'[252] (see Figure 5.18). The flower illustrations continued with 'I love my love for her liquid eyes' to accompany 'The Crocus', the poem which prefaced Lucilla's first diary entry which she could see and write for herself (see Figure 5.19).[253] These women looked directly out from the page and were prioritized as the magazine's cover or frontispiece. The women reinforced the context for the sighted Lucilla's use of her own words in the text of her diary in the 21st, 22nd and 23rd instalments and they also faced outwards as Miss Finch was never allowed to do in the novel's illustrations. Finally, the eyes of the girl illustrating 'The Snowdrop', which acted as the cover to 'Lucilla's Journal Concluded', were downcast towards the flower 'Grasped in thy whiter hand', and Hughes's illustration for the same week showed Lucilla in a similarly downcast posture eight pages later (see Figures 5.20 and 5.21).[254] It was as if both women had been tamed, sanctified even, through their place in the periodical.

---

[250] Simon Houfe, *Dictionary of British Book Illustrators and Caricaturists (1800–1914)* (Woodbridge: Antiques Collectors Club, 1996), 128.

[251] Reid, 261; Barbara Onslow, *Press Women* (Basingstoke: Macmillan, 2000), 223; see also Skilton, 'The Centrality of Literary Illustration.'

[252] *CassM*, 16 December 1871, 242.

[253] The journal commences on page 318.

[254] *CassM*, 3 February 1872, 353; Lucilla is pictured on p. 361.

Fig. 5.17   (left) Mary Ellen Edwards, 'Stood at Gaze,' illustration for 'Over the Snow,' *CassM*, 2 December 1871, 209.
Fig. 5.18   (centre) Mary Ellen Edwards, 'Flower-crowned hair with the berries between,' illustration for 'Led Captive,' *CassM*, 16 December 1871, 241.
Fig. 5.19   (right) Mary Ellen Edwards, 'The buds of the crocus gay,' illustration for 'The Crocus,' *CassM*, 13 January 1872, 305.

"MISS BATCHFORD ROSE TO HER FEET."

"GRASPED IN THY WHITER HAND."

Fig. 5.20   (left) Mary Ellen Edwards, 'Grasped in thy whiter hand,' illustration for William Sawyer, 'The Snowdrop,' *CassM*, 3 February 1872, 353.

Fig. 5.21   (right) Edward Hughes, 'Miss Batchford rose to her feet,' Chapter 45, *Poor Miss Finch*, *CassM*, 3 February 1872, 361.

The illustrations and poems in the *Magazine* during the serialization of *Poor Miss Finch* demonstrate the technique of using intertextuality to reinforce respectability whilst allowing the *Magazine* to participate in the sensation trend. Hughes's illustrations for *Poor Miss Finch* were used to distract from or defuse the sensation of the serial but the Edwards women restored some of the dangerous elements of the sensation heroine in a technique which has been described as 'interpictoriality' or 'adjacency',[255] terms which apply to the effects observed here and in the *Cornhill* discussion above. Despite the respectable illustrations to the serial this 'counter narrative'[256] is made visible again when the text is seen with its original thresholds restored. As Patricia Anderson observes, it is the 'context for the picture which directs the reader-viewer's attention towards a specific message which may or may not be literally depicted'.[257] In *The Moonstone*, Gabriel Betteredge, Ezra Jennings and Miss Clack were allowed to narrate for themselves. In *Poor Miss Finch*, the competition between sensation and sanctification meant that Lucilla was allowed to see and then to narrate with the help of both Herr Grosse and the flower girls before she was re-assimilated into the 'domestic story' within *Cassell's Magazine*. At the same time, however, being saved from the wrong twin disguised the fact that it was her blindness which allowed her to pursue Oscar in the first place. Gladden describes the illness, foreignness and criminality in the novel as 'narratives of otherness'[258] but the counter narratives set against the serial in the magazine can be seen as further evidence of the competition between sales and respectability.

The overall effect of the serialization in *Cassell's Magazine* demonstrates how an invitation to publish collaboratively could permit taboo subjects to enter periodical discourse. The concepts of darkness and veiling and of women seeing and being seen are within the novel in its own right as well as being re-presented by the periodical text in which the original serial was embedded. The illustrations and poems operated 'interpictorially' to provide a competing commentary on sight and blindness. Both the novel and the magazine were concerned with the propriety of seeing, but further analysis discloses the tension generated by the amusement and instruction, sensation and sanctification which were the *Magazine*'s aims. In *The Moonstone*, alternate narrators are in competition for control of the narrative within an internally edited text. In *Poor Miss Finch*, narrative authority is

---

[255] See Linda K. Hughes, 'Inventing Poetry and Pictorialism in *Once a Week*: A Magazine of Visual Effects,' *Victorian Poetry* 48 (2010): 41–72.

[256] As discussed in Chapter 1, see Brian Maidment, *Reading Popular Prints 1790–1870*, 2nd ed. (Manchester: Manchester University Press, 2001), 9 and Judith L. Fisher, 'Image Versus Text in the Illustrated Novels of William Makepiece Thackeray,' in *Victorian Literature and the Victorian Visual Imagination*, ed. Carol T. Christ and John O. Jordan (Berkeley: University of California Press, 1995), 60–87.

[257] Patricia Anderson, *The Printed Image and the Transformation of Popular Culture 1790–1860* (Oxford: Clarendon Press, 1991), 58.

[258] Gladden, 483.

surrendered briefly to Lucilla Finch's diary before Madame Pratolungo restores the framework of control over the blind woman within which the sensation heroine nonetheless marries the man of her choice. *Poor Miss Finch* thus demonstrates the operation of the competitive discourses of sensation and sanctification set up by the serial in context. Although the volume edition of the novel originally published by George Bentley was un-illustrated, the sale of Cassell's single volume reprint of the *Magazine* in 1872 meant that in its time *Poor Miss Finch*, sanctified or not, was predominantly experienced and then reread in its serial context.[259] In 1875, the Chatto and Windus volume edition of *Poor Miss Finch* restored Hughes's original illustrations from the serial, and Lucilla was finally divorced from the competing illustrations and alternative intertextual gaze of the flower girls of *Cassell's Magazine*.

---

[259] See the discussion in Chapter 6.

Chapter 6
The Afterlife of the Serialized Novel

This final chapter examines the afterlife of the serialized novel by comparing the printed volume editions of the core novels and periodicals with their original serialized texts. The chapter concludes by proposing an outline model for examining the serial as narrative. The first two sections consider the existence of the novel after serialization, looking at the ways in which a serial became a collected piece of work. Among the core novels, this demonstrates a range of revisions as well as the re-visioning of the serials as closed texts. *Cranford* was issued in book form as if sequential despite the intervening timescales of the original publication, whilst *Poor Miss Finch* was sold as a single volume reprint containing 26 issues of *Cassell's Magazine* complete with all the original accompanying material.[1] Despite their original serial presentation, texts migrated into the market with some degree of reinterpretation. This might be demonstrated by the revisions of the author and editor as well as by new framing prefaces such as those of Craik and Collins, or through the future positioning of the novel in an outer facing series. That series might be grouped around an authorial identity such as that of Collins, Craik or Gaskell or be product-oriented such as the Barsetshire Chronicles.

The third section of the chapter moves on to discuss the volume edition of the periodical as another re-presentation of the serial through which the collected instalments might be read or reread. Again the collection might be grouped around the periodical itself or around the author, editor or series. Equally the series of both periodical and novel might represent a resale opportunity based on matching binding within a group of copyrighted works. In some cases a new product might emerge such as the memorial volume of *Good Words for 1862*. This has since become a significant text for visual studies based neither on the serial nor on the periodical but on the illustrations alone and, as will be demonstrated, it was an illustration as frontispiece which signalled the volume as a timed response to the first anniversary of the death of Prince Albert. The final section of the chapter briefly proposes an approach to the interpretation of the serialized novel as a narrative in its own right. This suggests ways in which access to periodicals broadens the study of the novel by reinstating its original material context.

Volume Editions: Gaskell, Collins and Dickens

Looking firstly at the immediate border between the serial and the volume, three well-known examples illustrate how a revised text could emerge from the process

---

[1]   The sequence of issues was originally dated 2 September 1871 to 24 February 1872.

of publishing a previously serialized work. *North and South, The Woman in White* and *Great Expectations* have migrated from their serialized form into the novels which are reprinted and re-edited today in ways which are indicative of the republishing process as a whole.

In a brief preface, Elizabeth Gaskell commended 'to the kindness of the reader' her two-volume edition of *North and South* published in 1855. She excused her revisions of the final chapters for the volume edition which had been rearranged from the text originally published in *Household Words*; in broad terms eight chapters of the novel were substituted for the last four chapters of the serial. *North and South* had been contracted as a serial to appear over a five-month period but a disagreement arose about how many weeks – and therefore instalments – this period comprised. In the event, 22 instalments ran from 2 September 1854 to 27 January 1855, two weeks longer than Dickens the editor had planned. The novel had been advertised on 26 August as a 'New Tale by the Author of MARY BARTON, to be published weekly in HOUSEHOLD WORDS.' It was clearly stated that '[t]he publication of this Story will be continued in HOUSEHOLD WORDS from Week to Week, and completed in Five Months.'[2] The author complained in private that Dickens had tried to limit the serial to 20 instalments but surviving letters indicate that Gaskell also struggled with the demands made by weekly publication. Only a few weeks before the final instalment was due to be published she wrote to Dickens on 17 December: 'What I send today is meant to be crammed and stuffed into Janry 20th; & I'm afraid I've nearly as much for Janry 27.' She asked the editor to shorten it for her without her involvement, for '[s]hortened I see it must be'; and in a postscript: 'Don't consult me as to the shortenings; only please yourself'.[3] She later told a friend that the space occupied by the novel was 'grudged' and that she was 'compelled to desperate compression'.[4]

Dickens, who had begun publishing the novel before the manuscript was completed, wrote to Wills as early as August 1854 that the serial's 'only means of being of service or disservice to us, mainly lay in its capacity of being divided at such points of interest as it possesses'.[5] This represented the very minimum formula for serialization on the 'pair of scissors' model criticized by the *British Quarterly Review*.[6] Gaskell wrote to a friend on 25 January 1855 that the management of *Household Words* had 'said "the public would expect me to keep my word" &c, – a

---

    2   *HW*, 26 August 1854, 24.

    3   Elizabeth Gaskell to Charles Dickens, 17 December 1854, Gaskell, *Letters*, 323. For a discussion of the disagreement, see J. Don Vann, 'Dickens, Charles Lever and Mrs Gaskell,' *Victorian Periodicals Review* 22 (1989): 64–71.

    4   Elizabeth Gaskell to Anna Jameson, January 1855, Gaskell, *Letters*, 328.

    5   Charles Dickens to W.H. Wills, 24 August 1854, R.C. Lehmann, *Charles Dickens as Editor* (London: Smith Elder, 1912), 145.

    6   See Chapter 3 for a discussion of 'Cheap Literature,' *British Quarterly Review*, 29 April 1859, 330–31.

word they had passed not I'.[7] This theme was echoed in her prefatory note to the volume; that 'this tale was obliged to conform to the conditions imposed by the requirements of a weekly publication, and likewise to confine itself within certain advertised limits, in order that faith might be kept with the public'.[8] To Maria James she vowed that she would never write for the periodical again and she bemoaned the 'pantomime figure' of her story. Her revisions for the volume edition fulfilled her declaration that she would 'try to add something to the separate publication to make it less unnatural, and deformed'.[9] She was seeing the serial or at least the weekly serial as an inferior art form despite its contribution to her reputation as a writer. At the same time she nonetheless mused whether the 'bounds and limits' imposed might not have produced a happy accident in bringing Margaret Hale and John Thornton together 'all smash in a moment'.[10]

Conversely, Wilkie Collins did not draw attention to the differences between the serialized and volume versions of his signature novel *The Woman in White* in the 1860 or 1861 volume editions. He had, of course, shown himself more amenable to the weekly format and proved that he was able to exploit its limitations to his advantage. The novel first appeared in *All the Year Round* from 26 November 1859 to 25 August 1860 but a chronological discrepancy of two weeks appeared in the meticulously plotted text. This affected the precise dating of Laura Fairlie's movements in the novel which crucially allowed her to be substituted for Anne Catherick after Anne's death. The date was so significant to Walter Hartright's case against Laura's husband Sir Percival Glyde that this error in dating should have caused the whole plot to unravel. E.S. Dallas commented in his review of the volume edition of the novel: 'A plot that is worked out of impossibilities, like that of robbing the almanac of a fortnight, may be treated as a jest; but we vote three cheers for the author who is able to practise such a jest with impunity.'[11] It would appear that the serial in *All the Year Round* had escaped the degree of scrutiny required to uncover Collins's error, and the volume edition at first replicated that error. The dating problem was then corrected in the 1861 edition and to this were added other adjustments made by Collins to suit a three-volume edition as opposed to the 32 breathless instalments in the periodical.

These examples from the work of Gaskell and Collins may be complemented by the much discussed case of *Great Expectations* whose serialized text was influenced even before its publication in *All the Year Round*. The serial concluded on 3 August 1861, a year after *The Woman in White*. Dickens had been persuaded by his friend, the author Edward Bulwer Lytton to replace the muted ending to the

---

[7]   Elizabeth Gaskell to Maria James, 25 January 1855, Gaskell, *Further Letters*, 123.

[8]   Elizabeth Gaskell, *North and South*, ed. Angus Easson and Sally Shuttleworth (Oxford: Oxford University Press, 2008), note after title page, 3.

[9]   Elizabeth Gaskell to Maria James, 25 January 1855.

[10]   Elizabeth Gaskell to Anna Jameson, January 1855.

[11]   *The Times*, 30 October 1860, 6. See Wilkie Collins, *The Woman in White*, ed. John Sutherland (1996; repr., Oxford: Oxford University Press, 1998), Appendix C, 662–8.

novel which he had already written. This unpublished ending would have caused Pip and the remarried Estella to remain apart after a chance meeting in London when she mistakes Pip's nephew for his son. The serial ending published on 3 August reunited Pip and Estella at Satis House, however, and the evening mists and the exit of the protagonists hand in hand famously echoed the end of *Paradise Lost*. Estella proposes that they 'will continue friends apart' and Pip concludes as narrator, 'I saw the shadow of no parting from her'.[12] Having first of all published an unchanged three-volume edition of the novel with Chapman and Hall in July 1861, Dickens amended the last line of the novel for a one-volume edition in November 1862 to read: 'I saw no shadow of another parting from her'. This implies that there will be a 'parting from her' but critics have not agreed that this rearrangement of the emphasis redressed the balance between the original progression of the novel in serial and its revised ending. E.D.H. Johnson observes that 'the original conclusion seems more commensurate with the novel's design'.[13] Biographer Michael Slater finds the pre-Lytton version a 'brilliantly economical downbeat ending ... resonat[ing] perfectly with this novel of ruined lives and lost illusions'. He owns that the revision might have retained some 'telling ambiguity' but that the "new" ending appeared on the surface romantic and conventional.[14]

These three examples from within the community of authors and editors discussed in preceding chapters indicate different strands of the afterlife of the serial revised outside the context of its station within a periodical. In the case of *North and South*, the serial was itself shaped to some extent by Dickens, not just in his selection of Gaskell for the novel portion of *Household Words* previously written only by himself but also in his demands as editor. As a result the serialization was a stepping stone to another version of the work represented by the volume edition. Gaskell was afterwards as we have seen an admirer of *Framley Parsonage* and its place in the lives of the readers of *Cornhill Magazine*, and her last novel *Wives and Daughters* proved to be more suited to monthly publication in the *Cornhill*. The serialized version of *The Woman in White* was effectively "found out" when the novel appeared as a bound volume; the serialization had disguised the flaw in its plot because the very format for reading had impelled subscribers forward and apparently given them no time or inclination for this level of critical evaluation. It was the volume edition which caused the serial to be revised as a result of the novel's being experienced in a different context although the original serial, of course, remained in place within the reprinted volume editions of the periodical. The instance of *Great Expectations* in *All the Year Round* demonstrates the influence of sales of the periodical over a serial in progress. The novel had been planned as a part work but appeared as a magazine serial in an attempt to revive flagging sales of *All the Year Round* in the wake of the conclusion of

---

[12]   *AYR*, 3 August 1861, 437.

[13]   E.D.H. Johnson, *Charles Dickens: An Introduction to His Novels (New York: Random House, 1969), 109.*

[14]   Slater, *Charles Dickens*, 495.

The Woman in White. The role of the editor has been discussed more fully in Chapter 3, but it is perhaps significant that Bulwer Lytton himself was the author of *A Strange Story*, the serial which succeeded *Great Expectations* in *All the Year Round* and thus that he had a vested interest in modifying the interface with his own contribution.[15] Dickens as editor himself could not apparently afford to ignore the potential problems of losing readers again through a misjudged ending at the interface between the closure of the novel, the open magazine content and the succeeding serial.

Volume Editions: the Novels

As Louis James points out, the book and the periodical demand a different form of commitment from the reader in terms of an investment in money and time.[16] Viewing the serial as a product on its way to being made whole as a reprinted bound novel, Mark Turner has observed that serialization is a marketing plan for a three-volume novel.[17] Turning specifically to those novels which have been discussed as collaborations in serial, it can be seen that the appearance of the volume edition of the novel and the volume edition or editions of the periodical impacted not only on sales but on the representation of the author, editor and text in the market.

The volume edition of *Cranford* was both a collection of sketches or papers and the consolidation of an act of memory and also a rehearsal for the much longer worked-out plot of *Wives and Daughters*. As Martin Dodsworth has observed: 'the two opening chapters was originally all that there was to be of *Cranford*; the rest is a happy accident'.[18] The volume editions of *Cranford* rewrite this process of evolution. The ninth occasional sketch, 'A Happy Return to Cranford', appeared in *Household Words* on 21 May 1853 and Gaskell herself revised the text for the book edition of June 1853. The original sketches which had appeared in four groups migrated into sixteen chapters with 'Friends in Need at Cranford' having its own chapter and 'The Great Panic at Cranford' becoming three chapters out of its two instalments; the other instalments became two chapters each. Gaskell also took the opportunity to rename her 'Miss Matey' as 'Miss Matty' and to restore the lost references to Dickens which the editor had substituted without her

---

[15]   *A Strange Story* by 'the author of "My Novel", "Rienzi", &c. &c.' appeared from 10 August 1861 to 8 March 1862.

[16]   Louis James, 'The Trouble with Betsey: Periodicals and the Common Reader in mid Nineteenth-Century England,' in *The Victorian Periodical Press: Samplings and Soundings*, ed. E.J. Shattock and Michael Wolff (Leicester: Leicester University Press, 1982), 351.

[17]   Mark W. Turner, *Trollope and the Magazines: Gendered Issues in Mid-Victorian Britain* (Basingstoke: Macmillan, 2000), 9.

[18]   Martin Dodsworth, 'Women Without Men at Cranford,' *Essays in Criticism* 17 (1963): 132.

permission in the manuscript of 'Our Society at Cranford' and later on in 'Stopped Payment at Cranford'.[19] Dickens's substitution of Thomas Hood, a contemporary writer who had died in 1845, for references to Boz and *Hoods Own* (published in 1838) for those to *Pickwick Papers* removed some of the original impact of Gaskell's tales in the voice of Mary Smith since Dickens was both more relevant as a living comparison with Dr Johnson and more current for the original readers of *Household Words*. In both serial and book Miss Jenkyns and the young Flora Gordon/Campbell read the volume edition of *The Rambler* at the end of the first instalment or second chapter, but Flora in the volume edition of *Cranford* has the opportunity to read *A Christmas Carol* supplied by Miss Matty rather than a poem by Hood as cited in the serial.[20] Miss Jenkyns and Captain Brown are both serial readers in their different ways but the Captain is highlighted as a reader in the moment when the *Pickwick* references are restored.

The collected edition of *Cranford* in turn omitted some of the linking passages which originally occurred at transitional points in *Household Words*. As discussed in Chapter 5, 'Our Society at Cranford' concluded with an exclamation from the narrator referring back to the Amazon discussion which opened it: 'Poor, dear Miss Jenkyns! Cranford is Man-less now.'[21] This gave some closure to the first instalment but was edited out of the volume. Mary Smith opened the second instalment with her 'latest intelligence of Our Society at Cranford' as the factual fiction writer of the periodical, and Gaskell excised this observation for the book version.[22] Typographical errors such as a 'fresh trait of villany (sic)' in the early sentences of the second chapter of 'The Great Panic at Cranford' were also amended, although that small error might have been perfectly characteristic of Miss Pole in her habitual exaggeration within the pages of the less formal magazine version.[23] What is notable is that this excision of material was a reverse of the practice commonly used when shorter pieces were collected from their original sources of publication. Wilkie Collins's *After Dark*, for instance, was published in 1856 with its newly composed framework of 'Leah's Diary'. Gaskell's own two-volume collection *Round the Sofa* was published by Sampson Low in 1859 and included *My Lady Ludlow*. For collected publication, the stories acquired a

---

[19]   In 'Stopped Payment', Mary Smith's father describes a Ladies' Committee using 'a passage in Hood, which spoke of a chorus in which every man took the tune he knew best, and sang it to his own satisfaction' (*HW*, 2 April 1853, 108). This was intended to be a reference to Chapter 32 of *The Pickwick Papers*.

[20]   In the original serial this was Hood's comic poem 'Miss Kilmansegg and her Golden Leg' (*HW*, 13 December 1851, 27) which did not have the localized resonance of Dickens's Christmas tale.

[21]   *HW*, 13 December 1851, 274.

[22]   *HW*, 3 January 1852, 349. As previously discussed, the term 'factual fiction' is used by Jennifer Phegley, 'Clearing Away "The Briars and the Brambles": The Education and Professionalisation of the *Cornhill Magazine*'s Women Readers 1860–65,' *Victorian Periodicals Review* 33 (2000): 25.

[23]   *HW*, 15 January 1853, 413.

framework of group storytelling around the sofa of the disabled Margaret Dawson who was already the narrator of *My Lady Ludlow* in its original serialized form.[24] *Cranford* retained some already existing transitional links provided by the periodical character of Mary Smith who had also evolved as narrator within the magazine. Instead of being a series of sketches within a complementary frame like *Round the Sofa*, however, *Cranford* migrated into the form of the standalone novella, its contextual linkages undone in being divorced from its place among the correspondents and subject matter of *Household Words*.

The reinstated references to Dickens and *Pickwick Papers* could not regain their potency since they were now divorced from the planned periodical context. Dickens's original editorial acts effectively undid the topical links which Gaskell was using to draw her story into the lives of periodical readers. In *Household Words* in December 1851 Miss Jenkyns rambled about *The Rambler* and about her part as Lucy in 'Old Poz' by Maria Edgeworth which was all that remained of the allusion to Boz. She mused: 'better than that strange old book, with the queer name, poor Captain Brown was killed for reading – that book by Mr. Hood, you know – Hood – Admiral Hood; when I was a girl; but that's a long time ago, – I wore a cloak with a red Hood.'[25] Aside from his own fears of over-exposure, Dickens may have been concerned at the time that the periodical audience was being confronted with an uncomfortable representation of its own reading practices. In the periodical as a whole, there was an ongoing tension between serialization and topicality within the safe bounds of nostalgia, and Gaskell's contemporary references would have put into *Household Words* some commentary on the contrast between reading styles and the consumption of texts. After all, Captain Brown, a railway reader, was cut down in the volume edition by his own heroic act after being engrossed in the latest episode of *Pickwick*. It must, however, be noted that even if 'Boz' was originally eliminated from the columns of the serial in *Household Words*, each page was headed throughout with the strapline 'Conducted by Charles Dickens'.

The immediate publishing afterlife of *Cranford* demonstrates the mingling of a new open text with a firmly closed one. Gaskell contributed 'The Cage at Cranford' to *All the Year Round* in 1863[26] as a sort of postscript to the serial but this piece was not collected into the last version of *Cranford* to be overseen by her which was published by Smith Elder in 1864. She had produced by this time the four-part *Cousin Phillis* for the *Cornhill* (November 1863 to February 1864) and *Wives and Daughters* was about to begin in the magazine in August 1864. These works signalled the beginning of the association of her publications with the illustrator George du Maurier who was employed by George Smith for both

---

[24]   *My Lady Ludlow* appeared in *Household Words* from 19 June to 23 September 1858 and was reprinted as Volume 1 of *Round the Sofa* in 1859.

[25]   *HW*, 13 December 1851, 274.

[26]   *AYR*, 28 November 1863, 332–6.

the serials.[27] The illustrated title page of the 1864 Smith Elder edition of *Cranford* firmly ruled *Household Words* out of the account by repackaging the novel with the image of Gaskell's new publisher. In fact, the illustration for the title page situated the publisher's address 'Smith Elder & Co. 65 Cornhill' quite literally within the Cranford street scene drawn by du Maurier.[28] Smith Elder would have been separating Gaskell from her Dickens connection with *Household Words*. Nonetheless, although Gaskell herself reused *Cranford* outside the periodical context, the account in Chapter 5 demonstrates how the novella and periodical are artistically interdependent.

Framley Parsonage was intrinsically linked with *Cornhill Magazine* from its first issue. This was the serial which helped to set the parameters of Thackeray's periodical with an enduring influence over its reputation. At the same time, the Barsetshire series became interlinked with the publishing house of Smith Elder. Looking back, Trollope provided a retrospective shape for the series of which this novel was a part when he wrote in his *Autobiography*: 'by placing Framley Parsonage near Barchester, I was able to fall back upon my old friends Mrs Proudie and the Archdeacon'.[29] The reuse of existing characters occurred throughout Trollope's novelistic career and those who followed his serials found this familiarity entertaining despite the negative response of some critics. Reviewing the volume edition in 1861 for instance, the *Examiner* observed prosaically that *Barchester Towers* was sequential to *The Warden* and *Framley Parsonage* was 'an appendix to them both'.[30] The reviewer in the *Saturday Review* denigrated those who take 'intellectual food ... monthly in the shape of magazines' and described *Framley Parsonage* as merely *BarchesterTowers* 'réchauffée'.[31] Trollope also explained in his *Autobiography* the reverse progression of his incidental series in that '*Barchester Towers* would hardly be so well known as it is had there been no *Framley Parsonage* and no *Last Chronicle of Barset*'.[32] The series eventually comprised *The Warden* (1855), *Barchester Towers* (1857) and *Dr Thorne* (1858) which appeared in volume format; *Framley Parsonage* (1861) and *The Small House at Allington* (1864) serialized in the *Cornhill* and *The Last Chronicle of Barset* (1867) in sixpenny monthly parts.

---

[27] See Thomas Recchio, *Elizabeth Gaskell's 'Cranford': A Publishing History* (Farnham: Ashgate 2009), 75–149. Hugh Thomson was later employed on the 1891 Macmillan edition and his work dominated the imagery associated with the novel through the twentieth century.

[28] See the reproduced frontispiece in *Cranford/Cousin Phillis*, ed. Peter Keating (1976; rep., London: Penguin, 1986), 35; this edition also reprinted 'The Cage at Cranford' as an appendix (327–38).

[29] Trollope, *Autobiography*, 142.

[30] *The Examiner*, 20 April 1861, 244–5; repr., *Trollope: The Critical Heritage*, ed. Donald Smalley (London: Routledge and Kegan Paul, 1969), 118.

[31] *The Saturday Review*, 4 May 1861, 451–2; repr., Smalley, ed., 121.

[32] Trollope, *Autobiography*, 104.

The Barsetshire association was in effect enough to make the pages of *Cornhill Magazine* a vehicle for Trollope's fiction for 30 monthly issues out of the first 52.[33] Having responded to the demands of his new contract in 1859 by 'falling back 'on his old friends, Trollope responded again to the never-ending seriality of Barsetshire by continuing the series with *The Small House at Allington* which appeared in the *Cornhill* from September 1862 to April 1864 on the *Framley Parsonage* model of three chapters per instalment.[34] The popularity of *Framley Parsonage* and its effect on the sales of the magazine gave Trollope additional leverage in negotiating the sale of the then unwritten novel since George Smith this time commissioned it directly from him.[35] It was arranged that rather than buying the copyright outright for £3,500 (a three and a half fold increase on the sum offered in 1859), Smith would pay Trollope £2,500 for *The Small House at Allington* and £500 for a licence to reprint the volume edition for 18 months after the serialization was completed. The serial had its outer-facing position as both the successor to *The Warden, Barchester Towers* and its other sequels and as one amongst other reading opportunities within the *Cornhill* as demonstrated in Chapter 5. Mark Turner comments that 'The intertextual relationship between *The Small House at Allington* and its Barsetshire predecessors, especially the most recent *Framley Parsonage*, would have comforted the readers who thought they knew exactly what they were getting'[36] but of course there was no happy resolution for the heroine of the later novel. Lily Dale stayed unmarried after being jilted in *The Small House at Allington* whereas Lucy Robarts in *Framley Parsonage* married Lord Lufton after her initial refusal. It would appear that as a result of his success in 1860–61 Trollope now had the confidence not to conform to romantic stereotypes although he later described his own creation (Lily) as a prig in his *Autobiography*.

In order to conclude this series which had begun with *The Warden* in 1855, Trollope and George Smith issued *The Last Chronicle of Barset* with illustrations by George H. Thomas as a sixpenny weekly in 32 parts between 1 December 1866 and 6 July 1867. Trollope had previously issued *Can You Forgive Her* in 20 monthly instalments of four chapters each between January 1864 and August 1865 and in his *Autobiography* he recalled that this was not a great success: 'The public finding that so much might be had for a shilling [i.e. in a magazine] in

---

[33] In fact, the very unsuccessful serial *The Struggles of Brown, Jones, and Robinson: By One of the Firm* appeared between August 1861 and March 1862 (a further eight months of the first 52) but the subject matter was very different. It did not appear in volume form until 1870 and in his *Autobiography* Trollope was candid about its failure.

[34] *Framley Parsonage* was completed in 16 instalments as opposed to 20 for *The Small House at Allington*. Trollope prevaricated in the *Autobiography* about whether the latter novel was part of the series.

[35] Smith wrote to Trollope on 24 June 1861 two months after the serialization of *Framley Parsonage* ended and the agreement was finalized on 6 July.

[36] Turner, *Trollope and the Magazines*, 20.

which a portion of one or more novels was always included, were unwilling to spend their money on the novel alone'. The sixpenny weekly parts did not prove 'altogether successful' either but the world of Barset had finally to be removed from the *Cornhill* influence in order to close the series with which both author and magazine had become so closely associated.[37] On the evidence of his *Autobiography*, Trollope felt like a murderer in narrating the sudden death of Mrs Proudie but at the same time he resisted any temptation to give his readers closure by having Lily Dale change her mind about marrying Johnny Eames. This pattern of character linkage and miscellaneous publishing arrangements was a feature of Trollope's authorial career. The linked Palliser series which also introduced characters and locations from Barsetshire had publication patterns ranging from weekly and monthly serialization to shilling monthly parts,[38] and John Sutherland has discussed how Trollope's own varied approach to copyright ownership gave him both the security of an income whilst also cheapening his own work through over-production.[39]

The three-volume edition of *The Moonstone* appeared as usual hard on the completion of Collins's serial within *All the Year Round*. In his Preface, Collins drew attention to his 'former novels' and thus his prior authorship by suggesting that he had 'reversed' his usual process of tracing 'the influence of circumstances on character'. He claimed that his new novel rather addressed 'the influence of character on circumstances', offering a succession or progression from his other novels. He also insisted that 'living authorities' had verified the opium experiment conducted by Ezra Jennings and that the diamond itself was only loosely based on the Koh-i-Noor.[40] These would appear to be issues questioned during the novel's serialization which were being anticipated and addressed for the volume edition. A letter to G.H. Lewes survives in which Collins describes the opium-induced re-enactment staged by Jennings as 'a certain physiological knot which threatens to start up in the texture of my new story' although it is unclear how Lewes assisted

---

[37]   The appearance of *The Last Chronicle of Barset* also overlapped with Trollope's last serialization within the *Cornhill*, *The Claverings* which appeared between February 1866 and May 1867 with illustrations by Mary Ellen Edwards.

[38]   *Can You Forgive Her* appeared in shilling monthly parts (January 1864 to August 1865) and in two separate volumes in October 1864 and June 1865. *Phineas Finn* was serialized monthly in *St Paul's Magazine* (October 1867 to May 1869) after the period of Trollope's own brief editorship. *The Eustace Diamonds* was serialized monthly in the *Fortnightly Review* (from July 1871 to February 1873); *Phineas Redux* was serialized weekly in *The Graphic* from 19 July 1873 to 10 January 1874; *The Prime Minister* appeared in eight shilling monthly parts (November 1875 to June 1876) and *The Duke's Children* was serialized in *All the Year Round* post-Dickens from 4 October 1879 to 24 July 1880.

[39]   See John Sutherland, 'The Fiction Earning Patterns of Thackeray, Dickens, George Eliot and Trollope,' *Browning Institute Studies* 7 (1979): 71–92. r

[40]   Wilkie Collins, 'Preface,' *The Moonstone*, ed. Sandra Kemp (London: Penguin, 1998), 3.

in this.[41] The difficulties in the composition process of *The Moonstone* are well known since Collins wrote a second preface to the one-volume edition of 1871 describing how the original serialization was affected by his own illness – with what he called 'rheumatic gout' – coinciding with the death of his mother. Like Gaskell and her 'faith ... kept with the public', Collins recalled his 'duty to the public [to his] good readers in England and in America whom I had never yet disappointed, [who]were expecting their regular weekly instalments of the new story'.[42] His new and returning readers three years on were invited to see how the act of composing the novel in serial form combined with their reading loyalty had affected his ability to carry on as a novelist: 'I doubt if I should have lived to write another book, if the responsibility of the weekly publication of this story had not forced me to rally'.[43]

Where Trollope used patterns of place and character to advertise the seriality of his authorship, Collins used the very serial experience of writing itself. He reminded his readers of their role in saving his life so that he could write more of the kind of novels they demanded. In writing to a plan and within the bounds of the serial, Collins was under contract for the book version and so anticipated the future appearance of the novel for which he offered his texts in a new frame for publication. His prefaces projected a revised reading experience at the same time as acknowledging the existence and importance of the serial version in marketing terms. In May 1871 when the second *Moonstone* preface was being written, he had already serialized *Man and Wife* in *Cassell's Magazine* and had agreed to supply *Poor Miss Finch*.[44] Whilst his ongoing authorship continued to be marketable, Collins was not successful in persuading George Smith that this one-volume edition of his last *All the Year Round* serial should feature a picture of the Moonstone itself on the cover so that the book might also be 'visible' on bookstalls.[45] Smith Elder did, however, take the precaution of reinforcing Collins's previous successes through the title page of 1871 where he was inevitably described as the 'author of "The Woman in White,"' but also of '"No Name," "Armadale," ETC. ETC.'[46] By this time the publisher owned the copyright of all four novels and both parties thus had a vested interest in identifying Collins firmly with those previous serials.[47]

Mistress and Maid appeared in two volumes published by Hurst and Blackett immediately after its serialization in *Good Words*. The text was divorced from its illustrations, an act which can be explained by the need for a lower price for the book version although the *English Woman's Journal* nonetheless bemoaned that it

---

[41] Wilkie Collins to G.H. Lewes, 20 April 1868, Collins, *The Public Face*, vol. 2, 112.

[42] Collins, *The Moonstone*, 5.

[43] Collins, *The Moonstone*, 5.

[44] *Man and Wife* concluded on 30 July 1870 and *Poor Miss Finch* commenced on 2 September 1871.

[45] Wilkie Collins to George Smith, 28 March 1871, Collins, *Letters*, vol. 2, 247.

[46] Collins, *The Moonstone*, 1.

[47] Smith Elder also produced the one-volume edition of *Man and Wife* in 1871.

was still 'beyond the reach of the maids, by whom it may be read with advantage'.[48] The twelve instalments were broken into these two volumes just before the August portion because, as we have seen, the May part was shorter and that for August longer by way of compensation. The longer section was also an opportunity to dissect the implications of Ascott's forgery and flight. The print size of the volume edition was larger and the volume itself smaller to encourage reading in snatched moments when light was poor and so that the book might be slipped into an apron pocket. In the Preface to Volume 1 Craik, under the aegis of 'the author of *John Halifax, Gentleman*', 'confesse[d]' that this was a book '"with a purpose"'. In her own respectable voice she expounded that purpose for writing which was implied but not explicitly stated in the serialized novel. She referred to the novel's original serialized version and asked that her tale be widely disseminated:

> that mistresses will send it down to the kitchen, that benevolent ladies who are Sunday school teachers and district visitors will lend it among the poor; ... It may thus reach the class for whom it was specially written, and with a view to whom it was originally published in "Good Words".[49]

The status and resonance of the periodical title were clearly part of her 'purpose' too.

Although the situation of the plot reflected some parts of her own life, Craik insisted in her preface that the 'incidents' of the novel were 'purely imaginary'. At the same time, she also used this personal statement to explain that the character of Elizabeth Hand was modelled on a real person. Whilst suggesting that her fiction could not do justice to the beautiful simplicity of the original, she excused the attempt as 'a tribute to the memory of the dead [and] as an incentive and ensample to the living'.[50] In the volume edition, of course, this description of 'a faithful servant' leads directly into the opening of Chapter 1. The serial had a different intertextual impact since the text of the chapter in *Good Words* was interpolated with the first illustration physically depicting Elizabeth in her interview with the Leaf sisters.[51] This differentiation between ostensibly identical texts continued at the end of the serial and of the second volume of the book where Elizabeth was described in both texts as still alive and unmarried. For the book she was thus being fictionalized based on the memorial tribute in the Preface. The novel's ending as a serial, however, – 'Elizabeth is still living' – retained the factual fiction approach carried over from Craik's persona in *Chambers's Edinburgh Journal*.

As corrected, refocused and continuous texts, the republished volumes represent some undoing of coherence for the serial which re-emerges full-length, fixed and uninterrogated by its original context. At the same time, the authors use prefatory material to remind readers of their original engagement with that serial.

---

48   *English Woman's Journal*, 2 February 1863, 427.
49   [Dinah Craik], *Mistress and Maid* (London: Hurst and Blackett, 1863), 1: v–vi.
50   [Craik], *Mistress and Maid*, 1: vi.
51   [Craik], *Mistress and Maid*, 1: 1.

Editors of modern editions supply indications of the serial breaks which help in the reconstruction of the instalment but this only goes as far as to recreate the serial as a part work. Since, however, the imprint of the serial remains on the novel once it becomes a full text outside the periodical, an important dimension of the original collaborative experience must still be recovered by revisiting that original context.

Volume Editions: the Periodicals

There was, however, another way in which the collected form of a serialized novel within a periodical could reappear and have an ongoing life: within the volume edition or editions of the periodical. The role of volume editions of monthly or weekly publications was to target a different audience and to bring together the collected issues as gifts or as demonstrations of learning. The newly bound volumes would enhance or replace the previously read issues in order to showcase the household's investment in reading over time. Thus, for instance, the 10 individual half-yearly volumes of *Household Words* had been 'neatly bound in Cloth' and priced at 5s, 6d since the periodical's launch in 1850.[52] On 20 January 1855, the magazine announced at the bottom of the final column: 'On the Third of February will be published, price 5s. 6d. cloth boards, THE TENTH VOLUME OF HOUSEHOLD WORDS. Containing, from No. 230 to No. 253 (both inclusive), and the Extra Christmas Number entitled THE SEVEN POOR TRAVELLERS'.[53] This material promised additional value for money to those collecting the matching bound volumes over time but with five years of publication completed, a new package of issues was also offered:

> [a]t the same time will be published, for greater convenience, and cheapness of binding, THE FIRST TEN VOLUMES OF HOUSEHOLD WORDS, IN FIVE HANDSOME VOLUMES, WITH A GENERAL INDEX TO THE WHOLE. Price of the Set, thus bound in Five Double instead of Ten Single Volumes, £2 10s. 0d.[54]

This would be a saving of five shillings over the half-yearly format and would create a uniform display for those who had not collected the earlier set.

Using the last of these five double volumes it would have been possible to read Dickens's *Hard Times* (in Volume 9) and Gaskell's *North and* South (just concluded in Volume 10) still embedded in the matter of the periodical. It must be debateable whether this was an easy task although not impossible for fireside reading aloud. When *Hard Times* was completed, an advertisement for the ninth

---

[52]   Advertised each time a volume was due; for instance *HW*, 28 February 1852, 552.

[53]   *HW*, 20 January 1855, 552.

[54]   *HW*, 20 January 1855, 552; repeated on 27 January.

volume drew attention to the fact that the novel was contained within it.[55] The same advertisement also announced the one volume edition of the novel 'revised and wholly reprinted' being published by Bradbury and Evans. On 20 January 1855 another 'Ten-volume' advertisement was headed rather tersely by the news that 'NORTH AND SOUTH By the AUTHOR OF MARY BARTON Will be completed in the next Number (no. 253)'.[56] The tenth volume was then never advertised as 'containing' *North and South* and although this might be the result of Gaskell's dispute with her editor, it may merely be explained by the fact that the volume edition of the novel was contracted to rivals Chapman and Hall.[57] The earlier *Cranford*, however, could only have been read within the volume by careful consultation of the new ten-volume index since the nine instalments appeared in four different volumes of *Household Words*. The first two sketches from Christmas 1851 appeared in Volume 4.[58] The third piece also appeared in Volume 4 but the second part of this second pair of sketches appeared in Volume 5[59] separated by a half-yearly and yearly division in volume terms although the originals were only three weeks apart in periodical time. This suggests once again how the sketches were intended to partake of the 'variety' of the periodical and could not yet be viewed as a reading whole.[60]

This process of advertising demonstrates how a publisher/editor would be keen to exploit all forms of the text – the weekly, monthly and half-yearly issues of the periodical, the volume editions of both novel and periodical – in order to encourage repeat purchases. Thus on 19 August 1854 the final column of *Household Words* also advertised 'the FIRST PORTION of a New Work of Fiction, called NORTH AND SOUTH. By the AUTHOR OF MARY BARTON ... [p]rice of each Weekly Number of HOUSEHOLD WORDS (containing, besides, the usual variety of matter), Twopence; or Stamped, Threepence'. It added that 'HOUSEHOLD WORDS, CONDUCTED BY CHARLES DICKENS, is published also in Monthly Parts and in Half-yearly Volumes.'[61] In a few lines were encapsulated the 'portion', 'number', 'part' and 'volume' as well as the authorial and editorial identities associated with the serialization and its 'variety of matter'. At this period, Dickens

---

[55] The final column on 19 August 1854 announced: 'The NINTH VOLUME of HOUSEHOLD WORDS (containing HARD TIMES), price 5s. 6d., was published on the 16th instant' (HW, 19 August 1854, 24).

[56] *HW*, 20 January 1855, 552; also, a week earlier, North and South '[w]ill be completed on the Twenty-Seventh of January' reiterating the extra two numbers which Gaskell had negotiated (*HW*, 13 January 1855, 528).

[57] The gesture was also not made towards Wilkie Collins's first serial *The Dead Secret* (which appeared in Volume 15 of *Household Words* before Collins's wider popularity in *All the Year Round*) although it was published as a novel by Bradbury and Evans themselves.

[58] Originally published on 22 March 1852 (*HW*, 13 March 1852, 600).

[59] Announced for publication on 20 September (*HW*, 4 September 1852, 596).

[60] The indexing of the Cranford sketches is discussed in Chapter 4.

[61] *HW*, 19 August 1854, 24.

himself manipulated the half-hidden monthly pattern with his ongoing *A Child's History of England* which appeared once a month, although not strictly at monthly intervals, between 25 January 1851 and 10 December 1853. The advertisement for the 'First Portion' announced that it 'will be continued, at regular intervals, until the History is completed'.[62] Collected volumes of the *History* were also announced which picked up the need for conformity of appearance and the display of acquired knowledge. Thus the first volume was ready by 10 April 1852 and the *History* would '*be completed in three Volumes, of the same size and price* .Collected and revised from "Household Words", With a Table of Dates' for added value.[63] It is interesting that the conclusion of this work as a serial demonstrates Dickens's double standard when later dealing with Gaskell's 'faith ...with the public'. The first 38 instalments 'at regular intervals' traced the history of England from the Ancient Britons to 1688 against the unfolding timescale of *Household Words* from week to week. The final instalment began 'I have now arrived at the close of my little history' and then brought history giddyingly, abruptly and rather tetchily up to date to 1853 with the closing words 'GOD SAVE THE QUEEN!'[64] A serial often concluded with a double-length instalment but by contrast this one was not even a quarter of the usual length and less than a page of the magazine, albeit in its customary final station. Michael Slater observes that Dickens had 'become tired of the thing' and that the collected issues did not sell well. [65]

The seriality of *Household Words* as a periodical was about the familiar elements and tone which each issue created for the contemporary reader. Fiction was less prominent and the tension created by the overarching relationship between reader and periodical was dependent on the weekly renewal of contact. *All the Year Round* increased and regularized the fictional content and relied, as Dickens famously stated at the end of the serialization of *A Tale of Two Cities*, on 'a continuous original work of fiction'.[66] He promoted the idea of making a contract with his readers by explaining that such a work would occupy 'about the same amount of time in its serial publication, as that which is just completed', and this was the immediate gateway to *The Woman in White* which would occupy the 'station' now vacated by Dickens's novel.[67] The first five novels in *All the Year Round* had varying impacts on the periodical's fortunes with *Great Expectations* brought in to rescue it when Charles Lever's *A Day's Ride* proved less popular as discussed in Chapter 3. Collins's *No Name* which would follow on from *A Strange*

---

[62]   *HW*, 18 January 1851, 408.

[63]   *HW*, 10 April 1852, 92. The second volume was announced in *HW*, 12 March 1853, 92.

[64]   *HW*, 10 December 1853, 360.

[65]   Slater, *Charles Dickens*, 360–61.

[66]   *AYR*, 26 November 1859, 95.

[67]   *AYR*, 26 November 1859, 95; this boundary is discussed in Chapter 3 and in Catherine Delafield, *Women's Diaries as Narrative in the Nineteenth-Century Novel* (Farnham: Ashgate, 2009), 108–9.

Story starting on 15 March 1862 was promised over six months before its eventual appearance so that Collins's work once again appeared at a significant boundary.[68] These novels (apart from *A Strange Story*) overlapped within issues of *All the Year Round* and each one spanned two volumes of the periodical. *A Tale of Two Cities* ended in the issue when *The Woman in White* began on 26 November 1859. *The Woman in White* and *A Day's Ride* overlapped for two issues on 18 and 25 August 1860. *A Day's Ride* was then removed from first station when *Great Expectations* took over on 1 December 1860 but carried on in tandem for 17 more instalments until 23 March 1861. *A Tale of Two Cities* could be read in Volumes 1 and 2 of *All the Year Round*, *The Woman in White* in Volumes 2 and 3, *A Day's Ride* in Volumes 3 and 4, *Great Expectations* in Volumes 4 and 5 and *A Strange Story* in Volumes 5 and 6.

These are clearly tactics to encourage the ongoing purchase of the periodical issues and volume editions, and to fulfil the public duty which Dickens imposed on serializing authors. An advertisement for the seventh volume of *All the Year Round* also demonstrates how much more potent the extra fiction content was in promoting the volume editions. On 13 September 1862 with *No Name* half completed, the advertisement read:

> *The Six preceding Volumes are always to be had. They include the following Novels:*—A TALE OF TWO CITIES, AND GREAT EXPECTATIONS. BY CHARLES DICKENS. THE WOMAN IN WHITE. BY WILKIE COLLINS. A DAY'S RIDE, A LIFE'S ROMANCE. BY CHARLES LEVER. A STRANGE STORY. BY SIR EDWARD BULWER LYTTON.[69]

With *Great Expectations* moved forward in the list, the three novels which made *All the Year Round* successful could be prioritized over the two from which it had to be rescued.

The weekly pattern under Dickens seems more to suggest a serial building into a completed novel whilst the monthly equivalent is presented as a completed novel divided into sixteen or twenty serialized parts. Trollope's novels spanned at least three volumes of the *Cornhill*, and this was partly because the fiction serial portion of the six-monthly collected volume was meant to be equivalent to one volume of a book edition. A publisher would be looking at this transmutation into hard covers as part of the original negotiation as George Smith was with Trollope over *Framley Parsonage*. The extent to which the volume edition of the periodical interacted with the rereading of the novel as a serial within that periodical is difficult to gauge. At the time of serialization, of course, *Framley Parsonage* appearing monthly was still being composed, contrary to Trollope's subsequent practice. Factual serials could also, however, be collected in the volumes of the *Cornhill* such as Lewes's 'Studies in Animal Life', Sala's 'William Hogarth' and

---

[68]   *AYR*, 3 August 1861, 437.
[69]   *AYR*, 13 September 1862, 24.

Thackeray's 'The Four Georges'.[70] Thackeray's editorial 'Roundabout Papers' which concluded many numbers of the magazine appeared bi-monthly until July 1860 for collection into Volume 1, then monthly for the second volume up to December 1860. The collected edition of 32 'Roundabout' sketches was reordered for publication in 1863 but the pieces retained the character of 'factual fiction', reflecting their original timed and topical appearance in the periodical.[71] The *Cornhill* also offered a second piece of fiction to accompany *Framley Parsonage* as has been shown in Chapter 5.[72] Although Thackeray's *Lovel the Widower* could be acquired in one volume of the periodical – the first – along with the first series of 'Studies in Animal Life', the volume still did not represent a convenient way to revisit the serial especially when the demands of production or the need for balance and variety within a single issue disrupted patterns of presentation. Instead the volume acted as a sign of fidelity to the chosen title, reminding readers of their educational and aspirational goals as consumers and as partakers around Thackeray's 'table'.

Mistress and Maid was timed to appear exactly within the volume edition of *Good Words for 1862* in 12 monthly instalments. The embedded illustrations by Millais which always appeared on the opening page reinforced the pattern of the serialization but this was disrupted for the final instalment in December 1862. The repositioning of the twelfth illustration is a marker of the re-composition of the volume edition of *Good Words* as a highly topical memorial or themed text overarching the individual numbers. The text of the novel had acted as a consistent thread across the issues but that final instalment with the repositioned illustration participated in the wider retrospective project of mourning Prince Albert. Rather than depicting an incident in the closing chapters of the novel or advertising its broader content, this illustration effectively acted as the boundary to a new composition or marketable commodity which memorialized the Prince.[73]

Topical elements of *Good Words* month by month were retained in their original form but the effect of the reprint was to accumulate the readings, poems and prayers into this new product when the whole was reproduced as an annual. In chronological sequence, the poem 'Our Widowed Queen' had appeared as a

---

[70] 'Studies in Animal Life' (CM 1, January to June 1860) was published in volume form in 1862; 'William Hogarth' (CM 1, February to June 1860; CM 2, July to October 1860) appeared with illustrations in 1866 and 'The Four Georges' (CM 2, July to October 1860) originated as an American lecture tour and was published with illustrations in 1861.

[71] W.M. Thackeray, *Roundabout Papers: Reprinted from 'The Cornhill Magazine'* (London: Smith Elder, 1863).

[72] Alongside *Framley Parsonage* were Thackeray's *Lovel the Widower* (*CM* 1, January to June 1860) and *The Adventures of Philip* (*CM* 3, January to April 1861; concluding in *CM* 4, August 1862). See Chapter 5 for a discussion of the order of presentation over the sixteen instalments.

[73] This is also discussed in Catherine Delafield, 'Marketing Celebrity: Norman Macleod, Dinah Mulock Craik, and John Everett Millais in Alexander Strahan's *Good Words*,' *Victorian Periodicals Review* 46 (2013): 267–71.

supplement within the issue of January 1862, immediately after the concluding serial item 'Our Sunday Evenings: *A Series of Papers for Family Reading*'.[74] This was very timely following the death of the Prince only a few weeks earlier on 14 December 1861. In May 1862, a poem by Alexander Smith was published recalling the Prince's visit to Scotland and in August the article 'On Solitude' referred again to the prince 'whom we so recently lost'.[75] In June, Craik herself bemoaned 'the want of that guiding Head' which was provided by the Prince for the Great Exhibition eleven years earlier, and she concluded her article with a peroration on 'the originator of it all, now a disembodied soul'.[76] *Good Words for 1862* was then published close to the first anniversary of the Prince's death. The twelfth illustration for the final instalment of *Mistress and Maid* was bound in as a frontispiece and was thus coincidentally brought into proximity with the poem originally published in January (see Figure 6.1).

This illustration clearly had a funereal subject and was meant to appear in serial time in December. In the annual volume it was physically positioned before the first instalment of the novel which originally appeared in January 1862. This image of a mourning woman would certainly have jarred if it had been positioned as usual on the first page of the serial's final instalment which had opened in December 1862 with the words: 'Let us linger a little over this chapter of happy love'.[77] Based on the content of this final instalment, the illustration for that month's issue should have depicted Elizabeth Hand mourning Tom in Kensal Green cemetery. In the serial, the servant reflected on the happiness in the Leaf family at Ascott's return '[b]ut happy as everybody was, there was nothing so close to Elizabeth's heart as the one grave over which the snow was now lying, white and peaceful, out at Kensal Green' and thus befitting a December instalment.[78] The woman pictured, however, is neither the physically solid, round-faced Elizabeth nor indeed the bereaved Queen Victoria but rather the slim and conventionally beautiful Hilary mourning her sister Selina at her Stowbury monument. As discussed in Chapter 5, this is not an incident in the novel. Craik and more specifically Millais have created a heroine who is beautiful and statuesque despite her struggles with poverty and family responsibilities, and it is she who is pictured in the frontispiece of the volume. This can be demonstrated by comparison with earlier images throughout the serialization, images which were still to come in this reprint of the year's issues.[79] The use of the repositioned illustration as a frontispiece which is both part of the serial but also set apart reinforces the billing of Millais on the facing title

---

[74]   *GW* 3 (1862): 64.

[75]   Alexander Smith, 'Wardie – Springtime,' *GW* 3 (1862): 273; Aeneas Sage, 'On Solitude,' *GW* 3 (1862): 473.

[76]   [Dinah Craik], 'Five Shillings' Worth of the Great World's Fair,' *GW* 3 (1862): 327.

[77]   *GW* 3, 737.

[78]   *GW* 3, 751.

[79]   See the February 1862 illustration of Hilary teaching Elizabeth to read (*GW* 3, 97, *DMVI*, MM003) for a direct comparison.

MISTRESS AND MAID.

Fig. 6.1   J. E. Millais, Frontispiece to *Good Words for 1862*.

page and is also a sign of the re-presentation of the volume edition as a memorial which partakes of the monarch's grief.

Good Words for 1862 thus disrupted the pattern of editorials and timed scripture readings for every evening in order to respond to the timing of a particular event. It was also targeting a new audience: one which could both afford the collected issues and read the subtext of loyal sympathy to the Queen channelled through Hilary in mourning. Exerting control over her own boundaries, Craik used the Preface to the two-volume book edition of the novel to describe Elizabeth Hand as an 'ensample to the living ... literally and faithfully painted'.[80] This 'faithful painting' was distorted for the volume edition of the periodical to fulfil the demands of the publisher. It was the book edition of *Mistress and Maid* that re-emphasized the original 'purpose' and focus of Craik's novel by using as its frontispiece a steel-engraved version of the February serial illustration of Hilary and Elizabeth which was a direct depiction of mistress and maid.

In the case of *Poor Miss Finch*, the ongoing existence of the novel in the volume edition of the periodical for 1872 was a significant factor in the afterlife of the serial. George Bentley published the three-volume un-illustrated book edition on 26 January 1872, five weeks before the final instalment of the serialized version appeared in *Cassell's Magazine* on 24 February. Collins supplied an elaborate dedication to this edition addressed to his old friend Frances Elliott (*née* Dickinson). Her unconventional lifestyle was glossed over by her actual address, 'Mrs Elliott (of the Deanery, Bristol)' which was the literal heading to the preface.[81] Collins used this dedication to insist that he was 'exhibiting blindness as it really is' as opposed to its sentimental portrayal in other fiction.[82] He had received letters from people wanting to be put in touch with the surgeon Herr Grosse and at the time he wrote to Arthur Locker, editor of *The Graphic*: 'The vile periodical system of publication is partly to blame for the vain hopes which I have innocently raised.'[83] In periodical time Lucilla has had her operation on 9 December 1871 and then relapsed into total blindness eight weekly instalments later on 3 February 1872. In his preface Collins claimed that he aimed to console blind people through the now finished book by demonstrating that 'happiness can exist independently of bodily affliction' and that in fact Lucilla's 'blindness and her happiness are made to be conditional'.[84] He thus differentiated again between the serial and the book since the unfolding story in *Cassell's Magazine* did not have a published ending

---

[80]   [Craik], *Mistress and Maid* (1863), 1: vi.

[81]   Catherine Peters suggests that this was a private joke in public (*The King of Inventors: A Life of Wilkie Collins* (London: Minerva Press, 1991), 332).

[82]   Wilkie Collins, *Poor Miss Finch*, ed. Catherine Peters (1995; repr., Oxford: Oxford University Press, 2000), xxxix. See the discussion of Bertha Plummer in *The Cricket on the Hearth* and Muriel Halifax in *John Halifax, Gentleman* in Chapter 5.

[83]   Wilkie Collins to Arthur Locker, 18 January 1872, Collins, *The Public Face*, vol. 2, 314–15.

[84]   Collins, *Poor Miss Finch*, xl.

at the time of her "cure" whereas the book appeared as a whole, incorporating the outcome of the relapse.

As with the 'physiological knot' in *The Moonstone*, Collins nonetheless used the *Poor Miss Finch* book preface to reinforce the events of the novel by claiming 'competent authorities of all sorts' for Lucilla's experience. He referred obliquely to his ongoing disputes with Cassell, Petter and Galpin when he described his observation of character as 'misunderstood – sometimes even resented – in certain quarters.'[85] The removal of a 'damnit' from an early instalment of *Man and Wife* had been the beginning of some unease on the part of Cassell, Petter and Galpin over the conduct of their new star novelist within the family magazine.[86] It seems likely that his allusions to Elliott's marital complications were part of this same confrontation and of his approach to his own authorial persona. He had already dwelt on marriage irregularities in *Man and Wife* and in his intervening novella *Miss or Mrs?* written for *The Graphic* Christmas number in 1871. In the 1872 Preface, he actually threatened his public and his publisher with manuscripts currently locked in a drawer which might fictionalize Elliott's story.

There was also a more significant disagreement with the publisher about the volume edition of *Poor Miss Finch*.[87] Where *Man and Wife* had spanned the first two volumes of *Cassell's Magazine*, *Poor Miss Finch* was contained within Volume 4 and it was thus that Cassell, Petter and Galpin were able legitimately to produce their own single volume reprint of *Poor Miss Finch*. The serial presented in volume form within the periodical was accompanied by the 'matter' of the magazine, retaining its weekly appearance. In Volume 4 the first episode was dated 2 September 1871 but the remaining issues of the *Magazine* ran on without further dating. The sales of this volume at 4s, 6d undermined those of the book version of *Poor Miss Finch* which cost 27 shillings more at a guinea and a half. Cassell's special edition of the novel in serialized format complete with illustrations and poems was the version available in Smith's Circulating Library which waited until March 1872 to buy *it* rather than the edition Collins had contracted with Bentley. Mudie's Library bought from Bentley on less favourable terms and Collins was forced to offer to revert to commission and to agree to a less profitable one-volume edition published in 1873 at six shillings.[88] As a collected text *Poor Miss Finch* was therefore still being widely consumed in its magazine format accompanied by editorial matter dictated by the periodical publishing house. The sanctification of

---

[85]   Collins, *Poor Miss Finch*, xxxix.

[86]   As discussed in Chapter 2, there are letters extant disputing contracted payments for *Poor Miss Finch* in which Collins grandly claimed that he deserved as much money for the shorter serial (Wilkie Collins to Cassell, Petter and Galpin, 25 September 1869, Collins, *The Public Face*, vol. 2, 152).

[87]   Wilkie Collins to Cassell, Petter and Galpin, 30 September 1871, Collins, *The Public Face*, vol. 2, 291.

[88]   Wilkie Collins to George Bentley, 22 March 1872, Collins, *The Public Face*, vol. 2, 335. See also Peters, *The King of Inventors*, 330.

the *Magazine* with its 'edification by weekly instalments' could therefore pervade the novel even after Collins was released from his contract with Cassell's.[89]

The periodical volume had varying impacts on the afterlife of the serial. These ranged from the preserved original reading format of *Poor Miss Finch* in *Cassell's Magazine* to the reframed memorial of *Good Words* and Dickens's usefully indexed 'greater convenience, and cheapness of binding'. The marks of seriality were written on the text of the novel itself but that text was also affected by the 'matter' in which the novel was still embedded. New features appeared as a result of exterior re-presentation in the collected volumes of the periodical. *Poor Miss Finch* thus reappeared as an embedded text with its wrappings intact because of Cassell's reprinted version. Alexander Strahan harnessed the illustrated serial to exploit his editor Macleod's royal connections in the periodical volume, but *Mistress and Maid* appeared as a novel shorn of its links with topical material and illustrations in order to focus on Craik's 'purpose' and to make the novel available to a target audience. Any study of a novel which appeared in serial form thus benefits from the ability to read around the text of the novel itself and to act like Trollope by 'falling back' or revisiting the serialized novel reconstructed within the volume edition of the periodical.

The migration into the novel format which excised the serial from other matter is worthy of examination in understanding the original material text of the serial. As we have seen, the original book editions were often prefaced by some accounts of the serial experience such as Collins's with blind people or of Gaskell's with her own editor. This final chapter has suggested ways in which an understanding of the collaborative and sometimes competitive serialization process should complement that of the re-readings which have followed. A consideration of the afterlife of the serialized novel as a published volume indicates how the serialized and volume formats should be differentiated in the study of the nineteenth-century novel.

Studying the Serialized Novel

The novel serialized within the nineteenth-century periodical had a timed and temporal existence before its appearance in volume form, and the novel can be recovered and reread as a text within other texts, as a narrative with multiple narrators, as fiction within the fictionalized facts of periodical discourse. Restoring the novel to its original context means that a range of questions can be answered about the narrative form of the serial within a periodical. This final section reviews serialization as a factor in the narrative form and briefly sums up the process of serialization encoded by its dialogic, intertextual and contextual forms.

Until the pioneering work of the Internet Library of Early Journals, access to the original form of the serialized novel in paper form was through the volume collected in a library. It was not always possible because of cataloguing or other

---

[89]   [D.E. Williams], *The Athenaeum*, 17 February 1872, 202–3; see the discussion in Chapter 3.

storage irregularities to find volumes of a periodical intact or in easily readable condition. Access is now being greatly increased by the availability of digitized versions of the periodicals such as those provided by the Dickens Journals Online project and the Internet Archive. Background material can be more readily accessed through other sample resources such as the Nineteenth-Century Serials Edition, SciPer and the Database of Mid Victorian Illustration. Large-scale digitization is being undertaken by ProQuest and Cengage, and this opens up the field of periodical studies in general and illuminates the serial in many guises. As a result, serial fiction can now be read in what Mark Turner calls 'a cultural framework of institutions and material conditions',[90] and the possibility of revisiting and (re)interpreting the novel in context is thus becoming more readily available to students and scholars.

Serialization and the Novel in Mid-Victorian Magazines has used the timed existence of the nineteenth-century serialized novel within a dated periodical to unlock re-readings and reinterpretations of the novel as a commodity of its time. Laurie Garrison points out that 'the periodical as a genre can offer opportunities for expression between the lines and in the margins of its pages'.[91] The periodical can be viewed through the bibliographic placement of text on a page through its columns, breaks, headings, advertisements, borders and boundaries. The serialized novel partook of these material conditions and was given form within the publisher's mission, the periodical's goals, the author's career and the topicality of the original issue. A model for the study of the serialized novel within the nineteenth-century periodical should therefore interrogate the influence of the editor and publisher in addition to that of the author. *Serialization and the Novel in Mid-Victorian Magazines* has highlighted these participants in the serial along thematic lines in Chapters 2–4 although some liberties have been taken with the elusive characteristics of the readers' response.

A four-part approach can then be extrapolated from the analysis conducted here, looking at the periodical frame, the function of authorship, the overall rhythm of production, and the intertextual patterns within and between numbers of the periodical. It is firstly important to identify the immediate periodical thresholds or 'paratexts' within which the serialized novel was presented in order to establish what Hughes and Lund have termed the 'specific material framework that shaped response'.[92] Secondly the function of authorship both outside and within the periodical should be considered, taking into account the practice of naming and anonymity and the roles of the editor and publisher as collaborators. Thirdly, detailed consultation of the periodical as published (although usually in volume

---

[90]   Turner, *Trollope and the Magazines*, 238.

[91]   Laurie Garrison, 'Seductive Visual Studies: Scientific Focus and Editorial Control in *The Woman in White* and *All the Year Round*,' in *The Lure of Illustration in the Nineteenth Century*, ed. Laurel Brake and Marysa DeMoor (London: Palgrave Macmillan, 2009), 182.

[92]   Linda K. Hughes, and Michael Lund, *The Victorian Serial* (Charlottesville: University Press of Virginia, 1991), 9.

form only) should demonstrate the means by which the serial was embedded in that periodical including the intertextual patterns, competing and complementary, set up by other serials and articles. This must be combined with an understanding of the 'station' of the novel instalments within the periodical to assess both the valorization of the serial in context and its dialogic impact as an embedded text. Finally, the model should also account for the effect of the serial's progression, including the influence of divisions between instalments on plotting within novel and periodical, the rhythm of the instalments whether weekly or monthly and the impact of the advertised and actual timeframe of completion. Elizabeth Gaskell thought that *North and South* was 'deformed' by the process of composition in weekly parts but the 'advertised limits' offered both the promise of a continuation and the expectation of an ending, a serial always 'to be completed' at a date contracted by the publisher with the audience 'that faith might be kept with the public'.

The intertextuality of the serial within the periodical enhances an understanding of the cultural significance of the text as the discussion in Chapter 5 has demonstrated. The availability and accessibility of online versions of the periodicals is illuminating that dimension of the novel as a serial which can be recovered and re-examined using the additional evidence of contextual material, illustrations and editorial strategy. The "inferior" form of the serial may have unfolded without the sanction of library or bookseller. It may then have been corrected by a volume edition which could fix the novel between hard covers, safe from the ongoing timeframe of serialization. A modern edition may now regard the serial version of the novel as a bibliographical curiosity, to be discussed in a further preface and consigned to the footnotes. *Serialization and the Novel in Mid-Victorian Magazines* has demonstrated, however, that the serial should not be afforded the status of an imperfect original but rather identified as a creative collaboration between author, editor and periodical. The understanding of the novel can be both revisited and enriched at this intersection of reading, serialization and the periodical publication of fiction.

Appendices

Appendix 1   Selected Serialized Novels

Novel	Periodical	Serialization	Frequency (No. Instalments)	Illustrated By (No.)
Cranford	*Household Words*	13 December 1851; 3 January, 13 March, 3 April 1852; 8 & 15 January, 2 April, 7 & 21 May 1853	Intermittent in weekly publication (9)	
Bleak House	Part work	March 1852–September 1853	Monthly (20)	Phiz (38)
Hard Times	*Household Words*	1 April–12 August 1854	Weekly (20)	
North and South	*Household Words*	2 September 1854–27 January 1855	Weekly (22)	
The Dead Secret	*Household Words*	3 January–28 March 1857; 11 April–13 June 1857	Weekly (23)	
My Lady Ludlow	*Household Words*	19 June–23 September 1858	Weekly (14)	
A Tale of Two Cities	*All the Year Round*	30 April–26 November 1859	Weekly (31)	
The Woman in White	*All the Year Round*	26 November 1859–25 August 1860	Weekly (40)	
Great Expectations	*All the Year Round*	1 December 1860–3 August 1861	Weekly (36)	
Framley Parsonage	*Cornhill Magazine*	January 1860–April 1861	Monthly (16)	John Everett Millais (6)
Mistress and Maid	*Good Words*	January–December 1862	Monthly (12)	John Everett Millais (12)
No Name	*All the Year Round*	15 March 1862–17 January 1863	Weekly (44)	

Appendix 1 (continued)

Novel	Periodical	Serialization	Frequency (No. Instalments)	Illustrated By (No.)
The Small House at Allington	Cornhill Magazine	September 1862–April 1864	Monthly (20)	John Everett Millais (18); also 19 vignettes
Cousin Phillis	Cornhill Magazine	November 1863–February 1864	Monthly (4)	George du Maurier (1)
Our Mutual Friend	Part work	May 1864–November 1865	Monthly (20)	Marcus Stone (40)
Wives and Daughters	Cornhill Magazine	August 1864–January 1866	Monthly (18)	George du Maurier (18)
Armadale	Cornhill Magazine	November 1864–June 1866	Monthly (20)	George Housman Thomas (20); also 20 vignettes
The Last Chronicle of Barset	Part work	1 December 1866–6 July 1867	Weekly (32)	George Housman Thomas (32; also 32 vignettes
The Moonstone	All the Year Round	4 January–8 August 1868	Weekly (32)	
Man and Wife	Cassell's Magazine	20 November 1869–30 July 1870	Weekly (37)	William Small (37)
Poor Miss Finch	Cassell's Magazine	2 September 1871–24 February 1872	Weekly (26)	Edward Hughes (26)
The Law and the Lady	The Graphic	26 September 1874–13 March 1875	Weekly (25)	William Small, Sydney Hall, Henry Woods

Appendix 2 Selected Periodicals Serializing Fiction

Periodical	Publishing	Frequency/Price	Publisher	Editor (Nineteenth Century)
Household Words	30 March 1850–28 May 1859	Weekly (2d) Monthly (9d)	Bradbury and Evans	Charles Dickens
All the Year Round	30 April 1859–95	Weekly (2d)	Charles Dickens	Charles Dickens (1859–70; Charles Dickens Jr. (1870–95)
Once a Week	1859–79	Weekly (3d)	Bradbury and Evans	Samuel Lucas (1859–65); Edward Walford (1865–69; E. S. Dallas (1869–73); George Manville Fenn (1873–79)
Cornhill Magazine	1860–1975	Monthly (1/-)	Smith Elder	W. M. Thackeray (1860–62); Editorial board (George Smith/Frederick Greenwood/G.H. Lewes/Edward Cook (1862–71); Leslie Stephen (1871–82); James Payn (1883–96); John St Loe Strachey (1896–97); Reginald Smith (1897–1916)
Good Words	1860 1861–1906	Weekly (1½d) Monthly (6d)	Strahan & Co.	Norman Macleod (1860–72); Donald Macleod (1872–1905)
Cassell's Magazine	1867–74	Weekly (1d)	Cassell, Petter & Galpin	William Moy Thomas (April 1867–March 1868); John Lovell (April 1868–March 1869); Hugh Reginald Haweis (April 1869–May 1870); George Manville Fenn (April 1870–November 1874)
Previously *Cassell's Illustrated Family Paper*	1853–67	Weekly		John Cassell and others
Afterwards *Cassell's Family Magazine*	1874–97	Monthly		Henry George Bonavia Hunt (December 1874–November 1896)

Appendix 3 Bleak House and Cranford (see Chapter 2)

Bleak House Instalment	Date/Chapter		Narrator	Title (selected chapters)	Household Words	Cranford
					13 December 1851	'Our Society at Cranford'
1	March 1852	1–2	Anon			
		3–4	Esther			
2	April 1852	5–6	Esther		3 January 1852	'A Love Affair at Cranford'
		7	Anon			
					13 March 1852	'Memory at Cranford'
3	May 1852	8–9	Esther		3 April 1852	'Visiting at Cranford'
		10	Anon			
4	June 1852	11–12	Anon			
		13	Esther	'Esther's Narrative' (13)		
5	July 1852	14–15	Esther			
		16	Anon			
6	August 1852	17–18	Esther	'Esther's Narrative' (17)		
		19	Anon			
7	September 1852	20–22	Anon	All Anon		
8	October 1852	23–24	Esther	'Esther's Narrative' (23)		
		25	Anon			
9	November 1852	26–29	Anon	All Anon		
10	December 1852	30–31	Esther	'Esther's Narrative' (30)		
		32	Anon			
11	January 1853	33–34	Anon		8 January 1853	'The Great Cranford Panic I'

Appendix 3 (continued)

Bleak House Instalment	Date/Chapter		Narrator	Title (selected chapters)	Household Words	Cranford
11 (cont.)					15 January 1853	'The Great Cranford Panic II'
		35	*Esther*	'Esther's Narrative' (35)		
12	February 1853	36–38	*Esther*	All *Esther*		
13	March 1853	39–42	Anon	All Anon		
14	April 1853	43–45	*Esther*	'Esther's Narrative' (43)	2 April 1853	'Stopped Payment at Cranford'
		46	Anon			
15	May 1853	47–49	Anon	All Anon	7 May 1853	'Friends in Need at Cranford'
					21 May 1853	'A Happy Return to Cranford'
16	June 1853	50–52	*Esther*	'Esther's Narrative' (50)		
		53	Anon			
17	July 1853	54–56	Anon	All Anon		
18	August 1853	57	*Esther*	'Esther's Narrative' (57)		
		58	Anon			
		59	*Esther*	'Esther's Narrative' (69)		
19	September 1853	60–62	*Esther*	'Esther's Narrative' (64)		
		63	Anon			
		64–65	*Esther*	'Esther's Narrative' (64)		
		66	Anon			
		67	*Esther*	'The Close of Esther's Narrative' (67)		

Appendix 4 *Cranford* in *Household Words* (see Chapter 4)

Household Words (selected)	Selected Articles (attribution from *DJO*)
29 November 1851	'A Roving Englishman: Benighted; Out Shooting' (I)
13 December 1851	'Our Society at Cranford'
20 December 1851	'A Roving Englishman: The Apple-Green Spencer; Glastein Baths' (II)
3 January 1852	'A Love Affair at Cranford'; 'What *I* Call Sensible Legislation'; 'The Roving Englishman: A Masked Ball; Advertisements' (III)
13 March 1852	'Memory at Cranford'; 'Fine Arts in Australia' (Dickens)
3 April 1852	'Visiting at Cranford'
19 June 1852	'The Schah's English Gardener' (Gaskell)
3 July 1852	'What to Take to Australia' (Samuel Sidney)
17 July 1852	'Off to the Diggings' (John Capper)
31 July 1852	'Transported for Life' I (William Moy Thomas)
7 August 1852	'Transported for Life' II (William Moy Thomas)
25 December 1852	'The Old Nurse's Story' (Gaskell) [Christmas number]
8 January 1853	'The Great Cranford Panic' I; 'A Child's History of England: Chapter 27'
15 January 1853	'The Great Cranford Panic' II; 'The Ghost of the Cock Lane Ghost Wrong Again'
22 January 1853	'Cumberland Sheep-Shearers' (Gaskell); 'The Roving Englishman: Travelling Servants; Yachting' (XV)
29 January 1853	'A Digger's Diary' (I); 'The Roving Englishman: Cares of State' (XVI)

Appendix 4 (continued)

Household Words (selected)	Selected Articles (attribution from *DJO*)
19 February 1853	'A Digger's Diary' (II)
2 April 1853	'Stopped Payment at Cranford'; 'The Roving Englishman: After the Boars' (XIX)
9 April 1853	'A Digger's Diary' (III)
30 April 1853	'Four-Legged Australians' (Samuel Rinder)
7 May 1853	'Friends in Need at Cranford'; 'The Spirit Business' (Dickens)
21 May 1853	'A Happy Return to Cranford'; 'Our Last Parochial War'
28 May 1853	'The Roving Englishman: Beautiful Naples' (XX)
18 June 1853	'The Roving Englishman: Diplomacy' (XXI)
3 September 1853	'A Digger's Diary' (IV)
10 September 1853	'First Stage to Australia' (John Capper)
17 September 1853	'Convicts in the Gold Regions' (Richard Horne)
19 November 1853	'Morton Hall' I (Gaskell)
26 November 1853	'Morton Hall' II (Gaskell)
10 December 1853	'Traits and Stories of the Huguenots' (Gaskell)
17 December 1853	'My French Master' I (Gaskell)
24 December 1853	'My French Master' II (Gaskell); 'The Roving Englishman: A Greek Feast' (XXV)
31 December 1853	'The Roving Englishman: Greek Easter at Constantinople; In Defence of Fleas' (XXVI)

Appendix 5 *Framley Parsonage* in *Cornhill Magazine* (see Chapter 5)

Cornhill Magazine	*Framley Parsonage* station	Illustration	Other Fiction (station)	Notes
January 1860	1		*LTW* (3)	Illustrated
February 1860	4		*LTW* (11)	Illustrated
March 1860	4		*LTW* (6)	Illustrated
April 1860	8	'Lord Lufton and Lucy Robarts'	*LTW* (1)	Illustrated
May 1860	1		*LTW* (7); *P*(11)	Illustrated (also *P*)
June 1860	6	'Was it Not a Lie'	*LTW* (2); *P*(4)	Illustrated
July 1860	4		*P*(7)	
August 1860	1	'The Crawley Family'		
September 1860	4			
October 1860	7	'Lady Lufton and the Duke of Omnium'		
November 1860	2			
December 1860	2			
January 1861	5	'Mrs Gresham and Miss Dunstable'	*Philip* (1)	Illustrated
February 1861	1		*Philip* (3); *HS* (8)	Illustrated
March 1861	8	'Mark, the Men are Here'	*Philip* (2); *HS* (4)	
April 1861	6		*Philip* (1); *HS* (3)	Illustrated

Key:

LTW: Lovel the Widower

P: The Portent

HS: Horace Saltoun

Bibliography

Primary Sources

[Alexander, Thomas]. '"Good Words": The Theology of Its Editor and Some of Its Contributors Reprinted from the "Record" Newspaper.' London: Record Office, 1863.

All the Year Round.

Cassell's Illustrated Family Paper.

Cassell's Magazine.

'Cheap Literature.' *British Quarterly Review* 29 (1859): 313–45.

Collins, Wilkie. *After Dark*. 2 vols. London: Smith Elder, 1856.

———. 'The Unknown Public.' *Household Words*, 21 August 1858, 217–22.

———. *The Woman in White*, edited by John Sutherland. 1996. Reprint: Oxford: Oxford University Press, 1998.

———. *No Name*, edited by Mark Ford. London: Penguin, 1994.

———. *Armadale*, edited by Catherine Peters. Oxford: Oxford University Press, 1989.

———. *The Moonstone*, edited by Sandra Kemp. London: Penguin, 1998.

———. *Man and Wife*. Stroud: Alan Sutton Publishing, 1993.

———. *Poor Miss Finch*, edited by Catherine Peters. 1995. Reprint, Oxford: Oxford University Press, 2000.

———. *The Law and the Lady*, edited by Jenny Bourne Taylor. 1992. Reprint, Oxford: Oxford University Press, 1999.

———. *The Letters of Wilkie Collins*, edited by William Baker and William M. Clarke. 2 vols. Basingstoke: Macmillan, 1999.

———. *The Public Face of Wilkie Collins: The Collected Letters*, edited by William Baker, Andrew Gasson, Graham Law and Paul Lewis. 4 vols. London: Pickering and Chatto, 2005.

Cornhill Magazine.

[Craik, Dinah Mulock]. *John Halifax, Gentleman*. London: Hurst and Blackett, 1856.

———. *A Woman's Thoughts About Women*. London: Hurst and Blackett, 1857.

———. 'To Novelists – and a Novelist.' *Macmillan's Magazine* 3 (1861): 441–8.

———. *Studies from Life*. London: Hurst and Blackett, [1861].

———. *Mistress and Maid*. 2 vols. London: Hurst and Blackett, 1863.

[Dallas, E.S.]. 'Popular Literature – The Periodical Press.' *Blackwood's Edinburgh Magazine* 85 (1859): 96–112; 180–95.

———. 'Popular Literature – Tracts.' *Blackwood's Edinburgh Magazine* 85 (1859): 515–32.

———. 'Popular Literature – Prize Essays.' *Blackwood's Edinburgh Magazine* 86 (1859): 681–9.

———. '*Great Expectations.*' *The Times*, 17 October 1861, 6.

'*David Copperfield* and *Pendennis.*' *Prospective Review* 7 (1851): 157–91.

Dickens, Charles. *The Pickwick Papers*, edited by Robert L. Patten. 1972. Reprint, Harmondsworth: Penguin, 1986.

———. *American Notes*, edited by Patricia Ingham. 2000. Reprint, London: Penguin, 2004.

———. *Bleak House*, edited by Norman Page. 1971. Reprint, Harmondsworth: Penguin, 1980.

———. *Our Mutual Friend*, edited by Stephen Gill. 1971. Reprint, Harmondsworth: Penguin, 1982.

———. *The Letters of Charles Dickens*, edited by Graham Storey, Madeline House and Kathleen Tillotson. 12 vols. Oxford: Clarendon Press, 1965–2002.

Gaskell, Elizabeth. *Cranford*, edited by Alan Shelston. Vol. 3 of *The Works of Elizabeth Gaskell*, edited by Joanne Shattock. 10 vols. London: Pickering and Chatto, 2005.

———. *Cranford/Cousin Phillis*, edited by Peter Keating. 1976. Reprint, London: Penguin, 1986.

———. *North and South*, edited by Angus Easson and Sally Shuttleworth. Oxford: Oxford University Press, 2008.

———. *Round the Sofa*. 2 vols. London: Sampson Low, 1859.

———. *The Letters of Mrs Gaskell*, edited by J.A.V. Chapple and Arthur Pollard. 1966. Reprint, London: Mandolin, 1997.

———. *Further Letters of Mrs Gaskell*, edited by John Chapple and Alan Sheldon. Manchester: Manchester University Press, 2000.

Good Words.

Household Words.

'Literature of the People.' *The Athenaeum*, 1 January 1870, 11–14.

[Mansel, Henry]. 'Sensation Novels.' *Quarterly Review* 113 (1863): 481–514.

[Oliphant, Margaret]. 'Sensation Novels.' *Blackwood's Edinburgh Magazine* 91 (1862): 564–84.

———. 'Mrs Craik.' *Macmillan's Magazine* 57 (1887): 81–5.

'On the Forms of Publishing Fiction.' *Tinsley's Magazine* 10 (1872): 411–14.

Salmon, Edward G. 'What the Working Classes Read.' *The Nineteenth Century* 20 (1886): 108–17.

Smith, George. 'Our Birth and Parentage.' *Cornhill Magazine* n.s. 10 (1901): 4–17.

'The Author of John Halifax.' *British Quarterly Review* 57 (1866): 32–58.

Thackeray, W.M. *Roundabout Papers: Reprinted from 'The Cornhill Magazine'*. London: Smith Elder, 1863.

Trollope, Anthony. *Barchester Towers*, edited by Robin Gilmour. 1982. Reprint, London: Penguin, 1994.

———. *Dr Thorne*, edited by Ruth Rendell. London: Penguin, 1991.

————. *Framley Parsonage*, edited by David Skilton and Peter Miles. 1984. Reprint, London: Penguin, 1988.

————. *Autobiography*. London: Oxford University Press, 1950.

————. *The Letters of Anthony Trollope*, edited by N. John Hall. 2 vols. Stanford: Stanford University Press, 1983.

Secondary Sources

Abbott, H. Porter. *The Cambridge Introduction to Narrative*. Cambridge: Cambridge University Press, 2002.

Allingham, Philip V. 'Robert Barnes' Illustrations for Thomas Hardy's *The Mayor of Casterbridge* as Serialised in *The Graphic.*' *Victorian Periodicals Review* 28 (1995): 27–39.

Altick, Richard D. *The English Common Reader: A Social History of the Mass Reading Public, 1800-1900*. Chicago: University of Chicago Press, 1957.

————. *The Presence of the Present: Topics of the Day in the Victorian Novel*. Columbus: Ohio State University Press, 1991.

Anderson, Patricia. *The Printed Image and the Transformation of Popular Culture 1790–1860*. Oxford: Clarendon Press, 1991.

————. 'Cassell and Company Ltd.' In *British Literary Publishing Houses 1820–1880*, edited by Patricia Anderson and Jonathan Rose, 72–82. Vol.106 of *Dictionary of Literary Biography*, London: Gale, 1991.

Ballaster, Ros, Margaret Beetham, Elizabeth Frazer and Sandra Hebron, eds. *Women's Worlds: Ideology, Femininity and the Woman's Magazine*. Basingstoke: Macmillan, 1993.

Bareham, Tony, ed. *The Barsetshire Novels*. London: Macmillan, 1983.

Barickman, Richard, Susan MacDonald and Myra Stark. *Corrupt Relations: Dickens, Thackeray, Trollope, Collins and the Victorian Sexual System*. New York: Columbia University Press, 1982.

Beetham, Margaret. 'Open and Closed: The Periodical as a Published Genre.' *Victorian Periodicals Review* 22 (1989): 96–100.

————. 'Towards a Theory of the Periodical as a Publishing Genre.' In *Investigating Victorian Journalism*, edited by Laurel Brake, Aled Jones and Lionel Madden, 10–32. Basingstoke: Macmillan, 1990.

Beetham, Margaret and Kay Boardman. *Victorian Women's Magazines*. Manchester: Manchester University Press, 2001.

Bell, Bill. 'Fiction and the Marketplace: Towards a Study of the Victorian Serial.' In *Serials and their Readers 1620–1914*, edited by Robin Myers and Michael Harris, 125–44. Winchester: St Paul's Bibliographies, 1993.

Bennett, Andrew, ed. *Readers and Reading*. Harlow: Longman, 1995.

Bennett, Scott. 'The Editorial Character and Readership of *The Penny Magazine.*' *Victorian Periodicals Review* 17 (1984): 127–41.

Berger, John. *Ways of Seeing*. London: Penguin, 1972.

Bernstein, Susan David. 'Dirty Reading: Sensation Fiction, Women, and Primitivism.' *Criticism* 36 (1994): 213–42.

Blain, Virginia, 'Double Vision and the Double Standard in *Bleak House*: A Feminist Perspective.' *Literature and History* 11 (1985): 31–46.

Blake, Andrew. *Reading Victorian Fiction: The Cultural Context and Ideological Context of the Nineteenth-Century Novel.* Basingstoke: Macmillan, 1989.

Brake, Laurel. 'Writing, Cultural Production and the Periodical Press in the Nineteenth Century.' In *Writing and Victorianism*, edited by J.B. Bullen, 55–72. Harlow: Longman, 1997.

———. *Print in Transition, 1850–1910: Studies in Media and Book History.* Basingstoke: Palgrave, 2001).

Brake, Laurel, Bill Bell and David Finkelstein, eds. *Nineteenth-Century Media and the Construction of Identities.* Basingstoke: Macmillan, 2000.

Brake, Laurel and Julie Codell, eds. *Encounters in the Victorian Press.* Basingstoke: Palgrave Macmillan, 2004.

Brake, Laurel and Marysa DeMoor, eds. *The Lure of Illustration in the Nineteenth Century.* London: Palgrave Macmillan, 2009.

Butt, John and Kathleen Tillotson. *Dickens at Work.* 1957. Reprint, London: Methuen, 1982.

Calinescu, Matei. *Rereading.* New Haven: Yale University Press, 1993.

Cantor, Geoffrey and Sally Shuttleworth, eds. *Science Serialized.* Cambridge, MA: MIT Press, 2004.

Case, Alison. 'Gender and History in Narrative Theory: The Problem of Perspective Distance in *David Copperfield* and *Bleak House*.' In *A Companion to Narrative Theory*, edited by James Phelan and Peter J. Rabinowitz, 312–21. Oxford: Blackwell, 2005.

Casey, Ellen. '"That Specially Trying Mode of Publication": Dickens as Editor of the Weekly Serial." *Victorian Periodicals Review* 14 (1981): 93–101.

Cayzer, Elizabeth. 'Dickens and his Late Illustrators: A Change in Style: "Phiz" and *A Tale of Two Cities*.' *The Dickensian* 86, no. 3 (1990): 131–41.

Chaudhuri, Brahma. 'Dickens's Serial Structure in *Bleak House*.' *The Dickensian* 86, no. 2 (1990): 67–84.

Cherry, Deborah. *Painting Women: Victorian Women Artists.* London: Routledge, 1993.

Colby, Robert A. '"Into the Blue Water": The First Year of the *Cornhill Magazine* under Thackeray.' *Victorian Periodicals Review* 32, (1999): 209–22.

Collin, Dorothy W. 'The Composition and Publication of Elizabeth Gaskell's *Cranford*.' *Bulletin of the John Rylands University Library of Manchester* 69, no. 1 (1986): 59–95.

———. 'Strategies of Retrospection and Narrative Silence in *Cranford* and *Cousin Phillis*.' *Gaskell Studies Journal* 11 (1997): 25–42.

Collins, Philip. *A Critical Commentary on 'Bleak House'.* London: Macmillan, 1971.

———, ed. *Dickens: The Critical Heritage.* London: Routledge and Kegan Paul, 1971.

Clarke, John Stock and Graham Law. 'More Light on the Serial Publication of *Tess of the D'Urbervilles.' Review of English Studies* 54 (2003): 94–101.

Cook, E.T. 'The Jubilee of the *Cornhill.' Cornhill Magazine* n.s. 28 (1910): 8–27.

Cooke, Simon. *Illustrated Periodicals of the 1860s: Contexts and Collaborations.* London: British Library, 2010.

Currie, Richard A. 'Against the Feminine Stereotype: Dickens's Esther Summerson and Conduct-Book Heroines.' *Dickens Quarterly* 16, no. 1 (1999): 13–23.

Daly, Nicholas. 'Railway Novels: Sensation Fiction and the Modernization of the Senses.' *ELH* 66 (1999): 461–87.

Dames, Nicholas. *The Physiology of the Novel.* Oxford: Oxford University Press, 2007.

David, Deirdre, ed. *The Cambridge Companion to the Victorian Novel.* Cambridge: Cambridge University Press, 2001.

Dawson, Gowan. 'The *Cornhill Magazine* and Shilling Monthlies in Mid-Victorian Britain.' In Geoffrey Cantor, Gowan Dawson, Graeme Gooday, Sally Shuttleworth, Richard Noakes and John R. Topham. *Science in the Nineteenth-Century Periodical: Reading the Magazine of Nature*, 123–50. Cambridge: Cambridge University Press, 2004.

Day, Matthew and John Hicks, eds. *From Compositors to Collectors: Essays on Book-Trade History.* London: British Library, 2012.

Delafield, Catherine. *Women's Diaries as Narrative in the Nineteenth-Century Novel.* Farnham: Ashgate, 2009.

———. 'Marketing Celebrity: Norman Macleod, Dinah Mulock Craik, and John Everett Millais in Alexander Strahan's *Good Words.' Victorian Periodicals Review* 46 (2013): 255–78.

Devitt, Anne. 'Moral Uses, Narrative Effects: Natural History in Victorian Periodicals and Elizabeth Gaskell's *Wives and Daughters.' Victorian Periodicals Review* 43 (2010): 1–18.

Dickens Journals Online. http://www.djo.org.uk.

Dodsworth, Martin. 'Women Without Men at Cranford.' *Essays in Criticism* 17 (1963):132–45.

Dolin, Tim. '*Cranford* and the Victorian Collection.' *Victorian Studies* 36 (1993): 179–206.

Dooley, Allan C. *Author and Printer in Victorian England.* Charlottesville: University Press of Virginia, 1992.

Drew, John. *Dickens the Journalist.* London: Palgrave Macmillan, 2003.

Easley, Keith. 'Dickens and Bakhtin: Authoring in *Bleak House.' Dickens Studies Annual* 34 (2004): 185–232.

Eddy, Spencer L. *The Founding of the 'Cornhill Magazine'.* Muncie, IN: Ball State University Press, 1970.

Ellegård, Alvar. *The Readership of the Periodical Press in Mid-Victorian Britain.* Göteburg: Göteburg Universitet, 1957.

———. 'The Readership of the Periodical Press in Mid-Victorian Britain.' *Victorian Periodicals Review* 13 (September 1971): 3–22.

Feltes, Norman. N. *Modes of Publication of Victorian Novels*. Chicago: University of Chicago Press, 1986.

Feltzer, Lynette. "'Delightfully Irregular": Esther's Nascent *écriture feminine* in *Bleak House.*' *Victorian Newsletter* 85 (Spring 1994): 13–20.

Fisher, Judith L. 'Image Versus Text in the Illustrated Novels of William Makepiece Thackeray.' In *Victorian Literature and the Victorian Visual Imagination*, edited by Carol T. Christ and John O. Jordan, 60–87. Berkeley: University of California Press, 1995.

Fletcher, LuAnn McCracken. 'A Recipe for Perversion: The Feminine Narrative Challenge in *Bleak House.*' *Dickens Studies Annual* 25 (1996): 67–89.

Flint, Kate. *The Woman Reader 1837–1914*. 1993. Reprint, Oxford: Clarendon Press, 2002.

Ford, George, H. *Dickens and his Readers: Aspects of Novel-Criticism since 1836*. 1955. Reprint, New York: Gordian Press, 1974.

Forster, John. *The Life of Charles Dickens*. 1872–1874. Reprint, The Charles Dickens Edition. 2 vols. London: Chapman and Hall, n.d.

Forster, Shirley. *Victorian Women's Fiction: Marriage, Freedom and the Individual*. London: Croom Helm, 1985.

Fraser, Hilary, Stephanie Green and Judith Johnston. *Gender and the Victorian Periodical*. Cambridge: Cambridge University Press 2003.

Frost, Thomas. *Forty Years' Recollections Literary and Political*. 1880. Reprint, New York: Garland, 1986.

Garrison, Laurie. 'The Seduction of Seeing in M.E. Braddon's *Eleanor's Victory*: Visual Technology, Sexuality and the Evocative Publishing Context of *Once a Week.*' *Victorian Literature and Culture* 36 (2008): 111–30.

Genette, Gérard. *Paratexts: Thresholds of Interpretation*. 1987. Translated by Jane E. Lewin. Cambridge: Cambridge University Press, 1997.

Gilead, Sarah. 'Trollope's *Autobiography*: The Strategies of Self-Production.' *MLQ* 47 (1986): 272–90.

Gladden, Samuel Lyndon. 'Spectacular Deception: Closets, Secrets and Identity in Wilkie Collins's *Poor Miss Finch.*' *Victorian Literature and Culture* 33 (2005): 467–86.

Glynn, Jennifer. *Prince of Publishers: A Biography of the Great Victorian Publisher George Smith*. London: Allison and Busby, 1986.

Goldman, Paul. *Victorian Illustration*. 1996. Reprint, Aldershot: Lund Humphreys, 2004.

———. *Beyond Decoration: The Illustration of John Everett Millais*. London: British Library, 2005.

Goldman, Paul and Simon Cooke, eds. *Reading Victorian Illustration, 1855–1875: Spoils of the Lumber Room*. Farnham: Ashgate, 2012.

Gravil, Richard, ed. *Master Narratives: Tellers and Telling in the English Novel*. Aldershot: Ashgate, 2001.

Gregor, Ian, ed. *Reading the Victorian Novel: Detail into Form*. London: Vision, 1980.

Griest, Guinevere L. *Mudie's Circulating Library*. Newton Abbot: David and Charles, 1970.

Grubb, Gerald Giles. 'Dickens' Pattern of Weekly Serialization.' *ELH* 9 (1942): 141–56.

Hack, Daniel. *The Material Interests of the Victorian Novel*. Charlottesville: University of Virginia Press, 2005.

Hall, Jasmine Yong. 'What's Troubling About Esther? Narrating, Policing and Resisting Arrest in *Bleak House*.' *Dickens Studies Annual* 22 (1993): 171–94.

Hall, N. John. *Trollope and his Illustrators*. Basingstoke: Macmillan, 1980.

Hamer, Mary. *Writing by Numbers: Trollope's Serial Fiction*. Cambridge: Cambridge University Press, 1987.

Harris, Janice H. 'Not Suffering and Not Still: Women Writers at the *Cornhill Magazine*, 1860–1900.' *MLQ* 47 (1986): 382–92.

Harvey, J.R. *Victorian Novelists and their Illustrators*. London: Sidgwick and Jackson, 1970.

Hayward, Jennifer. *Consuming Pleasures: Active Audiences and Serial Fictions from Dickens to Soap Operas*. Lexington: University of Kentucky Press, 1997.

Heller, Tamar. *Dead Secrets: Wilkie Collins and the Female Gothic*. New Haven: Yale University Press, 1992.

Hogarth, Paul. *Arthur Boyd Houghton*. London: V&A, 1975.

———. *Arthur Boyd Houghton*. London: Gordon Fraser, 1981.

Houfe, Simon. *Dictionary of British Book Illustrators and Caricaturists (1800–1914)*. Woodbridge: Antiques Collectors Club, 1996.

Huett, Lorna. 'Commodity and Collectivity: *Cranford* and the Context of *Household Words*.' *Gaskell Studies Journal* 17 (2003): 34–49.

———. 'Among the Unknown Public: *Household Words, All the Year Round* and the Mass-Market Weekly Periodical in the Mid Nineteenth Century.' *Victorian Periodicals Review* 38 (2005): 61–82.

Hughes, Linda K. 'Turbulence in the "Golden Stream": Chaos Theory and the Study of Periodicals.' *Victorian Periodicals Review* 12 (1989): 111–25.

———. 'Inventing Poetry and Pictorialism in *Once a Week*: A Magazine of Visual Effects.' *Victorian Poetry* 48 (2010): 41–72.

Hughes, Linda K. and Michael Lund. 'Studying Victorian Serials.' *Literary Research* 11 (1986): 235–52.

———. *The Victorian Serial*. Charlottesville: University Press of Virginia, 1991.

———. *Victorian Publishing and Mrs Gaskell's Work*. Charlottesville: University Press of Virginia, 1999.

Huxley, Leonard. *The House of Smith Elder*. London: Privately Printed, 1923.

Iser, Wolfgang. *The Art of Reading: A Theory of Aesthetic Response*. Baltimore: Johns Hopkins University Press, 1978.

Jackson, Arlene M. *Illustration and the Novels of Thomas Hardy*. Macmillan: Basingstoke, 1981.

Johnson, E.D.H. *Charles Dickens: An Introduction to His Novels*. New York: Random House, 1969.

Jordon, John O. and Robert L. Patten, eds. *Literature in the Marketplace: Nineteenth-Century British Publishing and Reading Practices*. 1995. Reprint, Cambridge: Cambridge University Press, 2003.

Keymer, Tom. 'Reading Time and Serial Fiction Before Dickens.' *Yearbook of English Studies* 30 (2000): 34–45.

King, Andrew. *'The London Journal', 1845–83: Periodicals, Production and Gender*. Aldershot: Ashgate, 2004.

Kuhn, Annette. *The Power of the Image: Essays on Representation and Sexuality*. 1985. Reprint, London: Routledge and Kegan Paul, 1992.

Langland, Elizabeth. *Telling Tales: Gender and Narrative Form in Victorian Literature and Culture*. Columbus: Ohio State University Press, 2002.

Lanning, Katie. 'Tessellating Texts: Reading *The Moonstone* in *All the Year Round*.' *Victorian Periodicals Review* 45 (2012): 1–22.

Latham, Sean and Robert Scholes. 'The Rise of Periodical Studies.' *PMLA* 121 (2006): 517–31.

Law, Graham. 'Wilkie in the Weeklies: The Serialization and Syndication of Collins's Late Novels.' *Victorian Periodicals Review* 30 (1997): 244–69.

———. *Serializing Fiction in the Victorian Press*. Basingstoke: Palgrave, 2000.

———. *Indexes to Fiction in 'The Illustrated London News' (1842–1901) and 'The Graphic' (1869–1901)*, Victorian Fiction Research Guides 29. St Lucia: University of Queensland, 2001.

———. 'A Tale of Two Authors: on the Short Fiction of Gaskell and Collins.' http://www.gaskell.jp/ronshu/16/16_01-14LAW.pdf.

———. 'The Serial Publication in Britain of the Novels of Wilkie Collins.' http://www.f.waseda.jp/glaw/arts/wcsp.pdf.

Lehmann, R.C. *Charles Dickens as Editor*. London: Smith Elder, 1912.

Leighton, Mary Elizabeth and Lisa Surridge. '"The Plot Thickens": Towards a Narratology of Illustrated Serial Fiction in the 1860s.' *Victorian Studies* 51 (2008): 65–101.

———. 'The Transatlantic *Moonstone*: A Study of the Illustrated Serial in *Harper's Weekly*.' *Victorian Periodicals Review* 42 (2009): 207–40.

Lonoff, Sue. 'Multiple Narratives and Relative Truths: A Study of *The Ring and the Book*, *The Woman in White* and *The Moonstone*.' *Browning Institute Studies* 10 (1982): 143–61.

———. *Wilkie Collins and His Victorian Readers: A Study in the Rhetoric of Authorship*. New York: AMS Press, 1982.

Lohrli, Anne. *'Household Words' A Weekly Journal 1850–1859 Conducted by Charles Dickens*. Toronto: University of Toronto Press, 1973.

Lori, Anne Loeb. *Consuming Angels: Advertising and Victorian Women*. Oxford: Oxford University Press, 1994.

Lund, Michael. 'Clocking the Reader in the Long Victorian Novel.' *Victorian Newsletter* 59 (1981): 22–5.

McCormack, W.J. '"Never Put Your Name to an Anonymous Letter": Serial Reading in the *Dublin University Magazine*, 1861–1869.' *Yearbook of English Studies* 26 (1996): 100–115.

Machor, James L., ed. *Readers in History: Nineteenth-Century American Literature and the Contexts of Response*. Baltimore: Johns Hopkins University Press, 1993.

Macleod, Donald. *Memoir of Norman Macleod*. 2 vols. London: Daldy, Isbister and Co., 1876.

Maidment, Brian. 'Entrepreneurship and the Artisans: John Cassell, the Great Exhibition and the Periodical Press.' In *The Great Exhibition of 1851: New Interdisciplinary Essays*, edited by Louise Purbrick, 79–113. Manchester: Manchester University Press, 2001.

———. *Reading Popular Prints 1790–1870*. 2nd ed. Manchester: Manchester University Press, 2001.

———. 'The Database of Mid-Victorian Wood-Engraved Illustration.' *Journal of Victorian Culture* 13 (2008): 108–113.

Martin, Carol A. *George Eliot's Serial Fiction*. Columbus: Ohio State University Press, 1994.

Martin, Michèle. *Images at War: Illustrated Periodicals and Constructed Nations*. Toronto: Toronto University Press, 2006.

Mason, Jackson. *The Pictorial Press: Its Origins and Progress*. London: Hurst and Blackett, 1895.

Mason, Michael. 'The Way We Look Now: Millais' Illustrations to Trollope.' *Art History* 1 (1978): 309–40.

Maunder, Andrew. '"Discourses of Distinction": The Reception of the *Cornhill Magazine* 1859–60.' *Victorian Periodicals Review* 32 (1999): 239–58.

———. '"Monitoring the Middle-Classes": Intertextuality and Ideology in Trollope's *Framley Parsonage* and the *Cornhill Magazine* 1859–60.' *Victorian Periodicals Review* 33 (2000): 44–64.

Mayo, Robert D. *The English Novel and the Magazine 1740–1815*. London: Oxford University Press, 1962.

Mitchell, Sally. 'The Forgotten Woman of the Period: Penny Weekly Family Magazines of the 1840s and 1850s.' In *A Widening Sphere: Changing Roles of Victorian Women*, edited by Martha Vicinus 29–51. 1977. Reprint, London: Methuen, 1980.

———. *Dinah Mulock Craik*. Boston: Twayne, 1983.

Muir, Percy. *Victorian Illustrated Books*. London: Batsford, 1971.

Nayder, Lillian. *Unequal Partners: Charles Dickens, Wilkie Collins and Victorian Authorship*. Ithaca: Cornell University Press, 2002.

Nowell-Smith, Simon. *The House of Cassell 1848–1958*. London: Cassell, 1958.

Orr, Mary. *Intertextuality: Debates and Contexts*. Cambridge: Polity, 2003.

Onslow, Barbara. *Press Women*. Basingstoke: Macmillan, 2000.

Oxford Dictionary of National Biography. http://www.oxforddnb.com.

Page, Norman, ed. *Wilkie Collins: The Critical Heritage*. London: Routledge and Kegan Paul, 1974.

Palmegiano, E.M. 'Women and British Periodicals 1832–1867: A Bibliography.' *Victorian Periodicals Newsletter* 9 (1976): 1–36.

Palmer, Beth. *Women's Authorship and Editorship in Victorian Culture: Sensational Strategies*. Oxford: Oxford University Press, 2011.

Park, Hyungji. '"The Story of Our Lives": *The Moonstone* and the Indian Mutiny in *All the Year Round*.' In *Negotiating India in the Nineteenth-Century Media*, edited by David Finkelstein and Douglas M. Peers, 84–109. Basingstoke: Macmillan, 2000.

Parker, David. 'Dickens, Edward Said and Australia.' In *Down Under with Dickens: Papers Selected from the International Dickens Conference Melbourne 2004*, edited by Alan Dilnot, 35–49. Melbourne: The Dickens Fellowship, 2006.

Patten, Robert L. *Charles Dickens and His Publishers*. Oxford; Clarendon, 1978.

Payne, David. *The Reenchantment of Nineteenth-Century Fiction: Dickens, Thackeray, George Eliot and Serialization*. Basingstoke: Palgrave Macmillan, 2005.

Pearce, Lynne. *Woman Image Text: Readings in Pre-Raphaelite Art and Literature*. Hemel Hempstead: Harvester Wheatsheaf, 1991.

Perkin, J. Russell. 'Narrative Voice and the "Feminine" Novelist: Dinah Mulock and George Eliot.' *Victorian Review* 18 (1992): 24–42.

Peters, Catherine. *The King of Inventors: A Life of Wilkie Collins*. London: Minerva Press, 1991.

Phegley, Jennifer. 'Clearing Away "The Briars and the Brambles": The Education and Professionalisation of the *Cornhill Magazine*'s Women Readers 1860–65.' *Victorian Periodicals Review* 33 (2000): 22–43.

———. *Educating the Proper Woman Reader: Victorian Family Literary Magazines and the Cultural Health of the Nation*. Columbus: Ohio State University Press, 2004.

Pykett, Lyn. *The Sensation Novel from 'The Woman in White' to 'The Moonstone'*. Plymouth: Northcote House Publications, 1994.

———. ed. *Wilkie Collins*. Basingstoke: Macmillan, 1998.

Raven, James, Helen Small and Naomi Tadmor, eds. *The Practice and Representation of Reading in England*. Cambridge: Cambridge University Press, 1996.

Recchio, Thomas. *Elizabeth Gaskell's 'Cranford': A Publishing History*, Farnham: Ashgate 2009.

Reid, Forest. *Illustrators of the Eighteen Sixties*. 1928. Reprint, New York: Dover, 1975.

Rimmon-Kenan, Shlomoth. *Narrative Fiction: Contemporary Poetics*. 2nd ed. London: Routledge, 2003.

Roberts, Lewis. 'The "Shivering Sands" of Reality: Narration and Knowledge in Wilkie Collins's *The Moonstone*.' *Victorian Review* 23 (1997): 168–83.

Rose, Jonathan. 'Rereading the English Common Reader: A Preface to a History of Audiences.' *Journal of the History of Ideas* 53 (1992): 47–70.

Routh, Jane and Janet Wolff, eds. *The Sociology of Literature: Theoretical Approaches*. Keele: University of Keele, 1977.

Sadleir, Michael. *Trollope: A Bibliography*. 1928. Reprint, London: Dawson, 1964.

Schachterle, Lance. '*Bleak House* as a Serial Novel.' *Dickens Studies Annual* 1 (1970): 212–24.

Schmidt, Barbara Quinn. 'Novelists, Publishers and Fiction in Middle Class Magazines 1860–1880.' *Victorian Periodicals Review* 17 (1984): 142–53.

———. 'The *Cornhill Magazine*: Celebrating Success.' *Victorian Periodicals Review* 32 (1999): 202–8.

Schor, Hilary M. 'Affairs of the Alphabet: Reading, Writing and Narrative in *Cranford.*' *Novel: A Forum on Fiction* 22 (1989): 288–304.

Shattock, E.J. and Michael Wolff, eds. *The Victorian Periodical Press: Samplings and Soundings.* Leicester: Leicester University Press, 1982.

Shattock, Joanne, ed. *Women and Literature in Britain 1800–1900.* Cambridge: Cambridge University Press, 2001.

Showalter, Elaine. 'Dinah Mulock Craik and the Tactics of Sentiment: A Case Study in Victorian Female Authorship.' *Feminist Studies* 2 (1975): 5–23.

Sillars, Stuart. *Visualisation in Popular Fiction 1860–1960: Graphic Narratives, Fictional Images.* London: Routledge, 1995.

Sinnema, Peter W. *Dynamics of the Printed Page: Representing the Nation in the 'Illustrated London News'.* Aldershot: Ashgate, 1998.

Skilton, David. *Anthony Trollope and his Contemporaries: A Study in the Conventions of Mid-Victorian Fiction.* 1972. Reprint, Basingstoke: Macmillan, 1996.

———. 'The Centrality of Literary Illustration in Victorian Visual Culture: the Example of Millais and Trollope from 1860 to 1864.' *Journal of Illustration Studies* 1 (2007). http://jois.uia.no/articles.php?article=30.

Slater, Michael. *Charles Dickens.* New Haven: Yale University Press, 2009.

Smalley, Donald, ed. *Trollope: The Critical Heritage.* London: Routledge and Kegan Paul, 1969.

Srebrnik, Patricia Thomas. *Alexander Strahan: Victorian Publisher.* Ann Arbor: University of Michigan Press, 1986.

Steig, Michael. 'The Iconography of the Hidden Face in *Bleak House.*' *Dickens Studies* 4 (1968): 19–22.

Suleiman, Susan R. and Inge Crosman, eds. *The Reader in the Text: Essays on Audience and Interpretation.* Princeton, New Jersey: Princeton University Press, 1980.

Sullivan, Alvin, ed. *British Literary Magazines: The Victorian and Edwardian Age.* Westpoint, CT: Greenwood, 1984.

Sutherland, John. *Victorian Novelists and Publishers.* London: Athlone Press, 1976.

———. 'Two Emergencies in the Writing of *The Woman in White.*' *Yearbook of English Studies* 7 (1977): 148–56.

———. 'The Fiction Earning Patterns of Thackeray, Dickens, George Eliot and Trollope.' *Browning Institute Studies* 7 (1979): 71–92.

———. '*Cornhill*'s Sales and Payments: The First Decade.' *Victorian Periodicals Review* 19 (1986): 64–71.

———. '"Chips off the Block": Dickens's Serializing Imitators.' In *Dickens and Other Victorians: Essays in Honour of Philip Collins*, edited by E.J. Shattock, 97–119. Basingstoke: Macmillan, 1988.

Tambling, Jeremy, ed. *Bleak House*. Basingstoke: Macmillan, 1998.

Taylor, Jenny Bourne. *In the Secret Theatre of Home: Wilkie Collins, Sensation Narrative and Nineteenth-Century Psychology*. London: Routledge, 1988.

Thomas, Sue. '*Cassell's Family Magazine*': *Indexes to Fiction*, Victorian Fiction Research Guides 12. St Lucia: University of Queensland, 1987.

Thompson, Nicola Diane. *Reviewing Sex: Gender and the Reception of Victorian Novels*. Basingstoke: Macmillan, 1996.

Tillotson, Kathleen. *Novels of the Eighteen-Forties*. 1954. Reprint, Oxford: Oxford University Press, 1961.

Tompkins, Jane P., ed. *Reader-Response Criticism: From Formalism to Post-Structuralism*. Baltimore: Johns Hopkins University Press, 1980.

Tracy, Robert. 'Reading and Misreading *Bleak House*.' *Dickens Quarterly* 20, no. 3 (2003): 166–71.

Treuherz, Julian. *Hard Times: Social Realism in Victorian Art*. 1987. Reprint, London: Lund Humphries, 1992.

Turner, Mark W. 'Gendered Issues: Intertextuality and *The Small House at Allington* in the *Cornhill Magazine*.' *Victorian Periodicals Review* 26 (1993): 228–34.

———. *Trollope and the Magazines: Gendered Issues in Mid-Victorian Britain*. Basingstoke: Macmillan, 2000.

Uglow, Jenny. *Elizabeth Gaskell: A Habit of Stories*. London: Faber and Faber, 1993.

Vann, J. Don. *Victorian Novels in Serial*. New York: MLA, 1985.

———. 'Dickens, Charles Lever and Mrs Gaskell.' *Victorian Periodicals Review* 22 (1989): 64–71.

Vann, J. Don and Rosemary T. Van Arsdel, eds. *Victorian Periodicals: A Guide to Research*. 2 vols. New York: MLA, 1978–1989.

———. *Victorian Periodicals and Victorian Society*. Aldershot: Scolar Press, 1994.

Warmbold, Marie E. 'Elizabeth Gaskell in *Cornhill* Country.' *Victorian Periodicals Review* 33 (2000): 138–49.

Waters, Catherine. *Commodity Culture in Dickens's Household Words: The Social Life of Goods*. Aldershot: Ashgate, 2008.

Wellwood, John. *Norman Macleod*. Edinburgh: Oliphant, Anderson and Ferrier, 1897.

White, Gleeson. *English Illustration 'The Sixties': 1855–70*. 1897. Reprint, Bath: Kingsmead, 1970.

Wiener, Joel H., ed. *Innovators and Preachers: the Role of the Editor in Victorian England*. Westport, CT: Greenwood Press, 1985.

Wiles, R.M. *Serial Publication in England before 1750*. Cambridge: Cambridge University Press, 1957.

Worton, Michael and Judith Still, eds. *Intertextuality: Theories and Practices*. Manchester: Manchester University Press, 1990.

Wynne, Deborah. *The Sensation Novel and the Victorian Family Magazine*. Basingstoke: Palgrave, 2001.

Index

Note: Page numbers for illustrations are in
bold

Albert, Prince 36, 60, 161, 177–80
Alexander, Thomas 69
All the Year Round 21, 24, 26, 30, **31**, 32,
    48, 56–8, 64–6, 80–81, 82, 83, 137,
    144–5, 188
    advertising 13, 32, 64–6, 136–7,
        145–7, 162, 176
    fiction 2, 13, 44, 71, 142, 186–7; *see
        also Great Expectations*, *The
        Moonstone*; *No Name*; *A Tale of
        Two Cites*; *The Woman in White*
    non-fiction 138–40, 142
    volume edition 37, 176
Altick, Richard D. 10, 93
American Notes (Charles Dickens) 146, 149
Anderson, Patricia 87n71, 88n79, 89–90,
    159
Armadale (Wilkie Collins) 15, 41, 43, 44,
    53, 156, 187
The Athenaeum 53, 54, 143, 148, 182,
authorship 8, 20, 22, 52, 77, 82–3, 94, 121,
    146, 171
    and branding 23, 41–5, 74
    group authorship (periodical) 20–21,
        23, 29–30, 33–7, 42, 45, 78, 135
    group authorship (serial) 23, 37–41, 135
    and naming 20, 23, 24–6, 27, 30,
        32n31, 33, 35, 36–7, 51, 66, 83,
        104, 123, 183
    prior authorship 23–32, 41, 42, 43–4,
        51, 79, 123–4, 170
Autobiography (Anthony Trollope) 18, 29,
    42, 58, 101–2, 119, 168–70

Barchester Towers (Anthony Trollope) 29,
    104, 168, 169
Beetham, Margaret 4n10, 16n53, 93,
    100n39

Bentley, George 17, 54, 160, 180, 181
Bird's Eye Views of Society (Richard
    Doyle) 104, 113, 119
Blackburn, Jemima 25, 84
Blackwood's Edinburgh Magazine 9, 15,
    42–3, 62
blindness 148–51, 155, 156, 159–60, 180,
    182
Bleak House (Charles Dickens) 12, 38–40,
    186, 189–90
Bradbury and Evans 48, 57, 81, 174, 188
Braddon, Mary Elizabeth 45, 55
Brake, Laurel 1, 4n9, 8, 10, 24, 26, 33, 54
British Quarterly Review 41, 45, 65, 88,
    89, 162
Burbury, Edwina Hicks 87, 89

Cassell, John 21, 24–5, 47, 54, 60, 61–3,
    86–9, 188
Cassell's Family Magazine 13, 63–4, 90,
    91, 188
Cassell's Illustrated Family Paper 17,
    61–2, 65, 69, 86–90, 91, 101,
    147–8, 188
Cassell's Magazine 24–5, 30, 32, 43, 48,
    52–6, 63–4, 69–70, 73, 89–91, 181,
    188
    fiction 86, 147–60, 187; *see also Man
        and Wife*; *Poor Miss Finch*
    illustration 17, 18, **151**, **152**, **153**, 156,
        155, **157**, **158**, 159
    non-fiction 69, 88–90
    poetry 148, 149, 150–51, 155–6, 159
    volume edition 17, 90–91, 161, 180,
        181–2
Cassell, Petter and Galpin 30, 48, 52–3,
    62–4, 86, 148, 181
Chambers's Edinburgh Journal 14, 73, 80,
    81, 87, 172; *see also Studies from
    Life*; *A Woman's Thoughts About
    Women*

Chapman and Hall 48, 94, 101, 164, 174
'Cheap Literature' 65, 88, 89, 162
A Child's History of England (Charles
   Dickens) 75, 96, 98, 174–5, 191
The Claverings (Anthony Trollope) 156, 170
Codell, Julie 1, 33, 54
Collins, Wilkie 43–4, 45, 52–4, 70,
   135, 156, 170, 181n38; *see also*
   Armadale; *The Dead Secret*; *The
   Law and the Lady*; *Man and Wife*;
   The Moonstone; No Name; *Poor
   Miss Finch*; *The Woman in White*
   in *All the Year Round* 135–47, 174n57
   as 'the Author of *The Woman in White*'
   23, 30, 32, 37, 45, 171
   in *Cassell's Magazine* 91, 147–8
Cooke, Simon 19, 86, 125, 134
Cornhill Magazine 2, 11, 20, 24, 32,
   33–5, 44–5, 48, 49–50, 55, 58–60,
   66–7, 70–71, 74, 80, 81–3, 101–20,
   168–70, 188
   advertising 49, 81
   fiction 13, 104, 164, 177, 186–7; *see
   also Armadale*; *The Claverings*;
   Framley Parsonage; *Lovel the
   Widower*; *Philip*; *The Portent*; *The
   Small House at Allington*; *Wives
   and Daughters*
   illustration 16, 17–18, 104, 107, 110,
   108–9, 111–12, 113, **114–17**
   non-fiction 49–50, 105–6, 118, 139,
   156; *see also Bird's Eye Views
   of Society*; *The Four Georges*;
   Roundabout Papers; *Studies
   from Life*; *Studies in Animal Life*;
   William Hogarth
   poetry 103, 110–11, 113
   volume edition 176–7
Craik, Dinah Mulock 20–21, 33, 41, 121,
   123–4, 149, 182; *see also John
   Halifax Gentleman*; *Mistress and
   Maid*
   as 'the Author of *John Halifax
   Gentleman*' 14, 23–8, 32, 35, 41,
   51–2, 68, 123, 172
   journalism 28, 36, 41, 68, 178; *see
   also Studies from Life*; *A Woman's
   Thoughts About Women*
   poetry 27, 134; *see also* 'Unto Her Death'

Cranford (Elizabeth Gaskell) 13, 14, 22,
   29, 33, 44
   and *Bleak House* 38–40, 189–90
   in *Household Words* 74, 75, 76–80,
   93–101
   volume edition 161, 165–8, 174

Dallas, E.S. 9–10, 15, 62, 163, 188
Dalziel Brothers 128, 134
A Day's Ride (Charles Lever) 64, 80–81,
   175, 176
The Dead Secret (Wilkie Collins) 15, 30,
   74, 80, 138, 149, 174n57, 186
Delafield, Catherine 44n89, 52n19,
   68n110, 175n67, 177n73
detection 38–9, 138–40
Dickens, Charles 10, 13, 25, 33, 48, 55, 70,
   71, 146, 149, 180, 188; *see also
   American Notes*; *Bleak House*;
   A Child's History of England;
   'George Silverman's Explanation';
   Great Expectations; *Hard Times*;
   'Holiday Romance'; *Oliver Twist*;
   Our Mutual Friend; *The Pickwick
   Papers*; *A Tale of Two Cities*
   as Boz 25, 65, 167
   as editor of *All the Year Round* 56–8,
   64–6, 80–81, 82, 83, 135–6, 144,
   145–7, 165, 175, 176
   as editor of *Household Words* 14,
   29–30, 56, 73, 75–6, 78, 94, 100,
   162, 165–7, 175
Dickens Journals Online 73, 79, 183
'A Digger's Diary' (see Horne, Richard)
Dr Thorne (Anthony Trollope) 29, 118,
   168

editors 1–3, 11, 12, 23, 33, 45, 47,
   54–71, 188; *see also* Cassell, John;
   Dickens, Charles; Fenn, George
   Manville; Haweis, Hugh Reginald;
   Macleod, Norman; Thackeray,
   William Makepiece
Edwards, Mary Ellen 90, **152**, 156, **157**,
   158, 159, 170n37
Eliot, George 7–8, 16

Fenn, George Manville 63, 70, 89, 188
Fisher, Judith L. 16, 17

Forster, John 38n58, 56–7, 94, 96
The Four Georges (William Makepiece
    Thackeray) 22, 34, 176–7
Framley Parsonage (Anthony Trollope)
    in Barsetshire Chronicles 29, 104–5,
        117, 118, 161, 168–70
    in *Cornhill Magazine* 1, 14, 22, 28–9,
        34–5, 42, 49–50, 101–20, 168, 169,
        176, 177, 186, 193
        illustrations 17–19, 107, **109**, 110,
            112, 113, **114**, 193

Gaskell, Elizabeth 1, 30n28, 34, 35,
        75–7, 78, 94, 166–7, 191–2; *see
        also Cranford*; *My Lady Ludlow*;
        'Lizzie Leigh'; *Mary Barton*; *North
        and South*; *Wives and Daughters*
de Gasparin, Countess 51
Genette, Gérard 19–20, 21, 26, 71n121
'George Silverman's Explanation' (Charles
    Dickens) 136–7, 144
Glynn, Jennifer 49, 50, 58n48, 59n60,
        60n62, 67n103
Grenville-Murray, Eustace (The Roving
    Englishman) 75, 78–80, 96–7, 138,
        140, 191, 192
Good Words 2, 13, 20–21, 25, 28, 35–7, 41,
        48, 50–52, 55–6, 60–61, 64, 67–9,
        74, 81, 82, 83–6, 88, 120–35, 141,
        172, 188
    advertising 25, 27, 68–9, 84
    fiction 60–61, 84, 121, 186; *see also
        Mistress and Maid*
    illustration 17–18, 25, 84–6, **126**,
        129–30, **132–33**, 161, 172
    non-fiction 26, 28, 36, 51, 68–9, 85,
        121–2, 123, 125, 128, 178
    poetry 27, 36, 85–6, 122, 123, 125,
        128, 131, 134, 177–8
    volume edition 161, 177–80
Graphic, The 14, 15, 28, 52, 170n38, 180,
        181, 187
Great Expectations (Charles Dickens) 9,
        26, 64–5, 80, 162, 163, 164–5, 175,
        176, 186

Hamer, Mary 8, 14n45, 87, 107n79
Hard Times (Charles Dickens) 44, 80, 96,
        173–4, 186

Haweis, Hugh Reginald 63, 70, 188
'Holiday Romance' (Charles Dickens)
        136–7, 144
Horne, Richard 75, 78, 79, 98, 192
Household Words 21, 24, 30, 32, 33, 34, 40,
        44, 48, 55, 56–8, 71, 73–80, 81, 82,
        83, 166, 167, 175, 186, 188, 191–2
    advertising 30, 57, 74, 95, 96, 162,
        173–5
    and Australia 78, 79, 96, 97, 98, 191–2
    fiction 65, 74–5, 93–101; *see also
        Cranford*
    non-fiction 38–40, 70, 75–80 , 97–101,
        138; *see also A Child's History
        of England*; Grenville-Murray,
        Eustace; Horne, Richard; Sala,
        George
    poetry 97–9, 166
    volume edition 57, 173–5
Hughes, Edward 90, **151**, **153**, 155, 156,
        158, 159, 160, 187
Hughes, Linda K. 4, 10, 11n36, 96n17,
        183, 159n255
Hunt, Henry George Bonavia 64, 150–51,
        188

illustration 3, 15–20, 81, 82, 84–86, 90,
        93, 102, 103, 105, 107–18, 119,
        124–35, 148, 150–51, 154–6,
        159–60, 177–8, 180, 193; *see also*
        Blackburn, Jemima; Edwards,
        Mary Ellen; Hughes, Edward;
        Millais, John Everett; Sandys,
        Frederick
    and poetry 36, 110, **111**, 113, 131, **133**,
        150–51, **152**, 155, **157–8**, 181
India 85, 97, 122, 137

James, Henry 42, 102, 119
James, Louis 12, 33, 165
John Halifax Gentleman (Dinah Mulock
    Craik) 14, 26–7, 123, 149; *see
    also* Craik, Dinah Mulock, as 'the
    Author of *John Halifax Gentleman*'

Keddie, Henrietta (*see* Tytler, Sarah)
King, Andrew 4, 10, 26
Knight, Charles 50, 76
Knox, James (The Scotchman) 77–8, 97, 140

The Last Chronicle of Barset (Anthony
    Trollope) 13, 107n81, 168, 169,
    170n37, 187
The Law and the Lady (Wilkie Collins)
    52, 187
Law, Graham 15, 43n87, 87–8
Leighton, Mary Elizabeth 16, 17n61
Lever, Charles (*see A Day's Ride*)
Lewes, G.H. 20, 60, 170–71, 176, 188; *see
    also Studies in Animal Life*
'Lizzie Leigh' (Elizabeth Gaskell) 29, 30,
    74–5
London Journal, The 26, 73
Lovel the Widower (William Makepiece
    Thackeray) 22, 59, 67, 103, 107,
    108, 177, 193
Lund, Michael 4, 10, 11n36, 96n17, 183
Lytton, Edward Bulwer 65, 163, 165, 176

Macleod, Donald 60n64, 61, 188
Macleod, Norman 60–61, 67–9
    as clergyman 21, 25, 55, 121, 122, 182
    as editor of *Good Words* 20–21, 25,
        27–8, 33, 35, 41, 55–6, 64, 71,
        83–5, 120–23, 124, 188
Macmillan's Magazine 14–15, 82, 89
Maidment, Brian 17, 18,
Martineau, Harriet 76, 98
Man and Wife (Wilkie Collins) 13, 18n66,
    25–6, 30, 43, 44, 52–4, 70, 148,
    154–5, 171, 181, 187
Mansel, Henry 42–3
Mary Barton (Elizabeth Gaskell) 14,
    29–30, 44, 149, 162, 174
Marryat, Florence 55
Maunder, Andrew 2, 11n38, 20n79, 81, 82,
    83n49, 93, 102
Millais, John Everett 17–19, 25, 107, **109**,
    110, **111**, **112**, 113, **114**, 115–16,
    118, 120, **126**, **129**, 131, **132**, 134,
    149, 177–8, **179**, 186
Mistress and Maid (Dinah Mulock Craik)
    13, 14, 26, 28
    in *Good Words* 22, 25, 27, 36, 51, 85,
        120–35
        illustrations 18, 85, 125, **126**,
            127–8, **129**, 131, **132**, 134, 178
    volume edition 17, 171–3, 177–80, 182

The Moonstone (Wilkie Collins) 14, 15, 17,
    21, 43–4, 143–4, 147, 159
    in *All the Year Round* 30, **31**, 32,
        37–38, 65–6, 135–47, 187
    and the Road Murder 138–40
    volume edition 170–71
Morley, Henry 76, 94, 98, 99–100
Mulock, Dinah Maria (*see* Craik, Dinah
    Mulock)
My Lady Ludlow (Elizabeth Gaskell) 29,
    77, 166–7, 186

Nayder, Lillian 144, 147
No Name (Wilkie Collins) 30, 65n91, 171,
    175–6, 186
North and South (Elizabeth Gaskell) 14,
    30n28, 44, 74, 80, 96, 162–3, 164,
    173–4, 184, 186
Nowell-Smith, Simon 52, 63n86, 91

Oliphant, Margaret 41n72, 42–3
Oliver Twist (Charles Dickens) 13, 48n3,
    94, 98, 100, 145–6
Our Mutual Friend (Charles Dickens) 6–7,
    187

Patten, Robert L. 3, 6, 15, 33
periodicals 2–4, 12, 13–14, 16, 26, 33–7,
    47, 73–91, 183–4, 188; *see also
    All the Year Round; Blackwood's
    Edinburgh Magazine; Cassell's
    Illustrated Family Paper; Cassell's
    Magazine; Chambers's Edinburgh
    Journal; Cornhill Magazine; Good
    Words; Household Words*
    editorials 64–71
    and fiction 8, 9–10
    paratexts and thresholds 5, 15–16, 45,
        47, 57, 65, 68, 69, 71, 91, 102, 147,
        159, 183; *see also* Genette, Gerard
    volume editions 173–82
        and indexing 23, 32, 78, 94–5, 173,
            174, 182
Peters, Catherine 147, 150n233, 180n81
Philip (William Makepiece Thackeray)
    107, 177n72, 193
The Pickwick Papers (Charles Dickens)
    6–8, 16, 75, 80, 166, 167

Poor Miss Finch (Wilkie Collins) 15, 25–6, 37, 44
  in *Cassell's Magazine* 22, 32, 52–4, 89, 147–60
    illustrations 148, 149, 150, **151**, **153**, 154, **158**, 159, 187
    volume edition 17, 53–4, 90–91, 161, 180–82
The Portent (George Macdonald) 113, 115, **117**, 193
publishers 2, 6, 9, 20–22, 24. 26, 45, 47, 48–54, 183; *see also* Bradbury and Evans; Cassell, Petter and Galpin; Chapman and Hall; Smith, George; Smith Elder; Strahan, Alexander; Strahan & Co

reading 4, 6, 9, 27, 35, 38, 61, 70–71, 75, 83, 86–8, 102, 120–22, 148, 167, 171, 172, 177
  and illustrations 107–18, 124–35, 150–54, 156–60
  and periodicals 1–2, 4, 11–14, 19–20, 22, 25, 47, 64, 68–9, 77–8, 94, 96, 100, 105–7, 169, 173
  and serialization 1–2, 4, 10–11, 13, 17, 42–3, 50, 119, 143, 174
Recchio, Thomas 101, 168n27
Road Murder, the (*see The Moonstone*)
Roundabout Papers (William Makepiece Thackeray) 2, 18, 55, 58–60, 66–7, 71, 103–7, 177
'Roving Englishman, The' (*see* Grenville-Murray, Eustace)
Ruskin, John 49–50, 94

Sala, George 20, 34, 42, 67, 76, 98–9, 105–6; *see also William Hogarth*
St John, Percy B. 65n93, 88–9
Sandys, Frederick 36, 85–6, 113, 115, **117**
Saturday Review, The 28, 35, 37, 44, 59, 119, 168
Schmidt, Barbara Quinn 81, 110–11
'Scotchman, The' (*see* James Knox)
sensation fiction 42–3, 45, 55, 69, 91, 148, 154, 159–60

serialized fiction
  and illustrations 15–20, 107–18, 124–35, 150–54, 156–9
  in magazines 1–4, 10–15, 21–2, 37–9, 52–3, 80, 84–5, 87–9, 102–7, 119–20, 120–24, 135–44, 148, 150–54, 155, 159–60, 182, 184, 186–7; *see also* selected titles listed in *Appendix 1*
  and narrative 20n81, 21n85, 182–4
  in parts 5–10, 186–7; *see also Bleak House*; *The Last Chronicle of Barset*; *Our Mutual Friend*; *The Pickwick Papers*
  volume reprints 3–4, 161–73, 180–82
serialized non-fiction 18, 49–50, 52, 58, 71, 79–80, 85, 88, 102, 105–6, 113, 176–7; see also *The Four Georges*; *Roundabout Papers*; *Studies from Life*; *Studies in Animal Life*; *William Hogarth*; *A Woman's Thoughts About Women*
Skilton, David 19, 102, 116n90, 156n251
Slater, Michael 13n41, 38n58, 146n214, 164, 175
The Small House at Allington (Anthony Trollope) 105, 107n81, 168–9, 187
Smith, George 1, 18, 25, 33–4, 49–50, 55, 58–60, 71, 82, 101–2, 113, 169, 171, 176, 188
Smith, John Frederick 89
Smith Elder 48, 49, 54, 67, 81, 167–9, 171, 188
Srebrnik, Patricia Thomas 25n4, 50n12, 51n13, 55n31, 69n116, 83n51, 84
Stevenson, William Fleming 28, 68, 121
Strahan, Alexander 20–21, 26, 28, 33, 41, 48, 50–52, 54, 55, 60–61, 68, 71, 83–6, 120, 122, 124, 125, 128, 182
Strahan & Co 177–80, 188
Studies from Life (Dinah Mulock Craik) 27n9, 36, 128
Studies in Animal Life (G.H. Lewes) 105, **115**, **116**, 176, 177
Surridge, Lisa 16, 17n61
Sutherland, John 8, 170

A Tale of Two Cities (Charles Dickens) 2, 32, 57, 64, 80, 175–6, 186
Thackeray, William Makepiece 8, 18, 71; see also *The Four Georges*; *Lovel the Widower*; *Philip* as editor of *Cornhill Magazine* 33–4, 49–50, 54–5, 58–60, 64, 66–7, 71, 81, 82, 101, 102, 177, 188; see also *Roundabout Papers*
Thomas, George Housman 169, 187
Thomas, William Moy 63, 188, 191
Tillotson, Kathleen 11, 38–9
Trollope, Anthony 4, 7, 14, 19n73, 20, 24, 28–9, 32, 42, 44, 69, 81–2, 101, 171, 176; see also *Autobiography*; *Barchester Towers*; *The Claverings*; *Dr Thorne*; *Framley Parsonage*; *The Last Chronicle of Barset*; *The Small House at Allington*
Turner, Mark 2, 11, 165, 169, 183
Tytler, Sarah (author of 'Papers for Thoughtful Girls') 51, 123

'Until Her Death' (Dinah Mulock Craik) 27, 36, 85

Victoria, Queen 60–61, 123, 127, 144, 177–80

Waters, Catherine 74, 80
Wellwood, John 61, 84
Westminster Review 7, 119
William Hogarth (George Sala) 34, 176–7
Wills, W.H. (William Henry) 38, 48, 56, 71, 73, 76, 94–5, 98, 162
Wives and Daughters (Elizabeth Gaskell) 14, 41, 44–5, 142, 164, 187
A Woman's Thoughts About Women (Dinah Mulock Craik) 27–8, 36, 120, 123
The Woman in White (Wilkie Collins) 15, 30, 32, 37, 40, 64, 79, 140, 163, 164–5, 175–6
Wood, Ellen 55
Wynne, Deborah 2, 4

For Product Safety Concerns and Information please contact our EU
representative GPSR@taylorandfrancis.com
Taylor & Francis Verlag GmbH, Kaufingerstraße 24, 80331 München, Germany

www.ingramcontent.com/pod-product-compliance
Ingram Content Group UK Ltd.
Pitfield, Milton Keynes, MK11 3LW, UK
UKHW020956180425
457613UK00019B/714